Welcome to the EVERYTHING® se

These handy, accessible books give you all you need to tackle a difficult project, gain a new hobby, comprehend a fascinating topic, prepare for an exam, or even brush up on something you learned back in school but have since forgotten.

You can read an *EVERYTHING*® book from cover-to-cover or just pick out the information you want from our four useful boxes: e-facts, e-ssentials, e-alerts, and e-questions. We literally give you everything you need to know on the subject, but throw in a lot of fun stuff along the way, too.

We now have well over 100 *EVERYTHING*® books in print, spanning such wide-ranging topics as weddings, pregnancy, wine, learning guitar, one-pot cooking, managing people, and so much more. When you're done reading them all, you can finally say you know *EVERYTHING*®!

FACTS
Important sound bytes
of information

ESSENTIALS
Quick handy tips

ALERT
Urgent warnings

QUESTIONS?
Solutions to
common problems

THE EVERYTHING Series

Dear Reader,

I still remember my shock when the secretary called me into the mental health clinic's waiting room and introduced me to my first patient a quarter of a century ago. The patient was about as tall as my knees, and he couldn't talk! I was so caught off-guard, I actually asked the secretary what I was supposed to do with him. "You're supposed to be the psychologist. I type," she said curtly.

Because my patient couldn't tell me what was troubling him, I set about trying to decipher his facial expressions, body postures, play, and style of relating to his parents and me in hopes of unraveling the mystery of his many fears and tantrums. As I came to understand his nonverbal communications, I realized that this was the key to understanding human beings of all ages. When people are troubled, they often lack the words needed to express themselves. The combination of errors, distortions, deceptions, and simple misunderstandings means that much is lost in the translation. And before someone can be helped, they must be clearly understood.

In this book I relay what youngsters have taught me over the years about their feelings, wants, problems, and needs. Once adults understand the words toddlers cannot say, parenting can be more straightforward and joyful.

Dr. *[signature]*

THE EVERYTHING® TODDLER BOOK

From controlling tantrums to potty training, practical advice to get you and your toddler through the formative years

Linda Sonna, Ph.D.

Adams Media Corporation
Avon, Massachusetts

EDITORIAL
Publishing Director: Gary M. Krebs
Managing Editor: Kate McBride
Copy Chief: Laura MacLaughlin
Acquisitions Editor: Allison Carpenter Yoder
Development Editor: Christel A. Shea

PRODUCTION
Production Director: Susan Beale
Production Manager: Michelle Roy Kelly
Series Designer: Daria Perreault
Layout and Graphics: Arlene Apone,
Paul Beatrice, Brooke Camfield,
Colleen Cunningham, Daria Perreault,
Frank Rivera

An Everything® Series Book.
Everything® and everything.com® are registered trademarks of Adams Media Corporation.

Published by Adams Media Corporation
57 Littlefield Street, Avon, MA 02322. U.S.A.
www.adamsmedia.com

ISBN: 1-58062-592-4
Printed in the United States of America.

J   I   H   G   F   E   D

Library of Congress Cataloging-in-Publication Data
Sonna, Linda 1950-
The everything toddler book : from controlling tantrums to potty training :
practical advice to get you and your toddler through the formative years / by Linda Sonna
p.   cm.
Includes bibliographical references and index.
ISBN 1-58062-592-4
1. Toddlers. 2. Toddlers–Care. 3. Child rearing. I. Title.
HQ774.5 .S59 2002
649'.122–dc21   2001055270

The information contained in this book is designed for educational purposes only and is not intended to provide medical advice or other professional services. The information should not be used for diagnosis or treatment or as a substitute for professional care. If your toddler has a medical or behavioral problem, or you suspect such a possibility exists, consult your health care provider. All case studies are composites designed to reflect common behaviors and situations. Information has been changed to protect parents' and children's identities.

This publication is designed to provide accurate and authoritative information with regard to the subject matter covered. It is sold with the understanding that the publisher is not engaged in rendering legal, accounting, or other professional advice. If legal advice or other expert assistance is required, the services of a competent professional person should be sought.
—From a *Declaration of Principles* jointly adopted by a Committee of the American Bar Association and a Committee of Publishers and Associations

Illustrations by Barry Littmann.
Interior Illustrations by Eulala Conner.

This book is available at quantity discounts for bulk purchases.
For information, call 1-800-872-5627.

Visit the entire Everything® series at everything.com

Acknowledgments

Thanks to the many who helped with this project, especially
Brandy Corry, Lois Mark, Irene Duncan, Akemi Rush, Susan Malone,
Jessica Quintana, Colleen Finley, Mary Gugino, Michele Potter,
Lauren Bjorkman, Kimber McDonald, Claire Brandenburg,
Jean Westland, Kathleen Knoth, Mauna Richardson, Dan Ritchey,
Elena Aguirre, Mark Sonna, Kobe Bellis, Michael Majors, and my
agent, Peter Rubie.

Special thanks to foster children Zion, Michele, Timmy, Shea,
Ruben, and Christina for reminding me of what it's like to be little
in a big people's world.

Contents

INTRODUCTION xi

CHAPTER 1 *One Giant Leap for Baby* 1
    An Infant Reborn 2
    Free at Last 2
    The First Classroom 3
    Ballerinas, They're Not! 4
    Concentration Counts! 8
    Shoes 'n Socks 9
    Stepping into Tomorrow 10

CHAPTER 2 *Communication Coups* 11
    The Language Ladder 12
    From the Mouths of Babes 13
    Speaking Parentese 19
    First Sounds 20
    Life Lessons 21
    First Words 23
    First Sentences 24
    Parents as Teachers 28
    Stuttering 31
    Language Disabilities and Speech Defects 33

CHAPTER 3 *Growing Bodies* 35
    Developing Physical Skills 36
    Misunderstandings and Misbehavior 41
    Clumsy Kids 42
    The Pincer Grasp 43
    Work Those Facial Muscles 44
    Brand-New Teeth 45
    "Where Do I Come From?" 47
    Gender Issues 47
    Toddlers Are Sexual Beings 51
    Sexual Abuse 54

CHAPTER 4 *Brain Power* **57**

Absorbent Minds 58

Daily Living Skills 58

Building Self-Esteem 62

The Art of Teaching 63

The Concept of Categories 66

Memory Bank Deposits 71

Boosting IQ 76

CHAPTER 5 *The Road to Independence* **77**

The Roller Coaster Years 78

A Growing Trust 79

The Parenting Challenge 81

Stranger Anxiety 83

Contact Comfort 84

Comfort Objects 86

Feelings 101 88

Developing Initiative 91

Delaying Gratification 93

The Road to Independence 98

CHAPTER 6 *Potty Proud* **101**

Early Learning 102

The Lowdown on Diapering 102

Fearless Potty-Training 104

On Your Mark 109

Get Set 111

Go! 111

Bed-Wetting 116

Bowel Problems 117

Bathroom Explorers 120

CHAPTER 7 *Safety First* **121**

Instant Trouble 122

Safety at Home 122

Be Prepared! 127

Buckle Up . . . Carefully 131

Swimming Pools 133

Fire Safety 133
Keeping Your Cool 135
Lifesaving Skills 136
First-Aid Kit 141
Medication Safety 142

CHAPTER 8 *Doling Out Discipline* 145
Little Disciples 146
Teaching about No-No's 146
Dangerous Situations 151
The Problem with Praise 153
Praising Accomplishments 155
Time-Out 156
Spanking 157
Handling Tantrums 159

CHAPTER 9 *Food Fiesta* 163
The Toddler Appetite 164
When to Wean 164
Introducing Solids 165
Minimal Diets 167
Good for You 168
Special Bodies, Special Needs 174
Healthy Appetites 177
Broadening Culinary Horizons 178
Food Struggles 181
High Chairs and Booster Seats 186
Restaurant Survival 187

CHAPTER 10 *Sleepy Time* 189
Counting the ZZZs 190
The Battle of the Bed 193
From Crib to Toddler Bed 197
Bedrooms as Jails? 202
Winding Down 202
Sleep Cycles 206
Nighttime Rituals 207
Recipes for Insomnia 212
Exhausting Work 214

CHAPTER 11 *Fun and Games* **215**
  The Best Toys 216
  At-Home Favorites 219
  Forbidden Toys 227
  Outdoor Play 227
  Check It Out! 228
  Toys, Toys Everywhere 229
  Birthday Parties 232

CHAPTER 12 *Parenting Tricks and Tactics* **233**
  Misbehavior Management 234
  Hyperactivity 237
  Approaches to Discipline 238
  Other Problems 245
  Dealing with Death 252
  More Quality Time? 253
  And Toddler Makes Three 254
  Parenting Styles 256

CHAPTER 13 *Super Toddlers* **259**
  The Magic of Books 260
  Books Versus TV 263
  The Road to Reading 264
  Gifted Tots 266
  Special Gifts 270

APPENDIX A *At This Age: What Toddlers Are Learning* **271**
  Age Twelve to Eighteen Months 272
  Age Eighteen to Twenty-four Months 273
  Age Twenty-four to Thirty Months 274
  Age Thirty to Thirty-six Months 275

APPENDIX B *Resources* **277**
  Books and Magazines 278
  Web Sites 279
  Videos 280
  Programs and Associations 281

INDEX **282**

Introduction

If many parents find the toddler years the most challenging, they also agree that nothing is quite as gratifying as being present through this special stage. Even though an hour spent coping with a cranky toddler can seem like a year, the opposite is also true: those twenty-four months from ages one through three pass in the blink of an eye.

While each stage of childhood contains special joys, the intensity of the toddler years offers more emotional highs than any other stage, if parents can open their hearts to the blessings of the many precious moments. Toddlers' enthusiasm as they discover the world is infectious. Parents can re-experience the miracle of life in all of its fascinating manifestations.

These are the years to relive the thrill of leaves blowing in the wind. To marvel at fingers and toes turning to prunes in a bathtub. To revisit the wondrous lands of Itsy Bitsy spiders, London Bridge, and Winnie the Pooh. To again delight in the mystery and beauty of butterflies, earthworms, and dandelions.

These two short years offer parents the chance to revel in their child's long string of victories: Building a block tower and sending it crashing to the floor. Getting a bite of egg from plate to mouth with a fork. Sleeping in a big bed. Zipping a zipper and using a potty. This time offers parents the chance to experience the warmth of a spontaneous kiss, the comfort of a consoling hug, and the reassurance of knowing they are special, important, and oh-so needed.

This book contains tips for every aspect of guiding youngsters through these critical years of rapid intellectual, physical, emotional, and moral development. It summarizes the best available information on everything from diet to safety, from discipline to fun and games.

My best advice to parents shepherding a young one through this special stage of life can be summed up in a nutshell: Relax. Smile. And enjoy!

CHAPTER 1
One Giant Leap for Baby

There are so many "firsts" in a baby's life, and each one is a miracle—part and parcel of that gradual unfolding into humanness through which a helpless infant becomes an independent person. But of all the "firsts," none is as momentous as when a baby lets go of a protective hand or solid piece of furniture and puts one small foot in front of the other.

An Infant Reborn

On taking that first independent step, the expression that crosses a toddler's face is one of amazement. If the youngster appears as startled as if he were entering the world for the first time, it may be because, in one sense, that is exactly what he is doing.

FACTS

Like baby kangaroos that finish developing in their mother's pouch, human babies aren't ready to be born until they can walk, according to some scientists. Infants' oversized heads dictate that they leave the womb long before they could possibly survive on their own; in that sense, all babies are born prematurely. It's not until little ones can walk that they become full-fledged members of the human race!

Although it is impossible to know exactly what is happening inside their minds as they take those first tentative steps, there are indications that toddlers realize they have undergone a remarkable transformation. Most of their faces reflect ecstatic joy and wonderment, and they immediately set about perfecting their new skill. Some youngsters, however, are frightened by the dramatic change in perspective and quickly retreat to the safe, familiar world near the furniture or floor. It takes them a few days or weeks to risk more unassisted steps, as if they need more time to prepare to enter this new stage.

Free at Last

Walking is a life-altering accomplishment. Just as an upwardly mobile youngster's expanded reach frees her body, walking frees her mind. Given their rudimentary verbal skills, babies are limited in their ability to make sense of the world via *indirect* learning, which occurs from asking questions and listening to explanations. Therefore, they need to experience the world *directly*, by using their senses to unravel the thousands of mysteries that surround them.

To comprehend objects and understand the relationships between them, toddlers need to touch, taste, and smell those objects. Crawling enabled them to begin unraveling some of the world's mysteries; walking opens the way to discovering areas far from their mother's side.

Once toddlers get the hang of walking, they'll probably want to practice all day and may protest loudly at bedtime. Although they do need to go to bed whether or not they want to, try to indulge their desire for exercise during the day. They need to keep practicing!

WALKING STATISTICS

SKILL(S)	AGE OF MASTERY FOR 90% OF TODDLERS
Walks holding on	12.7 months
Stands alone briefly	13.0 months
Stands alone well	13.9 months
Walks well	14.3 months
Begins to run	18.0 months
Walks up steps	22.0 months
Runs with ease, stands on tiptoe, steps backward	24.0 months
Jumps, kicks a ball forward, balances on one foot, climbs a low ladder, leans forward without losing balance, pedals a tricycle	30.0 months
Jumps 15 inches, hops, uses alternating feet when walking up and down stairs	36.0 months

The First Classroom

Educators have long insisted, "a child's play is his work." Now accumulated research proves that if a child's job is to learn, the educators are definitely correct! Still, it can be hard for parents to understand that their toddler is having an important educational experience when their child stumbles into the living room, retrieves a toy ball from under the sofa, and licks the plastic. Or when the child spends fifteen minutes drumming on pots and pans with a wooden spoon.

Parents may think toddlers are merely making useless mischief. But by getting to know the unique texture of plastic or the sound a spoon makes hitting a pot, toddlers are actually gathering data, developing hypotheses, conducting experiments, analyzing the results, and drawing conclusions. Imagine! Every time the spoon hits the pot, Mom yells! A spoon's ability to make noise come from the pot *and* Mom's mouth is amazing to a toddler.

ALERT

Although you often have to curtail your toddler's explorations because they are too dangerous or messy, try to accommodate his or her urge to explore. It's important to accept the fact that your house won't be as tidy as it was before your tot became mobile.

Prodding, poking, tasting, and smelling are crucial for children's long-range intellectual development. Researchers have long known that toddlers with fewer opportunities to use their senses end up less intelligent than peers who are given freer reign.

More recently, scientists have used imaging equipment to study toddlers' brains to find out exactly what happens when they engage in various kinds of play activities. The results are nothing short of amazing. Different areas of the brain respond when children engage in different kinds of exploration. When toddlers manipulate objects, brain cells and those all-important connections between them can be seen in the act of being born. They appear, grow, and proliferate. When a child is deeply engrossed in a toy, the growth of this rootlike structure speeds up, and a complex web of long thin cells emerges. As children continue to play, those cells deepen until they make permanent creases in the gray matter of the brain.

Ballerinas, They're Not!

Toddlers aren't particularly graceful when they're learning to walk. In fact, they are very awkward until they figure out how to coordinate so many body parts at once. Few youngsters master the smooth heel-to-toe motion until age two. Until then, don't be surprised if you notice your child:

- Lifting her knees so high she appears to be goose-stepping. She may put a lot more energy into stepping about than needed until she realizes that walking doesn't have to be such a big deal.
- Pointing his knees and toes out instead of forward. This wider base provides him with a better sense of balance.
- Walking on tiptoes. As she gains confidence and her balance improves, she should settle to the ground. However, tiptoe walking can also stem from the heel cords being too short or tight. To check, see if your youngster can keep her feet flat on the floor when she's squatting. If she can't, call your pediatrician.

Pigeon Toes

Walking with the toes pointed in, or pigeon-toed, helps toddlers balance by compensating for their flat feet. If the angle doesn't interfere with your toddler's ability to walk, and if the movements of the foot are smooth rather than rigid, there's no need for corrective action. Alert your pediatrician if the angle of the feet is severe enough to hamper walking, if the feet aren't straight when at rest, or if they don't straighten out before age three. Encourage toddlers to sit cross-legged or with their feet stuck straight out in front. Some experts believe that sitting with their feet tucked underneath their bodies or turned out in a W shape can cause the legs to curve. Most children outgrow being pigeon-toed, but some never do. An estimated 8 or 9 percent of adults walk with their toes pointing in.

Baby Walker

If you are using a baby walker to help a late walker develop the skills needed to walk alone, don't bother! Doctors say walkers do *not* help children learn faster. Crawling teaches more about balance and coordination than gliding through the house in a walker. And if you are using a baby walker for its entertainment value, you need to be aware of how seriously dangerous they are. An estimated 29,000 children each year have an accident in rolling walkers serious enough to send them to the emergency room! If you decide the risks are worth it, it's important to supervise your child every moment and to walker-proof your house.

- Level all bumps in the floor! Children moving fast can be ejected if they hit a bump; this is how many of the more serious accidents happen.
- Protect floor lamps that could be knocked over, hitting the toddler in the head or breaking and starting a fire.
- Stabilize wobbly stoves and tables so they can withstand a hard bump without spilling hot food or liquid on a child's head.
- Be aware of hot oven doors that can burn the palm of a tender hand and of burner knobs that are within reach.
- Make sure the refrigerator door handle is too high for a toddler to open, or that glass jars and heavy containers can't be pulled off the shelves.
- Be sure the safety gate at the top of the stairs is sturdy enough to survive a crash. Spring-action gates will not withstand the force of a walker in motion; wall-mounted gates are best.
- Don't use a walker with springs or coils within reach of little fingers. They can pinch!

Since an upright child's reach is much longer than a crawler's, objects on end tables, bookshelves, windowsills, and sofas become a threat. That includes the dog hunkered down in the recliner and the cat curled up in the rocking chair. Pets have been known to bite the little hands pulling their fur and yanking on their tails!

QUESTIONS?

What is tibial torsion?
Tibial torsion is a condition that can cause pigeon toes. The leg bone is turned from having been squeezed inside the uterus. The angle of the feet should straighten out as the shinbones become properly aligned (usually by eighteen months).

Little Athletes and Einsteins?

The truth is, there is no relationship between walking and athletic ability *and* intelligence. In fact, early walking does have its drawbacks.

It complicates emotional development because younger ones more often wander from Mom or Dad's side and then become terrified at finding themselves alone in another room.

ESSENTIALS Did you know that the brains of children who don't play much are actually 20 to 30 percent smaller than normal? And that what toddlers learn as they poke and prod and lick and chew and sniff actually becomes part of the brain itself?

Larger youngsters may have more trouble with balance, and coordination can be a problem if their joints are highly extensible (that is, the knee bends more than 180 degrees). Until these toddlers develop more muscles to support their unsteady joints, walking will be difficult. Delays can be up to six months.

Whether your child is off and running, or taking his time, there are things you can do to make things a little easier for him and reduce some risks. Open up space in the rooms of your house so toddlers don't have to navigate an obstacle course as they waddle about. Be careful to do the following:

- Remove furniture from high-traffic areas.
- Keep toys picked up.
- Put towels over skid areas to prevent rug burn.
- Pad hard edges of furniture to guard against head injuries.

Don't trip them up! Make sure toddler's shoes fit properly, and avoid buying shoes with soles that are sticky or slippery. Allow toddlers to go barefoot inside whenever possible.

Stairs

Stairs are as dangerous as they are intriguing for toddlers. Until they can negotiate them safely on their own, place a safety gate at the top *and* bottom of the stairway. Remember: What goes up can also fall down! To prevent stairway-related injuries:

- Keep steps and landings free of clutter.
- Secure the edges of carpeting.
- Place skid-proof mats on slippery hardwood and linoleum.
- Keep the stairs well illuminated.
- Place guards on railings, windows, and patios above the first floor.

Finally, when your youngster is old enough to begin practicing climbing up and down (around age two), move the bottom gate up to give her an opportunity to practice on the first few stairs.

Bathroom Safety

Between the cramped space, slippery floors that invite falls, and the unforgiving porcelain fixtures that hurt so much in a crash, bathrooms need special attention to protect wobbly toddlers.

Use skid-proof flooring and mats on your bathroom floors, and be sure to place decals or a skid-proof mat on the bottom of the tub and shower. Stick decals on the rim of the tub and shower walls, too. In the event of a slip, that bit of friction may help break a fall. And, last but not least, if your youngster can climb out of his crib and doesn't have a bed yet, put night-lights in the bedroom and bathroom to create a well-lit trail.

ESSENTIALS

Mother Nature constructed toddlers to withstand some pretty heavy-duty spills. Their layer of baby fat functions like a built-in cushion, while their still-soft skeletons absorb the kinds of shock that would cause the brittle bones of older folks to fracture and break.

Concentration Counts!

Balancing a head and torso on two tiny moving feet is no small task; so walking requires a beginner's undivided attention. Tots are too busy figuring out how to coordinate their movements to think about—much less avoid—an obstacle looming ahead, so it's important to smooth the bumps in the rugs and clear some paths.

Don't assume your child is defiant because she doesn't slow down when you warn her that she's about to crash or doesn't return when you call her. She may not have heard a word you said. And if she did, she probably didn't understand what you meant.

FACTS

When freedom and independence become overwhelming, toddlers may retreat to the more predictable world of babyhood. If your toddler is too heavy to carry, offer to hold his hand; perhaps that additional security will be enough. After outings, offer some extra TLC and temporarily scale back some of your demands for more mature behavior at home. And next time, take the stroller!

Shoes 'n Socks

Toddlers don't need to wear shoes except for warmth and protection. Nonskid socks provide traction as well as warmth. Prewalkers have sturdier fabric or soft-leather soles, so they provide protection for walks outdoors. They should fit snugly enough that they don't slip, but the fit is larger than a regular shoe.

When buying regular shoes, however, the fit is very important. Shoes must fit correctly at the outset because soft baby feet can't break them in. It's normal that your child's feet might be slightly different in size. Your child needs a pair that fits the *larger* foot; a shoe that is too small can inhibit the foot's development. The fit on regular shoes must be checked frequently since toddlers grow so fast. With a good fit:

- The heel shouldn't slip. Your pinky finger should fit between the back of the shoe and the child's heel.
- There should be enough room for the toes to wiggle, which requires about a half inch of space from the longest toe to the tip of the shoe.
- The height should be adequate, so there is room to wiggle the toes up and down. To test, press down on the top of the shoe over the big toe. You should feel space between the shoe and the toe.

- When you pinch the side of the shoe at the widest point, you should get a little bit of shoe. If you can't pinch any leather, the shoes are too narrow; if you can get hold of a good-size piece, they're too wide.
- After your child walks (or is walked) in the shoes for a few minutes, make sure they haven't left any red marks on your child's feet.

Baby feet can be so sensitive that even the seam of a sock can cause them pain. Stretch socks are the easiest to fit and last the longest. Socks that are too big will wrinkle and bunch up, which can cause blisters; if they're too small, they'll leave red marks and can cause cramping.

Stepping into Tomorrow

With the increased independence that comes with walking, toddlers experience a surging desire for autonomy. Combine this desire with the changes that walking introduces into their lives, and it is typical for their behavior to deteriorate a bit. Expect more crying, defiance, and trouble getting your child to go to sleep.

CHAPTER 2

Communication Coups

The toddler years are a time of astounding language development. At twelve months, 50 percent of youngsters can say six or more words. When the toddler years end, speaking vocabulary has ballooned to 1,000 words; three-year-olds can combine them to express thousands of ideas! At this age it's the ability to comprehend speech that influences how adept children will be at language skills later in life.

The Language Ladder

It doesn't work to apply the averages to individual toddlers, of course, because the age at which a child begins talking is governed by physical maturation. Typically, however, the language progression is:

- Cooing
- Gurgling
- Babbling
- Gibberish
- Individual words
- Two-word sentences
- Complex sentences

The most common progression is for children to begin with one word, gradually add others, and then combine them into two-word sentences before creating more complex sentences. This is not the only pattern, however.

FACTS

When it comes to saying those first dozen words, researchers say that simply practicing doesn't make speaking perfect. Toddlers will be able to get the words out when the speech centers of the brain mature. But vocabulary comprehension grows quickly. Don't judge your toddler's progress with language by her ability to speak, because the amount youngsters *understand* is a much better predictor of later language ability. Just keep talking to your toddler, even if you don't receive a reply!

Some youngsters mouth rapid-fire streams of gibberish. Their voices rise and fall as if they were expounding on the state of the universe. Their facial expressions are as serious and their gestures as dramatic as Shakespearean actors, yet they don't utter a single recognizable word. This apparent delay can be worrisome to parents, but when toddlers finally start saying words people can understand, they usually begin with short sentences rather than individual words, and continue to progress rapidly. Einstein didn't begin talking until he was almost three!

On average, girls start talking at an earlier age than boys do, if only by a few months. Some children speak later than others because there is simply no need for them to talk—their parents and older siblings are all too adept at figuring out the meanings of their grunts and whimpers. They fulfill their toddler's requests without letting them know that there are other, better ways to communicate.

The best way to encourage youngsters to use words rather than gestures to communicate is to demonstrate the correct way to ask for an item. For instance, when your toddler points at a glass of water and grunts, you can respond, "Water? Can you say 'water'?" After a brief pause to let the question sink in, hand over the water whether or not he attempts to say the word. Your child may be unable to speak because his brain is not sufficiently mature. Trying to force him will only make him feel bad. Pushing toddlers is a definite "no-no." There will be plenty of times when you find yourself using the "just tell me what you want" line when you really don't know what your toddler is trying to communicate. But there's no point in creating a scene when you do understand the gesture.

Children who have delays in several areas, such as premature babies often do, may have language delays, too. Parents can expect toddlers with slower overall development to begin talking later rather than sooner. There's no need to be concerned about *exactly* when children start talking as long as the child is younger than two, or the following signs are present:

- Gibberish and babbling continue
- Attempts to imitate sounds continue
- Comprehension continues to improve
- Responds to your hearing tests (see page 25). Still, if you can't shake the feeling that something's wrong, talk to your pediatrician.

Cooing seems to be innate. Even deaf infants coo. But if babies cannot hear their parents' responses and feedback, instead of progressing to gurgles, babbles, and gibberish, the coos will gradually disappear. Even if your state mandates newborn hearing evaluations, seek a second opinion from a speech and language expert!

From the Mouths of Babes

It's never too soon to begin conducting language lessons—within the context of daily interactions, that is. By understanding the fine points of human communication, parents can provide a rich learning environment and better verbal stimulation. Acquiring speech is a two-step process that involves (1) listening to language being spoken, and (2) practicing talking. You can engage your youngster in her first conversation by placing your face close to hers and alternate between talking to her and mimicking the noises she makes. This is the time to giggle, tickle, tease, snort, crow like a rooster, quack like a duck, moo like a cow, and make every kind of funny noise you can think of!

The give-and-take of sounds encourages your youngster to mimic you, thereby engaging in the work that is essential for good language development: listening carefully to sounds and trying to reproduce them. When she's had enough, she'll signal her desire to stop by turning her head away. When she wants to continue, she'll again make sustained eye contact. Be sensitive to your child's readiness to play language games, as well as to her desire to quit. Failing to at least back off for a while leads to overstimulation and toddler stress.

Talking Hands

To speed communication, many parents now teach some basic sign language to their toddlers. And they're having great success! Baby sign language started as an experiment at Ohio State University's laboratory school. It was so successful that children as young as nine months old were able to communicate some of their basic needs by signing, thereby eliminating a lot of crying on the part of the little ones because the staff could more readily determine their needs. Some older toddlers could sign up to thirty words.

You don't need to conduct any kind of special drills to teach sign language. Simply make the sign for "more," "down," "potty," "stop," and so on, while *saying* the word (don't forget to keep talking!). In time, your child will mimic your motions. There's no need to know American Sign Language, and it's okay to invent signs rather than using the standard gestures, as long as you are consistent.

However, a definite advantage to using the standard signs is that toddlers can then readily communicate with people other than their parents. It is becoming increasingly common for toddlers and the adults who work with them to know some sign language. And if caregivers don't know sign language, you can facilitate communication by providing them with a photocopied page of the signs your toddler knows, right along with the list of emergency numbers and other important information.

FIGURE 2-1: All gone/Done
Right hand, palm down, sweeps across top of left hand.

FIGURE 2-2: Down
Point index finger down.

FIGURE 2-3: Drink
Shape right hand as if holding a glass, bring to mouth.

FIGURE 2-4: Eat
Pinch right hand fingers together, bring to mouth.

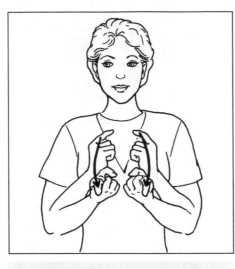

FIGURE 2-5: Go
Hold hands at chest, with index fingers pointing up. Rotate hands forward, so index fingers point out.

FIGURE 2-6: More
Pinch fingers of both hands, then bring hands together.

FIGURE 2-7: No
Hold right hand with thumb out and index and middle finger straight up. Bring fingers to thumb in pinching motion.

FIGURE 2-8: Now
Keeping hands palm up and bent at fingers, lower hands slightly.

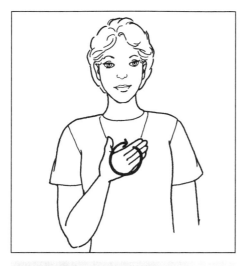

FIGURE 2-9: Please
Move hand over heart in circular motion.

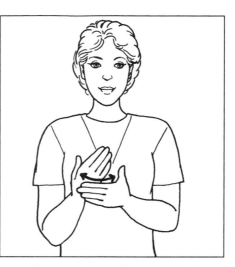

FIGURE 2-10: Share
Hold left hand palm open and thumb up. Sweep right hand, also palm open, along side of index finger of left hand.

FIGURE 2-11: Sit
Tap index/middle fingers of right hand on index/middle fingers of left hand.

FIGURE 2-12: Stop
Right hand comes down on palm of left hand in "cut" motion.

FIGURE 2-13: Thank you
Open palmed right hand starts with fingertips at mouth, then moves forward.

FIGURE 2-14: Tired/Bed
Right hand, flat palmed, is alongside tilted head.

FIGURE 2-15: Toilet
Make a fist with right hand, thumb between index and middle fingers, and shake right to left.

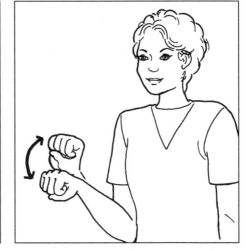

FIGURE 2-16: Yes
Make a fist with right hand, thumb across fingers. Bend up and down at wrist.

Fine-Tuning Listening

Seize opportunities to encourage your toddler to tune in to the world of sound. For example, when you're in the car, point out the shriek of a police siren, the blare of a horn, or the whistle of a train. When you go for a walk around the neighborhood, help your toddler notice the tweet of a bird, the rustle of leaves, or the whoosh of the wind. In the house, listen together to the crackle of a fire, the hiss of a kettle, or the ring of a kitchen timer. Use your voice as well; hum, whistle, and sing to your little one. She won't care if you can't carry a tune. And, by all means, play music.

Careful listening helps toddlers to reproduce the sounds needed for speech today, to recognize the subtle differences in sound needed for speaking tomorrow, and to sound out words when they're learning to read in the years to come.

Words, Words, Words

Besides normal hearing and listening in general, children need to hear words spoken in context. I hope you've been uttering streams of them since Day 1, so by twelve months your toddler has had continuous exposure to millions of words. Otherwise, begin now to make up for those lost months.

Unfortunately, the TV won't provide the kind of exposure to words that toddlers need. Pediatricians warn that TV dialogue drifts by in a blur. The crucial ingredient is missing: the association of the sounds of language with the objects to which those sounds refer. In fact, the TV shouldn't even be playing in the background since the noise can keep toddlers from hearing language that is being spoken. For young toddlers, the TV really is a squawk box!

Speaking Parentese

Highly educated parents often pride themselves on not using baby talk with their little ones, believing that they can speed language development by using normal adult speech. It turns out, however, that the high-pitched singsong voice adults typically use when addressing babies has a name, *parentese*. It actually involves subtly emphasizing important syllables, lengthening the vowels, and often simplifying or eliminating the pronouns, such as saying "he" or "she" or the child's name instead of "you," even when speaking directly to the youngster.

ESSENTIALS

Baby talk actually makes language more comprehensible to youngsters. To get a feel for this kind of speech, imagine a relative picking up a baby and speaking directly to it while saying things like, "Oh, look at this precious little cutie pie! Oh, he's sooo tired. Does Edward wanna go sleepy-bye now? I think he does!"

Adults all over the world naturally use parentese when addressing babies. Research shows that little ones respond by listening longer and more intently to baby talk than to normal adult speech. This is true even if parentese is spoken in a language the baby isn't familiar with! However, language experts say that there's one aspect of parentese that does not help toddlers: parents referring to themselves as "Mommy" or "Daddy" instead of as "I" or "me," and to their child by saying his or her name instead of saying "you." Toddlers have a hard enough time with personal pronouns. Don't complicate it by saying things like "Mommy is going now" and "Does Susie want some milk?" Say, "I am going now" and "Do you want some milk?"

Although speaking parentese to young toddlers facilitates learning, it's probably a good idea to use correct sentence structure, especially correct pronouns, with increasing frequency as your child's comprehension improves.

First Sounds

The first discernable sounds embedded in English-speaking youngster's gibberish are *b, p, m, t, d, n, h, k, g.* Although parents celebrate the arrival of the word they've been longing to hear—"Mama" or "Dada"—they usually first occur by accident, as random sounds tucked in the youngster's babbling. It may take several more months for toddlers to use the words consciously and attach meanings to them.

During the gibberish phase, some parents have been known to exclaim, "He's speaking a different language!" There is an element of truth to this. Babies are born with the capability to learn any language and emit sounds from every language in the world. As they imitate adults and receive praise for repeating certain sounds while other sounds are ignored, the variety of the sounds they make diminishes. They gradually lose their ability to make the sounds needed to speak other languages. That is why learning to speak a foreign language like a native becomes harder after age six, and impossible for most after ages twelve to fifteen. Certainly the remarkable ability of young humans to go from completely nonverbal to fluent is the envy of any adult who has tried to learn a foreign language.

FACTS

Don't be surprised if a bilingual baby is somewhat behind in speech development. Her brain has more to process! The "window of opportunity" for foreign language fluency is up to six years old. Studies suggest that it's best to expose babies to the second language *before* they begin speaking. Starting the day they are born is best of all.

Life Lessons

Although maturation dictates when children will be able to talk, parents are crucial partners in helping to develop language skills. The *amount* of exposure to language toddlers receive is key, and it is associated with intelligence as measured by IQ tests at age three.

To spur your child's language development, verbalize your thoughts whenever your toddler is around, not just when you have something specific to say, like "Let's get your coat. We're going out now." Instead, try this: "It's about time to run errands. Let's see, I need to pick up some food for dinner, but where did I put my coupons? Oh, here they are. And I need to stop at the bank on the way to the grocery store to get some cash. Well, maybe I'll just use the debit card. Okay, let's get your coat. We're going now."

When parents speak their thoughts aloud in an ongoing, running narrative, youngsters hear words in context and in grammatically correct sentences. They are also exposed to a host of other important information. By hearing a parent think out loud as he gets ready to go to the gym, for example, the child learns how to prepare for this kind of outing, which actually involves quite a bit of planning and organizing: "Where is my gym bag? Oh, it must be in the closet. Oops—I forgot to wash these socks. No wonder this bag smells!" To teach children to think ahead, you need to show them, again and again, task after task, the kinds of things to think about.

Teaching Meanings

As you go through your day, dedicate yourself to helping your child grasp the meaning of individual words. Saying, "Do you want milk or juice?" while holding up a carton of milk and a bottle of juice is a way to teach children that different objects have different names. If your child points to the juice, only to get upset after taking a drink and frantically pointing to the milk, this isn't necessarily a sign he's being negative. He simply may not have learned to associate the word *milk* with the carton. By hearing their parent say a word and having the chance to experience the object, children learn what things are called.

First Conversations

Some parents have a hard time remembering how very important it is to continue talking to their child when they don't get a verbal response. Parents need to speak directly to toddlers about daily affairs, leaving pauses to teach them about the normal give-and-take of verbal exchanges—no matter that the tykes are still too inexperienced with language to hold up their end of the conversation. For example, you might say, "I was thinking I'd make tuna casserole for lunch. What do you think about that? . . . No, it looks as though I'm out of tuna. Perhaps we'll have tacos. Would you like tacos for lunch?"

A child's inability to respond with words doesn't mean that nothing is going on. It is quite the contrary. When the parent pauses, youngsters formulate responses in their minds long before they can demonstrate their knowledge by speaking.

Parents can focus their toddler's attention by getting down to their eyelevel and speaking directly to them. For instance, you might say, "We're going to visit Grandma. Do you want to show her your new hat? (Pause.) Come on, let's find your hat." Even if your tot doesn't know what a "hat" is at the beginning of the conversation, by the time you've said, "Here's your hat. Let's put it on you. It's cold outside. Your hat will keep you warm" (to teach about the purpose of a hat), and later, "Grandma, how do you like Jonathan's new hat? Jonathan, show Grandma your hat," he should associate the word with the object.

Explaining the World

As you go through your days, concentrate on telling your child about the world. "See the brown truck?" "That's called a stop light. When it's red, all the cars stop." "This is the aisle where they keep all the cereal." "The lady who rings up our groceries is called a cashier." "This yellow flower is a dandelion. See how it tickles your nose?"

And don't forget to repeat yourself . . . again and again and yet again. Toddlers love repetition. It makes them feel more secure because the world feels more predictable; when they hear about things they already know, it gives them a sense of mastery.

First Words

By the time toddlers can say twenty-five words, they can understand about 170. At that point, their spoken vocabulary is apt to consist of a few names of family members, foods, body parts, and animals; a smattering of actions like *[pick me]up* and *open*; some adjectives like *soft,* and *pretty*; the adverbs *where* and *there*.

When beginning speakers point at an object while saying its name, they usually mean "I want it." After youngsters are able to say about fifty words, somewhere between sixteen and twenty-two months, they realize that everything has a name. Then the pointing changes from a demand to a question. They don't want the item; they want to know what it is called. Suddenly their vocabulary explodes as they flit from object to object, asking to know the name of everything they see. Parents' responsiveness pays off in a big way. Toddlers going through this stage can master several new words each day.

First Sentences

After accumulating a store of individual words, the next developmental step is to combine them into sentences. At first toddlers use two words to create short sentences, such as "Want juice!" for "I want some juice" and "What dat?" for "What is that?"

QUESTIONS?

What does telegraphic speech mean?
Using two words to create short sentences, such as "What dat?" for "What is that?" is called "telegraphic speech." It dates back to when people used the telegraph for long-distance communication. They had to pay by the word, so they were very creative about using just a few words to convey an entire message.

Expanding Language Skills

When your toddler is able to signal her desire for a drink by saying "water," you can encourage her to take the next step to more elaborate sentences by saying, "Can you say 'Water, please'?" Or you can respond with a full sentence ("You want some water.") or with a grammatically correct question ("Do you want some water?") to help move her toward the toddler version of a complete sentence, "Want water." Again, you should hand over the cup even if the only reply is a nod, which means, after all, that she has heard and understood the question.

Similarly, if a toddler sees a cat and starts a conversation by pointing to it and saying, "Cat," a caregiver can engage in conversation by expanding on the subject he brought up. To do this, the adult might say, "Yes. It's a cat," or "Yes, it's a big, white cat. And look at its long tail!" By giving a verbal response as opposed to simply nodding when toddlers speak, adults encourage them to say more.

After all, if toddlers don't receive a response when they initiate a conversation, there is no reason for them to talk! By responding with longer, more complex, sentences, adults help build toddlers' vocabularies.

Pronunciation Errors

New speakers make many "errors of articulation"; that is, they mispronounce words in predictable ways. Although articulation problems may stem from hearing problems, cerebral palsy, cleft palate, or dental problems, all toddlers make many errors. The vast majority improves with a little time and a lot of practice.

By age three, strangers ought to be able to understand your child's speech. If they cannot, it's time to talk to your pediatrician about a referral for a speech and language assessment. By age eight, children should correctly produce all the sounds of the English language.

Common errors include (1) omitting sounds, saying "at" for "hat" or "muhk" for "milk"; and (2) substituting easier sounds for more difficult ones, saying "danks" for "thanks," "medsur" for "measure," "wabbit" for "rabbit." The letters *s, r,* and *l* are especially difficult for toddlers to pronounce, and many children take several years to get them right. It is not unusual to hear students say "wunning" for "running" in the early grades of school. The same goes for lisping—substituting the *th* sound for the *s* so that "sand" becomes "thand."

Do You Hear What I Hear?

Since children must be able to hear accurately to learn to speak correctly, even mild hearing losses can take a toll on speech. If people's words sound muffled to the toddler, his speech will take on a similarly muffled or slurred quality. You should regularly screen your toddler's hearing at home. To do this, be sure that:

She turns her head toward sounds. Youngsters should signal an awareness of sounds by turning toward the front door when someone knocks or the doorbell rings, toward the sky when a helicopter or airplane flies overhead, toward the phone when it rings, toward the dog when it suddenly begins to bark.

He hears sounds coming from behind or the side. Even little ones can learn to do some lip-reading, so it can be easy to miss the fact that a youngster has a hearing problem if he converses comfortably with people standing in front of him. A telltale complaint from parents of children who are hard of hearing is, "She ignores me unless I'm in her face. Otherwise, I have to yell at her to get her to mind."

She hears correctly. Strange responses to questions may indicate hearing loss. An example would be if you ask a simple question like, "Do you want strawberry or vanilla ice cream?" and you receive a bizarre answer, such as, "Yes, play outside."

Chronic ear infections, allergies, and upper respiratory infections interfere with hearing. They are the most common culprits behind delayed speech and poor pronunciation.

Correcting Errors

Children's mispronunciations are often so cute that it can be tempting to adopt their errors as part of the regular household vocabulary. Soon you are routinely saying things like, "Carolina want wa-wa with din-din?" This is not the way to teach toddlers to speak so that others will be able to understand them!

You must continually demonstrate the proper way to speak so your child has a good model to copy. At the other extreme, continually correcting toddlers can produce self-consciousness and frustration that increases shyness and reticence about speaking. After all, if a child says, "Wa-wa" and points, it's probably because he still lacks the physical ability to coordinate tongue, breath, and lips to produce all the sounds in the word *water.* So instead of saying, "It's not 'wa-wa'; it's 'water,'" which can discourage a beginning speaker, emphasize correct pronunciation and grammar by responding, "Do you want some *water?* Here you go—one glass of *water* coming right up." Producing the water lets your toddler know that he is successfully communicating, which encourages him to continue to speak to get his needs met. Repeating the correct word several times in grammatically correct sentences encourages toddlers to pay attention to correct pronunciation and usage.

ESSENTIALS

Teach vocabulary by saying an object's name while moving it, and toddlers learn the words faster, experts say. Somehow it helps to roll the toy truck when you say "truck," bounce the ball when you say its name, or make Barbie dance as you say "doll."

Most toddlers, just like adults, are sensitive about having their speech corrected. Hearing language spoken correctly and having opportunities to practice speaking is what improves verbal skills. After all, people receive more benefit from feedback telling them they have done something *right*, because then they know exactly what to do. Receiving feedback that they have done something wrong doesn't clue them in as to exactly what they *should* do. Being told, "It's not 'wa-wa'; it's 'water'!" doesn't tell a toddler how to make all the complicated mouth movements needed to say the word. But when he finally says "wah-tuh," point it out and encourage him to practice while the memory is fresh by exclaiming, "You did it! You said 'water'! Can you say it again? Wow! My baby's growing up!"

Naming Parts of the Body

Besides talking directly to your toddler, voicing your thoughts when your toddler is within hearing range, and responding when she initiates conversations, set aside some time for helping her learn specific vocabulary. A good place to start is naming the parts of the body. This is basic vocabulary that toddlers need to know, the words are easy to teach, and the lessons provide an opportunity for fun parent/toddler interaction.

Simply say, "This is Mommy's nose" while touching your nose. Then say "This is your nose" while touching your child's nose. Then ask, "Where is Mommy's nose? Here it is!" and place your child's hand on your nose. With repetition, children learn not only the word *nose* but also those important phrases: *this is, where is,* and *here it is.*

Once the nose has been mastered, begin adding other parts of the body, such as ear, mouth, hair, eye, hand, and foot. Once toddlers can talk, they can take turns asking their parents to point to different parts of the body. Keep it fun by incorporating these suggestions:

- Squeeze your nostrils when you say, "This is my nose," to make your voice sound nasally.
- Smack your lips when you say, "This is my mouth."
- Bat your eyelashes wildly when you say, "These are my eyes."
- After you ask, "Where is your tummy?" quickly answer your own question by saying "Here it is!" and giving your toddler a quick tummy tickle.

Parents as Teachers

As any school principal can tell you, the best teachers spend as much time entertaining as they do teaching. Developing a positive attitude toward language and learning and being receptive when a parent steps into the role of teacher is more important than any individual lesson. Learning (and teaching!) requires a clear head, so if your child can't attend to the task at hand or you're feeling frustrated, don't push it. Also, avoid drilling at all costs. Lessons should be enjoyable enough to make you both smile and short enough that you'll both look forward to playing again. If your toddler isn't finding it fun, forget it!

Here are some simple ways to boost your toddler's verbal skills:

- Let her talk to relatives on the telephone.
- Ask him to tell you about his favorite activity at day care.

- Write down the details of a trip or outing and read them back to her.
- Tell him a bedtime story instead of reading him one (and if the main character has the same name as your child, so much the better!).
- Turn off the TV at mealtime and talk.
- Turn off the radio in the car and recite nursery rhymes.

ESSENTIALS Teach vocabulary by asking your youngster to hand you clothing when you're dressing him ("Please hand me your sock."), kitchen items while you set the table ("Please get a cup."), things you need to go out ("Where is your diaper bag?"). Remember, it's never too early to teach manners, so include "please" and "thank you."

The "Where Is It?" Game

Another way to give vocabulary lessons is to play the "Where is it?" game with your child:

1. Place three familiar objects—such as a cup, a teddy bear, and a sock—on a table.
2. Point to each object while naming it. For example, "See? This is the cup."
3. Then ask your child, "Where is the cup? Please show me (or give me) the cup."
4. Provide prompts by pointing to or placing your child's hand on the correct object.
5. If she responds correctly, nod immediately and say, "Yes, that's the cup," to provide feedback and to reinforce correct answers. For wrong answers, say, "No, that's the sock. This is the cup. Can you say 'cup'?" Pause briefly after asking him to repeat a word, but then move on.

The goal of the "Can you say?" questions should be to call the child's attention to an object and to build the association between the object and the sound of its name. Don't try to get a toddler to actually say the names of the objects. Remember that vocabulary comprehension is more important than speaking ability for long-term development. Physical maturation will determine when children are able to speak.

Taking Turns

If your child is able to say the names of some household objects, vary the game by giving her a turn to call out a name and then respond by pointing to the object or handing it to her while saying its name. For instance, say, "Now it's your turn. Ask Mommy for the cup. Can you say 'cup'?" When she says, "cup," point to it or hand it to her and say, "Here is the cup." Then have her ask you for the sock. Continue providing prompts until she can call out the names of objects by herself. When she's successful with the first three objects, stop the game. Use different objects on another day.

Toddlers are really just babies in disguise, and it can be tough for them to grasp that this game doesn't involve banging the cup on the table, cuddling the teddy bear, or eating the sock! If your child lacks the maturity or ability to concentrate on the practice session, so be it. Let a month elapse before trying again. In the meantime, place a few of his toys around the room and ask him to bring each one back to you.

Bundles of Books

Books are excellent vehicles for teaching vocabulary. By pointing to pictures and saying the names, children learn to associate the sound with the visual image. Librarians and bookstore clerks can steer you toward books that are best for your child's developmental level. See Chapter 13, "Super Toddlers," for tips on reading to youngsters.

Most adults feel discounted when the person they're talking to turns his or her back. The same goes for toddlers. Be a good listener and engage your child. Get down to her level, maintain eye contact, and ask questions to show you're interested.

Grappling with Grammar

Many routine grammar errors may actually show that toddlers correctly comprehend very complex grammar rules of the English language. For instance, the past tense in English is usually formed by adding *-ed* to the present tense of the verb, as in *reach/reached; seat/seated; hope/hoped; jump/jumped*. When toddlers say, "She teached me," they demonstrate their grasp of this basic rule. The best way to teach the correct forms of irregular verbs is to correct the errors each time they occur by restating the sentence correctly.

Unlike trying to get toddlers to pronounce words properly, which may be impossible until they mature physically, correcting grammar is important to keep bad speech habits from developing. So, if your child says, "It's bended," respond by saying, "Yes, it's bent." You should respond to "I done it," with, "Yes, you did it."

Stuttering

To talk li-li-like this is a normal hesitation for young speakers. To-to-to talk like like like this is normal, too. Wh-wh-when th-th-ey t-t-talk li-li-like th-th-is, it's considered stuttering.

Most toddlers stutter because their thoughts are moving faster than their tongues, mouths, and cheeks. The great river of words rushes from their brains and crashes into those giant dams, their tongues, so only a slow trickle emerges from their mouths. When they become adept at coordinating the two, the stuttering will go away. In the meantime, their struggle to get the words out can be observed in the tension in their facial muscles.

The key to curing stuttering is to eliminate the child's need to get the words out fast. To this end, you must be patient in order to help your child relax. Yelling at a child to "slow down" certainly doesn't promote relaxation! Instead, it increases the rush of thoughts in the child's mind because in addition to the words he wants to say, he now must think about slowing down.

Discussing *how* the child is speaking while the child is trying to speak also makes the stuttering worse. Children naturally mimic their parents and copy their speech patterns, so an effective way to get them to slow down is to slow your own rate of speech to a snail's pace. If toddlers have a hard time getting a word in edgewise in a family of talkative extroverts, they may feel pressured to talk faster, so it's important to dedicate more time to uninterrupted listening.

The majority of sufferers—60 percent—eventually overcome stuttering without help from professional speech therapists. To help the process along, keep these tips in mind:

- Don't call attention to stuttering.
- Don't interrupt, even to help finish a sentence.
- Don't allow siblings to interrupt, tease, mimic, or comment about the stuttering.
- Serve as a model by slowing your own speech to the speed of TV's Mr. Rogers.
- Spend some undivided time each day talking a little and listening a lot.
- If your child is frustrated or upset about stuttering, provide reassurance: "I can understand you, and that's all that matters."
- Don't criticize *what* your child says or *how* it is said. Fear of being criticized increases anxiety, which increases stuttering.

If the stuttering persists more than a few months or other speech problems develop, consult your pediatrician.

FACTS

It is common for tykes to talk to themselves when they are playing, falling asleep, or lying awake in bed in the morning. Don't discourage them; they are practicing their language skills! Once they've got all the mouth movements down pat and have matured, they'll be able to *think* their words without getting on your nerves by saying them.

Language Disabilities and Speech Defects

The cause of most language disabilities is unknown, but here are some terms to be familiar with:

Developmental aphasia. A problem in developing language that can result in poor pronunciation, limited speech, and problems with grammar

Expressive language disorder. A limited ability to speak (comprehension may be normal)

Receptive language disorder. A limited ability to understand the spoken word (speech may be normal)

Elective mutism. The use of language only in certain situations due to emotional blocks

Echolalia. A limiting of speech to repeating what others have said

Autistic speech. An abnormal inflection and intonation that gives the voice a robotlike quality

Psychotic or disorganized language. Language content is bizarre and lacks context

Even if a child has a severe speech defect that makes it almost impossible for others to understand her, parents should still try to teach the basics of conversation by doing the following:

- Continuing to talk
- Leaving pauses so the toddler can respond
- Listening to the tone of voice and watching facial expressions and gestures for clues as to what is being said
- Listening respectfully
- Providing neutral responses that encourage talking, such as "Oh," "Really?" and "Tell me more."

Remember that even if you can't understand what your toddler is saying, she may well understand what *you* are saying. As long as you keep talking, she'll keep learning! For further information, contact the American Speech-Language-Hearing Association at (800) 638-8255.

CHAPTER 3
Growing Bodies

Physical development follows a path, beginning at the center of the body and leading out to the fingers and toes. Babies control their backs and necks to sit up before they can purposely grasp objects. Development also proceeds from head to foot. As infants, they lift their heads; as babies, they use their hands; and as toddlers, they develop enough control of their feet to walk.

Developing Physical Skills

Toddlers grow taller and their shapes change dramatically as they turn from babies at twelve months into little people at the lofty age of three. Nevertheless, physical growth has less to do with gains in height and weight, which slows dramatically after the first twelve months, and much more to do with the maturing of the central nervous system, which consists of the brain and spinal cord. As the central nervous system develops, toddlers gain increased control of their muscles, both large and small, and of some internal organs, like the bowel and bladder. This enables them to handle increasingly complicated physical tasks— everything from walking up stairs to buttoning buttons to potty training.

Unless there is a physical problem requiring special therapy, parents can support physical development in their children by letting nature take its course. Allow children to follow their natural inclination to move freely about the house during virtually every waking moment, provide an opportunity for vigorous outdoor play, and clear an area inside for vigorous play during inclement weather. Occasional trips to the park will be good for both of you, too, both physically and socially.

The Home Gym

The accent should be on having fun when helping toddlers with physical skills. In designing activities, it is important to provide a wide range of physical outlets to stimulate different areas of the brain, which develops rapidly from ages one to three. Lots of repetition is also important so they can master important skills.

Beginning walkers need to work on *balance*. Parents can help by encouraging them to do the following:

- Stoop to retrieve a toy from the floor
- Walk carrying an object in each hand
- Walk while pulling a pull-toy

- Chase a balloon or bubbles
- Walk on a strip of paper 5 feet long by 6 inches wide that has been placed on the floor as if it were a tightrope
- Lie tummy down, feet touching the ground, on an oversized ball and roll (Supervise this activity carefully. Toddlers are top-heavy and can easily land on their heads.)

To help with *flexibility*, try the following:
- Play "So Big." (Ask, "How big is baby?" and then sweep the toddler's arms up over his head and encourage him to respond, "So big!")
- Make a maze by cutting "doors" in several oversize cardboard boxes; push the boxes together and let toddlers crawl through them.
- Teach toddlers to dance the twist.
- Put a blanket over a table to make a tent to crawl around in.

To develop *agility,* it's helpful for toddlers to do the following:
- Walk in a large sandbox
- Run on grass
- Walk over a series of car tires that have been placed in the backyard and partially filled with sand or dirt
- Jump over puddles
- Jump into and out of a hoop lying on the grass
- Practice somersaults and log rolls
- Jump on a beanbag chair (on carpet or a pad to cushion falls)

Toddlers can be helped to develop *strength* by doing the following:
- Climb the steps of a slide (Be sure to stand behind your child so you can catch her if she falls!)
- Pedal a tricycle
- Pull a wagon
- Hold on for a merry-go-round ride
- Ride a bouncing toy or seesaw at the park
- Fill and tote small buckets of sand

Locomotion Skills

Locomotion skills use large muscle groups—including the arms, legs, torso, and head—to move in space. Not all children master locomotion skills in the same order, but the typical progression is:

Crawling. Not all babies crawl. However, the world looks different from the floor, and the worm's-eye view from this vantage point is thought to enhance visual-spatial organization. Therefore, crawling should be encouraged. To do this, you'll need to get down on all fours to demonstrate. Then have your toddler get down on all fours and help her move her arms and legs in the correct sequence.

Pulling himself up. A toddler should be able to pull himself up to a standing position using furniture, a leg, or whatever sturdy object is handy. From a kneeling position, place your child's hand on a coffee table for balance and help him position one foot on the floor and then the other.

Lowering herself to the ground. Adults know they can reach that toy at their feet without collapsing into a heap, but a toddler may not know how to manage without falling. Show her how to hold onto the edge of the end table for support (cover sharp corners and hard edges), and then help her bend first one knee and then the other to lower herself slowly.

Climbing. By twelve months, most babies can climb at least 12 inches at a time. Steps are a great place to practice. With a safety gate at the third step, put your baby into a crawling position at the bottom landing, an enticing toy at the top step, and show him how to extend his hands and slide his knees forward to climb up to it.

Alternating feet. To help a youngster master this skill needed for walking, have her straddle a scooter. Show her how to push her feet to make it move forward.

Cruising. Children make their way around the room using furniture to steady themselves. To encourage cruising, put an enticing toy on a coffee table a few inches beyond the reach of the child when he is standing up, holding onto the table.

Walking. Timid souls may be reluctant to let go of steadying objects, so they walk a bit later. While a toddler is standing up holding onto a piece of furniture, sit just out of reach and call her to you. Catch her before she falls and exclaim, "Wow! My baby's walking!" When she's confident enough to let go for half a step, expand the distance by a few inches.

Running. Clear an area in the house where the toddler can practice this important skill. Your decor may suffer if you must push furniture against the wall of a small living room to make space, but your child's development and safety is definitely more important! Eliminate the lumps from the carpeting and use nonslip area rugs to soften hardwood and tile floors.

Jumping. You may need to demonstrate and help your toddler until he figures out what, for him, is a complex movement. After demonstrating, grasp the child under the arms, lift him up a few inches, lower him until his feet touch the ground, and then quickly lift him back up. Repeat several times.

ESSENTIALS

If a sedentary toddler shuns physical activity, he may need some incentives to get proper exercise. Parents can enroll themselves and their toddler in a kiddie exercise class. Check the newspaper, local parenting magazines, private gyms and spas, and early childhood education programs for leads. Friends with toddlers are good sources of information, too.

Hopping. Use the same procedure as for jumping, except show her how to extend one leg and keep the other bent. Grasp her under the arms, and help her get the idea by bouncing her up and down. Don't expect her to hop or jump by herself. The aim should be practice, not mastery, at this stage.

Galloping. This is a more advanced skill for toddlers closer to age three. Do it in slow motion first. The trick to galloping is to make sure that one foot always lands flat on the ground while the other foot remains bent so the child lands on the ball of his foot, without pressing down on the heel. Show him how to step forward, place his whole foot on the ground, then move the other foot forward and step down on the ball of the foot before moving the first foot forward again.

Skipping. Skipping involves combining walking and hopping, so the motion is step-hop-step.

Stationary Gross Motor Skills

These skills include stretching, bending, turning, twisting. If not every day, at least once a week:

Play follow-the-leader. Encourage your toddler to copy you as you reach for the sky, touch your toes, move your arms like windmills, or turn to look behind you.

Put on a kiddie exercise video or encourage your toddler to dance with the kids on *Barney*.

Turn on some music and dance! Do it free style. Do the twist. Do it fast and slow and every which way to any music your child likes!

Manipulation Gross Motor Skills

A variety of activities help children improve their ability to coordinate their legs, feet, arms, and hands:

Kicking. Spare the furniture and his toys. Tie some rags together with string to make a large ball, and let the fun begin!

Striking. Besides kiddie tool kits and workbenches, try attaching empty spools of thread to a board with large nails. Instead of pounding the nails all the way in, provide a toy hammer so she can spend the next five years finishing the job herself. Alternatively, provide a plastic hammer she can use for pounding plastic golf tees into Styrofoam.

Throwing. Roll up a pair of socks to throw and set up a paper plate to use as a target. Or use a clothes hamper, shoebox, or pail for a beanbag toss. When you weary of socks and beanbags, toss lids from cottage cheese cartons into a pot. For a very young toddler, put the target on the floor at their feet. Continue to move it a few inches farther away as their skill improves.

Catching. Show your child how to extend and steady his arms while you toss a large soft ball into them from a distance of 1 to 2 feet.

Rolling. Sit on the floor facing each other and roll a foam rubber ball back and forth.

FACTS

When toddlers receive information via the senses, the spinal cord carries it to the brain. The brain interprets the information, decides how to react, and sends commands back down the spinal cord telling the muscles or internal organs exactly what to do. If an adult sees a toy on the floor, experience tells him the toy is an obstacle. A toddler doesn't have the benefit of such experience. He will need to trip over a few things before his brain can correctly interpret these kinds of threats.

Misunderstandings and Misbehavior

If toddlers avoid crashing into the chair but lose their balance and hit the floor, it may take a few seconds for their brains to interpret the pain signals, which are arriving from a different part of the body than they had expected. It will take another few seconds for their brain to communicate with their throat and eyes so they can let out a large wail and begin to cry. Don't conclude your child isn't hurt because he didn't start crying at once! If the child isn't injured, provide comfort by helping him up and telling him he's okay. Let him think through what just happened rather than admonishing him to "be more careful." To avoid collisions, clear an area of your home where your toddler can run safely or provide an opportunity each day to play outside.

Perhaps an example will help you understand just how a toddler's mind and body interacts. If a toddler is reaching for a freshly iced cake sitting on the table and hears his mother yelling, "Don't touch!" his natural response is to turn his face toward the sound. Then, when he sees that

Mother is addressing him, he must figure out what she's trying to tell him. Once he comprehends that her words refer to his hand reaching for the cake and realizes that she wants him to stop, he must figure out which muscles to contract and which to relax to get that little hand to drop to his lap. By then, the hand may well be covered with icing.

ALERT

If a child is approaching serious danger, such as heading toward a drop-off or the top of the stairs, grab her! She won't be able to comprehend a verbal warning in enough time to avoid the danger.

It's understandable that a parent who doesn't have a grasp of toddler development gets very upset in this situation. After all, she said, "Don't touch," and her toddler looked straight at her and stuck his hand in the cake. It's tough enough to have the problem of a ruined cake and an icing-covered toddler. The anger that comes from believing the toddler has purposely misbehaved can cause the mother to punish her child, which leaves the toddler feeling upset without even understanding what he did wrong. So instead of attributing evil intentions to toddler misbehavior, be considerate of their inability to process information quickly, and be patient!

Clumsy Kids

Difficulty coordinating large and small muscle groups and/or a lack of clarity about physical boundaries cause clumsiness—and both causes are basic characteristics of toddlers! The usual solution is years of practice. The school of hard knocks will teach them exactly where their body leaves off and the rest of the world begins.

However, some toddlers have a high threshold for pain, so the usual bumps and bruises don't teach them to stop before colliding with the chair, the end table, or the ground—or even with themselves. They step on their own feet and their own hand clunks them in the jaw. They may cry each time it happens, but they are so readily distracted that they forget to watch what they're doing and the same or similar accidents keep recurring. "Careful!" "Look out! "Don't hurt yourself!" "Next time, watch where you're going," their hapless parents repeat as these seeming daredevils continue to knock and scrape and batter themselves in their heedlessly rough-and-tumble play.

But children aren't daredevils if they don't comprehend the risk. Warnings work only if youngsters know what to do to prevent another injury. They learn from their mistakes only if their intellect enables them to remember what went wrong last time, to figure out what to do differently when the same situation arises, and to concentrate to avoid a repetition of the same problem.

If warnings and frequent bumps don't slow your youngster down, provide comfort after she's been injured, and then encourage her to repeat the same movement, but this time without hurting herself. Praise her for being successful. Multiplied over many situations, this kind of concentrated teaching can help toddlers tune into the position of their bodies and be more aware of the proximity of their limbs, head, and torso to other objects. Meanwhile, encourage better body awareness by combining song and movement, such as the Hokey Pokey.

FACTS

Some experts say swimming lessons before age four don't help children learn faster because of the limitations of their central nervous systems and muscle development. Still, water babies' classes can be lots of fun and encourage them to stretch their little muscles!

The Pincer Grasp

Fine motor coordination involves the muscles of the finger, hand, mouth, face, and throat. The pincer grasp—the ability to pick up small objects with the thumb and forefinger—is what separates humans from other animals. It enables children to do everything from button a shirt to manipulate a pencil.

Young toddlers begin developing their pincer grasp by picking up and manipulating toys and household objects in the course of normal play. Toddler toys are large not only to prevent youngsters from swallowing them, but also because poor coordination makes it difficult for them to pick up very small objects.

Provide toys in a variety of interesting colors, shapes, and textures to encourage your child to practice this important skill. By eighteen months, tots should be ready for more concentrated practice. The following toys and activities can help:

Play dough. Even twelve-month-olds will enjoy making designs in a play dough pancake by poking at it with straws and plastic spoons, so you may want to whip up a batch (see the recipe in Chapter 11, "Fun and Games").

Drawing. Toddlers' early artistic productions won't look like much. But they enjoy manipulating pencils, markers, and crayons and practicing fine motor coordination in the process. Don't praise their work. The point isn't what they did—it's the doing of it!

Tongs. Give your toddler a pair of kitchen tongs and show her how to pick up small toys and place them in a can or box.

Cheerios. Have your child feed herself dry Cheerios or fish crackers from a bag. Break off a small piece of cereal or cracker and hold it on your palm. To take it from you, she will have to use her thumb and forefinger.

Peas. Let your toddler eat his peas without help. Whether he picks them up and puts them directly into his mouth or uses a spoon, peas offer lots of concentrated practice to develop the pincer grasp.

ESSENTIALS Don't wager any money on whether you're raising a little leftie until age three. Even then you may lose, because many children don't settle on a hand preference for another few years. About 20percent never do. They remain somewhat ambidextrous.

Work Those Facial Muscles

Toddlers develop strength and coordination by chewing, vocalizing, and talking. If children are not yet talking, encourage them to babble.

Take turns making funny sounds. Making funny faces also encourages tots to use their facial muscles. This is a good time for lots of clowning!

Because the muscles in the face, mouth, and throat are poorly developed, even soft food can cause toddlers to choke if they stuff their mouths—and it's a given that sooner or later they will do just that. Taking a first-aid course that teaches abdominal thrusts could be one of the best decisions of your life! Doing them wrong can cause injury.

ESSENTIALS   The soft spot in the front of a child's skull shouldn't be noticeable after age eighteen months. The skull plates continue to grow as the brain increases in size. They don't fuse until brain growth slows at about age two.

Brand-New Teeth

Most children have some teeth when they enter the toddler years, and by age three, many have a full set of choppers (**FIGURE 3-1**). Beginning around age six months, the two lower middle teeth appear. Next the two upper middle teeth (the incisors) come in. Then the teeth on either side of the two front teeth appear (more incisors) followed by more bottom teeth. By age two, most children have sixteen sparkling teeth. However, both the timing and pattern can vary dramatically. Eventually they should end up with ten on top and ten on the bottom.

These baby teeth, also called milk teeth or primary teeth, will gradually be replaced by a set of permanent ones beginning after age five. The health of the baby teeth affects the permanent teeth, so they need to be well cared for!

Toddlers will need parents to brush their teeth for them until they are coordinated enough to make the proper motions. (At the first dental checkup, typically at age three, the dentist will give them a lesson.) To teach proper brushing techniques, parents can simply place their hand over their toddler's and guide them through the process. Expect toddlers to chew and otherwise mangle the toothbrush bristles. Here are some tips to make tooth brushing easier for you and your child:

FIGURE 3-1

A: Central incisors
(6–10 months)

B: Lateral incisors
(10–13 months)

C: Canine
(17–23 months)

D: First baby
molar
(14–18 months)

E: Second baby
molar
(23–31 months)

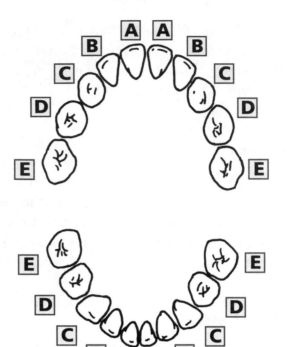

- Use a soft-bristled kiddie-size brush. If you buy several, you can let the toddler choose which to use at each brushing.
- Brush a doll or teddy's teeth first to give your toddler a chance to witness what is going on and become comfortable with the idea.
- Use your child's natural urge to mimic by brushing your teeth while she brushes hers.
- Provide a pea-size spot of toothpaste (choose a brand formulated for children; adult toothpaste is too strong) and try to keep her from swallowing.
- After she's finished, give her a once-over-lightly to make sure the job is done properly, especially at bedtime.
- Schedule a trip to the dentist, then cloak yourself in the voice of authority: Remind your child that the dentist said she must brush her teeth every day to keep them healthy.

"Where Do I Come From?"

One day, precocious thirty-three-month-old Jamie asked the question many parents dread: "Mom, where do I come from?" Jamie's parents had promised each other that when The Question arose, instead of resorting to the stork story, they would give an accurate recounting. And since Jamie was a boy, they decided his father would be in charge of teaching him the facts of life. With a red face and occasional stammer, Dad began fumbling through the tale of Daddy's seed and Mommy's egg, praying Jamie wouldn't ask exactly how Daddy puts the seed there. Mom listened for a bit, then interrupted. "Jamie, you come from Hawaii," she said. Jamie nodded and returned his attention to his toy piano.

There are three morals to this story:

1. Find out exactly what information your toddler is requesting before trying to answer his question.
2. In general, less information is better. Let toddlers ask if they want to know more.
3. Don't overwhelm either of you by serving up more information than your tyke is ready to hear.

Gender Issues

A few differences between the sexes seem to be innate. For instance, toddler boys tend to be more active and fussier than girls. Although boys don't actually cry more, their sleep tends to be more disturbed. As a group, girls' language skills develop faster than boys'. Girls also develop bladder and bowel control a few months earlier.

Of course, these are tendencies and group averages. The differences vanish when individual children are considered. There are lots of calm, moderate-energy boys who sleep soundly and are potty trained at an early age. Lots of active, fussy little female insomniacs reach their fourth or fifth birthday before they make it through the night without wetting the bed. Most differences are due to how boys and girls are raised. When twelve-month-old boys build towers out of blocks and zoom toy cars across the floor, for example, research has shown that parents nod, smile, and praise them more than when little girls do the same thing. The older boys get, the more support they receive for playing with "boy" toys, and the more they are subtly or actively discouraged from playing with Cinderella. Parents are less upset and react less intensely when girls cross the gender line in their choice of play activities.

FACTS

Adults typically talk to boys and girls very differently. They subtly encourage boys' independence, offering more support when they head off to explore and providing the kind of guidance that helps them solve problems themselves. In contrast, adults typically provide girls with fewer problem-solving tools by ignoring them more or by solving problems for them. Studies show that adults are more likely to use baby talk with girls than with boys, employing diminutive forms like "doggy" or "dolly" nearly twice as often.

Guys and Dolls: Teaching the Stereotypes

It is not possible to predict what sexual orientation a toddler will ultimately adopt. It is normal for toddlers of both sexes to imitate the behavior of both parents. Sensitive boys with tastes that run more to the artistic than the athletic will have a harder time developing comfort with their masculinity if their parents cannot accept these traits, and instead try to push them into more macho roles.

When children of either sex play with baby dolls, they are doing what they see parents, sitters, and day care staff do: take care of babies. Baby dolls can be helpful to boys as well as girls in several ways. They provide practice nurturing and taking care of a baby, enhance feelings of closeness to parents, and prepare toddlers for coping with uncomfortable situations. Dolls can also help older toddlers resolve their feelings about trying situations and traumas. After imagination has developed and before children can talk effectively about their problems, re-enacting upsetting events through play helps children work through anxieties and come to terms with troubling emotions. Playing with dolls doesn't turn boys into homosexuals any more than it turns girls into lesbians.

Core gender identity is formed during the toddler years. Children may go through phases of being a Mommy's boy or Daddy's girl and regularly mimic the behaviors of both men and women, but by age two they should have a conception of themselves as being male or female. Three-year-olds usually identify with the same-sex parent, which is often reflected in their stance, the way they walk, their gestures, and some of their speech patterns. Toddlers typically identify people's sex by their peripheral characteristics, such as clothing, hairstyle, or use of makeup; they don't have a real conception of what it means to be male or female. To increase identification, the same-sex parent should:

- Spend more time engaging in activities the child enjoys, since this can strengthen the parent-child bond.
- Be more accepting and less critical, since children emulate people they feel close to.
- Be kinder toward a spouse. (Children are protective of both parents and commonly align themselves with the one they feel is being picked on or unfairly attacked.)

Sugar and Spice

Most modern parents want to avoid raising their children in accordance with old gender stereotypes. They want their daughters to have a positive self-image, be comfortable asserting themselves, and have wider career aspirations. They want their sons to be able to express a range of emotions, nurture others, and cooperate as well as compete. However, researchers say it is almost a given that parents will pass on the sexism they've absorbed from the culture-at-large because so much of it is unconscious. Other research has demonstrated the following:

- Parents react differently to videotapes of toddlers engaged in routine play. For instance, subjects describe a child's response to a jack-in-the-box as "fearful" if they're told the little one is a girl, but "angry" if they're told the child is a boy.

- Most parents are now okay with little gun-toting Annie Oakleys and are far more comfortable than in decades past when little females oversee Tinker Toy, Lincoln Log, and building block construction sights. But many still get squirmy when a boy expresses more than passing interest in a doll or dresses up in a girl's clothes.
- Parents display more pleasure and spend more time interacting when their little boy tosses a foam rubber ball in the house than when their little girl does the very same thing.
- Girls get more encouragement for staging tea parties and playing house.
- When the daily dose of words and hugs are tallied, day care center teachers respond far more often to boys than to girls.
- Gender stereotyping on TV remains intense; it doesn't take kids long to figure out who is supposed to want My Little Ponies and Hot Wheels.
- In disputes over toys, adults commonly urge little girls to "share" and reprimand them for taking a boy's toy. Adults help little boys "protect their turf" by helping them fend off interlopers who try to take their toys.

That's So Cute!

The differences in the way adults respond to cutely dressed kids shows how subtle but powerful sexist stereotypes are transmitted. When one little miss entered a day care center dressed to the nines, the staff clucked, "Aren't you sweet!" "You're so cute!" "Isn't she darling!" The belle of the toddler crowd smiled and wiggled with delight. A moment later a little boy entered the very same center. He, too, was all dressed in a coordinated outfit. The same staff members clucked, "What a darling little sweater!" "Such cute pants." "Look at those cute elephants!" The little boy leaned over to study the embroidered elephants trudging across the front of his sweater. The messages conveyed to these children were clear: When she dresses up, *she* is cute; her clothes merge with her and together form her identity. When he dresses up, his *clothes* are cute, but the clothes remain separate from him and he continues being who he is.

Parents as Role Models

It's not just the differential treatment from adults that instills sexism at such a tender age, researchers say. All toddlers need to do is observe the daily household routine to see that mothers devote more time to food, clothing, cleanliness, and children's feelings while fathers are chiefs when it comes to maintaining yards, cars, and rules. (If spouses argue about who doesn't do enough of what around the house, watching who-does-what when their child starts playing house can settle it.)

> Given that most youngsters are exposed to adult sexuality via TV shows, music videos, and commercials, it isn't surprising that curiosity runs high, or that many try to mimic the behavior they see. This is yet another reason to monitor—and limit—children's TV viewing.

Even when "Mr. Mom" is responsible for the household and the mother is the breadwinner, men relate to children differently than women do. For example, women tend to carry infants facing in, toward their chest, while men more often carry them facing out so they can see the world.

It should come as no surprise that by twenty-four months toddlers are adhering to their sugar-and-spice versus puppy-dog-tail roles. If they're not, she's probably being labeled a "tough cookie," rather than a self-possessed little girl, while adults are probably running out of patience with his tendency to wear his heart on his sleeve and are searching for ways to help him develop a thicker skin.

Toddlers Are Sexual Beings

Taboos around childhood sexuality remain strong. The past practice of admonishing toddlers that touching "down there" would land them an eternity in hell has largely disappeared to be replaced by the myth that only youngsters who have been sexually abused engage in sexual exploration or activities or display a keen interest in sexual matters. Thus, instead of considering toddler's sexuality to be immoral, many view it as an indication of "sickness," a symptom of post-traumatic stress.

In truth, toddlers are sexual beings, though not in the adult sense. Their genitals are very sensitive, so they readily discover that the physical sensations produced by touching and rubbing are pleasant. Fondling the genitals for comfort is also common. Some youngsters may also hold themselves in hopes of stopping themselves from urinating. It also is common for little boys to have erections. When little girls see naked boys, many express concerns about their own lack of a penis. To reassure them, parents can simply explain that little girls have a clitoris and vagina instead. Girls grow into women, and only women can have babies. Babies grow inside the mother's body and pass through the vagina when they're ready to be born.

FACTS

Answer your toddler's questions in a straightforward manner:

Q: "Why is Daddy's penis so big and mine so small?"

A: "Daddy is bigger everywhere. When you grow up, your feet, hands, and penis will be big, too."

Q: "Why don't I have a penis like Daddy?"

A: "Girls have a vagina. Boys have a penis."

Q: "Where do babies come from?"

A: "They grow inside a mommy's uterus until they're big enough to be born."

Parents will have to handle sexual issues in accordance with their personal beliefs. The best approach seems to be to teach youngsters the social rules: masturbation is something to be done in private. Telling toddlers that they should only touch themselves when they are in the bathroom or bedroom and must refrain when around other people can be as straightforward as telling them it's not nice to belch at the dinner table. If parents can be calm and matter-of-fact in discussing sexual issues, children will feel freer to turn to them with future questions.

Let Me Be Naked!

Lots of toddlers decide clothes are something they'd rather do without. Every time parents turn around, they find their little one has managed to wriggle out of her clothes again. The dislike of clothing isn't surprising. If children are warm enough, they will feel much more comfortable with the freedom of movement that comes from being in bare skin. It may not be a problem if toddlers want to run around the house in their birthday suits, though this can get pretty messy if they're not toilet-trained. (That's an incentive some parents have successfully used with determined strippers: If you use the toilet, birthday suits are allowed at home.)

Regardless of what policies are in force at home, parents should insist that toddlers observe the social niceties of keeping their clothes on outside the house. Even if *you* don't care, other parents will be offended. Dressing toddlers in blouses that button up the back, pants with belts, and double-knotting shoelaces can slow down little strippers so parents can catch them before they completely disrobe.

However, there's no need to be upset or to shame them about it. Since they're too young to comprehend adult views on the subject, instilling guilt might make them feel that their body is bad or dirty. It should be enough to firmly state, "Undressing outside the house is a no-no!" and to put their clothes back on again and again until they get the message. Don't comfort them if they howl; there are times when staying dressed is non-negotiable. Also, avoid attempting to make re-dressing fun. Otherwise, they may conclude that removing their clothes is a way to initiate a great game.

Potty Mouth

Children only use words they have heard someone else say. If the naughty words have come from outside the household, the best strategy is simply to ignore them, which ups the odds that they'll go away. Otherwise, you'll spark your toddler's curiosity about the magic of a word to make you laugh or get angry, increasing the likelihood he'll use it more often. Even if naughty words don't bother you, they can upset teachers, other parents, and children enough to dampen your youngster's social life.

If the offensive words don't disappear on their own, or if she's using words she's heard at home, eliminate these no-no's from the family vocabulary before they become a habit. Tell your child that saying that word is a no-no and provide a brief time-out. To help yourself and other family members clean up their vocabularies, say, "Oops, somebody just said a no-no," and put your child in charge of walking the offender to his or her bedroom for a brief time-out.

Parental Nudity

There's nothing to indicate that young toddlers are in any way harmed by exposure to parental nudity. However, they will undoubtedly have questions and may want to touch, too, so be prepared.

As children approach age three, many become uncomfortable about witnessing the nudity of the opposite-sexed parent. Whether this is because they are experiencing conflict about their emerging sexual feelings toward that parent, as many psychologists believe, or because the societal taboos they have absorbed conflict with what is happening at home, it is important to respect their wish for boundaries. Eliminate joint father-daughter and mother-son baths, and close the bathroom door and oust little ones of the opposite sex from the room before changing.

Sexual Abuse

The definition of sexual abuse accepted by most child welfare professionals includes acts of exposing youngsters to sexual stimuli that are developmentally inappropriate. Parents place themselves at risk of being accused if they allow toddlers to witness parents having sex, touch parents' genitals, watch R-rated movies, or view pornographic materials. Symptoms commonly displayed by sexually abused youngsters include:

- Mimicking adult sexual behavior
- Possessing sexual knowledge and vocabulary beyond what is normal for the child's age

- Engaging in persistent sexual play (commonly with dolls, other children, pets, or themselves)
- Having abrasions, pain, bleeding, or swelling of the mouth, genitals, or anus
- Having an obsession with touching or poking objects into the genitals or anus
- Incurring unexplained urinary or vaginal infections
- Suffering from a sexually transmitted disease
- Making direct or indirect comments about having been molested
- Displaying a sudden, exaggerated upset over being touched when having a diaper changed, being bathed or helped to the potty, or during physical examinations
- Suddenly manifesting phobias or exaggerated fearfulness around particular people or in specific locations
- Experiencing frequent nightmares

If a parent suspects sexual abuse and there is no physical evidence, discovering the truth can be difficult. Given children's propensity for saying what they think parents want to hear, and the ease with which false memories are implanted, it's best to consult a professional with expertise in interviewing children and let him or her ask the questions.

ALERT

Youngsters need not be physically injured during molestation to suffer severe psychological repercussions. The aura of secrecy can be upsetting. Threats of retaliation against the child or a loved one for revealing what has transpired can produce significant trauma. If you suspect sexual abuse, consult a professional immediately.

Protection Against Sexual Predators

It is so easy for adults to manipulate and physically overpower toddlers that trying to teach them about bad people who hurt children won't enable little ones to protect themselves—and it can terrify them. In 90 percent of sexual molestation cases, the abuser is well known to the child.

FACTS

In most states, citizens are obligated to notify the authorities of any kind of suspected child abuse. Failure to report abuse is punishable as a misdemeanor. By making a report you are not acting as judge and jury. You can ask to remain anonymous. The police or child welfare workers will decide whether the reported suspicions warrant an investigation. For further information, or to obtain the phone number for reporting in your state, call ☎800-4 A CHILD (800-422-4453).

The concept of keeping secrets is hard enough for toddlers to grasp. Don't complicate it by urging them to keep secrets about birthday surprises or anything else. It will be impossible for them to differentiate secrets that are okay from secrets that are not okay. When youngsters are old enough to understand, they can be taught that some secrets are okay and others are not, and that they must inform you immediately if someone tries to get them to keep a secret from you. In the meantime:

- Keep track of his whereabouts at every moment and leaving him with trustworthy caregivers.
- Instruct your older toddler to be sure to tell you if anyone touches her in a way she doesn't like.
- Teach your child the correct names of all body parts, including "penis" and "vagina," so if something untoward does occur, he will have the words he needs to communicate.

Societies Differ

Exactly what constitutes abuse? In societies where families sleep in the same room, youngsters routinely witness parents' sexual intimacies without ill effect. However, children are born imitators, and their playground re-enactment of bedroom scenes may be a problem in countries with more conservative sexual norms.

In Western societies any unnecessary touching of genitals is regarded as abuse. When youngsters reach adolescence and reflect on what transpired, they realize that a sacred parent-child trust was broken. Many spend their lives trying to heal from the devastation.

CHAPTER 4

Brain Power

In this school of life, the most important learning takes place in the principal schoolhouse: the home. The textbooks are the objects around toddlers and the events that transpire as they make their way through each day. Parents and caregivers are the principal teachers. The majority of lessons occur via independent study. As toddlers look, listen, prod, poke, wave, clang, roll, tear, bang, pat, sniff, and mimic others, they learn. Field trips, including everything from walking down the block to accompanying parents on errands, enrich the curriculum by giving them glimpses of the greater world.

Absorbent Minds

Toddlers' ability to soak up vast quantities of information is legendary. Maria Montessori, the founder of the famous developmentally-based Montessori schools, calls the early childhood years, the time of the "Absorbent Mind." More brain growth occurs during these twenty-four months than during any other period. The combination of brain development and daily learning accounts for their dramatic gains in understanding, remembering, thinking, reasoning, and solving problems. In two short years, the foundation is laid for all future learning.

Daily Living Skills

Between twelve and thirty-six months, the educational curriculum for toddlers is focused on learning important daily living skills. These skills include washing their hands, eating, putting on their clothes, picking up their toys, brushing their teeth, and using the toilet.

But these important units of instruction constitute only a fraction of the daily living skills little ones work on. When toddlers wipe the end table with a small rag while an adult dusts, or follow a parent around the lawn with a toy lawnmower while yard work is being done, they are exposed to some of the general methods and specific skills they will need to care for an entire house one day.

ESSENTIALS

Toddlers' dedication to learning is so intense that they are veritable superstudents. Many are so enthusiastic they don't want to pause to eat, sleep, or even use the bathroom.

Parents: The Roles

Just as toddlers are born students who are genetically programmed to learn, parents are programmed to teach. Without even stopping to consider what they are doing, parents automatically begin imparting the knowledge needed to master a host of important daily living skills.

Just look more closely at exactly what you do to teach a skill like hand washing, and you will realize that you can teach toddlers almost everything they need to know:

1. You explain exactly what needs to be done. ("Let's wash your hands before you eat.")
2. You give instructions. ("Put your hands all the way under the water." "Let's get some soap on the backs of your hands, too.")
3. You set limits to reinforce the idea that people must continue caring for themselves whether they feel like it at a given moment or not. ("I know you don't want your hands washed right now, but they're sticky.")
4. You provide feedback. ("That looks good." "Oops, your hands still have some spots of chocolate. We need to get those off, too.")
5. You help when your child is having a hard time. ("Try rubbing your hands together." "Let's put on a little more soap.")

As toddlers progress, parents do less for them and spend more time monitoring and giving feedback to help them improve. Parents still need to participate actively in helping three-year-olds with basic self-care skills, but youngsters age one to three can make great progress in handling many self-care tasks.

Parents: The Responsibility

It's given that you will often feel less than enthusiastic about your endless teaching duties. Sometimes you will be as discouraged as a classroom teacher on a Friday afternoon in May. Even educators voted Teacher of the Year are sometimes overwhelmed by their students' apparent failure to grasp what they are trying to teach.

Doubts about having entered the child-rearing business may surface when a parent walks into the bathroom and discovers water all over the floor and dripping down the walls while a proud toddler stands in the middle of a puddle, drying her freshly washed hands. Or when the tot has decided to change clothes and is now clad in an inside-out shirt, mismatched socks, shoes that are on the wrong feet, and no pants.

At such moments it is easy to be so impressed by the extra work that the toddler has caused that her accomplishment is forgotten or, even worse, belittled. But it is important to acknowledge the toddler's initiative in tackling these kinds of self-assigned homework tasks, even if you don't feel inclined to award extra credit for a project so poorly done.

Making an A

Daily living skills are like math problems. Although there may be several routes to solving a problem and there may be more than one correct answer, there are definitely right and wrong ways to do things. The end result can be very good, satisfactory, mediocre, or very far from the mark.

Often students approach a math problem correctly and still get the answer wrong. With daily living skills, toddlers can go through all the right motions with soap and water, make a giant mess, and still not get their hands clean. Mistakes often occur because the task was simply too advanced for the toddler to handle alone or perhaps he misunderstood the directions or needed more instruction and more practice. You must remember that no toddler wants to fail or make a poor grade. In fact, every child wants to do things correctly, to make an *A* in his own, as well as in his parent's, eyes. When things go wrong, you need to affirm the toddler's efforts, decide what the toddler needs to learn to improve, and dedicate yourself to giving remedial instruction.

And of course, you will have to clean up many toddler messes. But since cleaning up is yet another daily living skill, be sure to enlist your toddler's assistance so he can begin learning how.

Problem-Solving Skills

Since there are right and wrong ways to wash hands, brush teeth, get dressed, pick up toys, and so on, parents must actively teach and constantly give feedback to help toddlers progress in mastering daily living skills. However, when it comes to mastering other intellectual tasks, it is important to let them do the work by themselves instead of giving them the answers.

When children manipulate blocks, they learn about size and shape, weight and mass. They solve a series of visual-spatial relationship problems and develop hand-to-eye coordination in the process. If an adult jumps in and maneuvers the toddler's hand to help stack his blocks, he is distracted from the important preliminary lessons he was working on. He may not yet be ready to tackle the more advanced problem of using mass to counter the effects of gravity to create a stack.

ALERT

Hands-on help with toys may seem to speed learning, but it actually deprives toddlers of the opportunity to develop the intellect that comes from figuring out how to solve problems, the self-confidence that comes from solving problems without help, and the educational benefit that comes from learning how to learn.

When a child is engrossed in a toy, try not to interrupt. What looks like "just playing" is actually a toddler working at his own pace on important work! However, if a child is sitting down with a toy and becoming restless or bored with it, this is a good time to provide a demonstration. Show the toddler how to operate the toy while she watches, but don't grasp your child's hand to help her manipulate the toy. Give multiple demonstrations if you wish, but don't try to get your toddler to imitate you. This way the child doesn't feel pressured to perform. She can continue to use the toy in her own way and work at her own pace. She is free to attempt to imitate your way when she is ready, but she will have used her own mind to figure out the solution to a problem when she eventually copies your demonstration.

Math Skills

Important math skills for toddlers are much more complex than learning to say, "One, two, three." To most toddlers, counting aloud is no more than a series of nonsense syllables that mean about as much to them as *"Zog, jib, oomp."* The keys to math include understanding spatial relationships, understanding cause/effect logic, and learning to solve problems with physical objects. When children can point to objects as they count them, they've accomplished a major feat!

Different play activities emphasize different intellectual skills. Children practice convergent thinking skills when they work on tasks that have one right answer, such as fitting a piece into a puzzle, sorting blocks by color, or organizing nesting toys so they fit inside one another. Children practice divergent thinking skills when they work on tasks with many solutions, such as building things with blocks or engaging in creative games, such as playing house. Be sure your child has lots of opportunity to practice both!

Building Self-Esteem

When a parent physically moves a toddler's hand to provide assistance with a toy and then gushes, "You did it," the parent is reinforcing the idea that this what the toddler is to do. When the toddler attempts to repeat the action on his own, she may fail. If so, that will undermine her self-esteem. Toddlers often show that they are feeling overwhelmed by suddenly abandoning the toy the parent has been trying to help them with.

Consider what would happen if a teacher placed a kindergarten student in a third grade arithmetic class and gave her the correct answers to ensure she passed the first test. It wouldn't take the student long to realize that she can't do long division problems on her own. At that point, she might want to give up on math altogether. Similarly, after a well-meaning parent tries to ensure that a toddler solves a problem he hasn't yet even fathomed, the tot is likely to become discouraged if he discovers he can't do it himself.

On the other hand, if a third grade student is trying to learn long division and is stuck, she certainly deserves more intensive assistance!

Provide hands-on help if your child is trying to achieve a particular goal and is becoming frustrated, or signals a desire for help.

The Art of Teaching

Successful teaching is as much art as science. It requires watching the child's struggles and reactions carefully to make better decisions about when to present new material, and when and how to intervene. Parents who are too quick to extricate the toddler's ball from under the sofa deprive her of figuring it out for herself. On the other hand, parents who hang back too long may find that the youngster gets upset, gives up, and moves on to a less challenging activity, thereby learning to handle difficult problems by avoiding them together.

Sorting out a student's needs is not easy. Some toddlers become more easily frustrated than others. They may need a lot of verbal encouragement and require more hands-on help than calmer, more easygoing youngsters. Some toddlers are more independent. They may find verbal encouragement more of a distraction than a learning aid, and may become frustrated when parents try to provide hands-on help.

Never wrestle toys away from a toddler or say "Just a minute" while the youngster begs for his toy so you can do a demonstration. This kind of bullying isn't helpful to young students!

Toddlers will react according to their moods, too, so the student who tends to become frustrated easily may continue to work independently when feeling especially mellow. Independent youngsters may collapse into balls of helplessness if they're having a difficult day. Watch your interventions and your toddler's reactions carefully to determine when to step in and when to back off. If you find yourself saying things like, "You've been just playing all day. It's time to do x, y, or z now," you're not grasping the mental effort that goes into toddler "play"!

Educational Toys

Ah, it would be so easy to move your toddler's arm or hand or finger to show her exactly what motions to make to operate a toy. But every toy is educational, so don't take the education out of the fun! Unless your child has a physical disability or is so frustrated that it looks as if she's about to give up, confine yourself to picking up the toy yourself and demonstrating. Then let your child tackle the problem again in hopes she can use her own mind to figure out how it works; for example:

- How much pressure must be used to push the button so the buzzer will sound
- How far to pull the string to make the doll talk
- How high to lift the mallet to make the xylophone notes play
- How to turn and position the puzzle piece to fit it into the slot
- How to turn the crank to make the jack-in-the-box pop up
- How to steady and balance the blocks to make a stack
- How to create enough friction to make a toy car zoom across the floor

When it comes to playing with toys, avoid saying, "Do it this way," followed by praise for doing it "right." Save those phrases for daily living skills.

Crafts: Not for Toddlers

Craft *materials* are great for toddlers to play with. So pull out the paste, sparkles, markers, paper, cotton balls, pipe cleaners, play dough, Popsicle sticks, paper plates, and paints. As they manipulate the textures and colors and sizes and shapes, they'll learn a lot. Just don't try to get your toddler to use them to create a craft *project* of your (or anyone else's) imagining. The finished product may mean a lot to you, but it probably won't mean much to him. Toddlers are oriented toward the "doing," not the "having done." Let them learn by interacting with the materials in their own way. Don't try to direct or control them.

"All Gone!"

It is hard for toddlers to grasp the concept of "all gone." For example, to a toddler, a peanut butter *jar* is the same thing as *peanut butter*. She can't comprehend that the empty jar means she can't have a peanut butter sandwich. To help her learn the difference:

- Let her explore the empty peanut butter jar.
- Try adopting her mindset and help her solve the problem by walking her through the steps: Hand her the peanut butter jar and a bread knife and let her work on it.
- Be sure to also provide an emotional outlet by helping the toddler to express her frustrations. This can help her loosen her mental grip on the concept "Mommy's mean and won't give me a peanut butter sandwich" so she can learn, "I'm angry because the peanut butter is all gone."
- Remain on your toddler's side when discussing this mini-disaster, and say, "Where's the peanut butter? You mean it's all gone? No more peanut butter! But my baby wants some! Wait! I know where it is. It's at the store. We need to go to the store to get peanut butter for you. But what are we going to do *now?* My baby wants peanut butter now! She could have some crackers. No? You only want peanut butter? It's all gone. We have to buy more peanut butter at the store."

If you react to your toddler's upsets by becoming upset and angry, you may only confirm her belief that you are purposely withholding the goodies. You need to be patient while explaining (again and again), "It's all gone." The combination of being allowed to look to see for herself and hearing a calm explanation will eventually help her realize that the problem isn't the parent's stubborn insistence on depriving her of what she wants.

The Concept of Categories

A lot of the intellectual work toddlers engage in involves learning to put objects and events into categories. For instance:

- Dogs, cats, birds, and fish belong to the category of animals.
- Dogs, neighbors, and classmates belong to the category of friends.
- Dogs, cats, mice, and horses belong to the category of four-legged animals.

Parents automatically teach categories all the time without even thinking about it. "What kind of vegetable should I serve for dinner?" they wonder aloud. "I think I'll cook some peas." This communicates that peas are vegetables, a category of food that is served at dinner. As toddlers learn the many different ways particular objects and actions can be categorized, they learn more about them. Understanding different ways that objects and events can be categorized forms the basis of abstract reasoning. Some educators consider abstract reasoning to be the highest form of intelligence.

FACTS

When people look at one object and can imagine other uses for it, they engage in the kind of creative thought that leads to innovations. Innovations have brought human beings from campfires to microwaves, from horses to jet planes. To help youngsters develop intellectually, parents should target their teaching efforts to helping them learn different ways to categorize objects.

For instance, when toddlers learn that shoes are worn on feet and hats cover heads, they learn specific facts about two concrete objects: shoes and hats. Once youngsters comprehend the basic way in which two objects are *similar*—they both belong to a category called "clothes"— they have learned an abstract concept. "Clothes" doesn't refer to any one thing, but to a group of objects that are alike in one important respect: they protect or adorn the body.

Once children grasp an abstract concept like "clothes," it suddenly becomes possible for them to engage in creative thought. They can imagine ways to transform other objects into clothes and can place an upside-down pan on their head to turn it into a hat. A small blanket tossed over the shoulders can become a cape.

At first, little ones may categorize all four-legged creatures as "dogs." When parents show them pictures of dogs, point out dogs on the street, and point out pictures of other four-legged animals and teach the names, toddlers are soon able to tell the difference between dogs and other animals. In fact, they will become so adept at categorizing that if they see pictures of different dogs that bear little resemblance to one another, they will still recognize that they are all dogs.

Any object can belong to many different categories. With help, toddlers eventually learn:

- That a dog and a cow both belong in the category of animals
- That a dog, a cat, and a parakeet are all pets
- That a dog can be a friend, a protector, a danger, or a nuisance, depending on the circumstances

Learning about higher-level categories that require finer differentiation and more specific knowledge will take place in school. The information that dogs, whales, and humans are all mammals usually isn't taught until third grade, though many toddlers would be capable of learning this if someone took the time to teach them.

By age three, toddlers should be familiar with many objects and a few concepts belonging to the following categories:

- Parts of the body
- Family members
- Clothes
- Rooms of the house
- Foods
- Toys
- Animals
- Colors
- Shapes

- Emotions (happy, sad, angry, scared)
- Physical states (tired, hungry, thirsty, sore throat, tummy ache)
- Occupations (doctor, teacher, bus driver, firefighter, police officer)
- Comparisons (different, the same, good, better, worse, more, less)
- Locations (up, down, under, over, inside, next to, near, far)
- Size (big, small)
- Quantity (many, a few, none)
- Time relationships (now, later, first, then, before, after)
- Temperature (hot, cold, warm, cool)

Learning from Books

One of the reasons that picture books are so important for toddler's intellectual development is that they give parents a convenient way to teach children about a wider variety of categories. By age twelve months, children are ready for books that have information about a particular topic, such as animals, nature, or transportation. For example, a book on transportation may have a picture of airplanes, cars, boats, helicopters, space ships, and so on, to help children understand that these different objects are alike in an important respect: they are machines that move people and objects from one place to another. By age two children are usually ready for books that have simple stories. A book about a trip on an airplane will teach children about related objects and activities, from pilots to seat belts and from takeoffs to landings.

Category Errors

Toddlers make some predictable errors in categorization. For instance, many youngsters put every grown man they see into the category of "daddy." To help them understand that "daddies" and "men" belong to two different categories, follow these tips:

1. Correct their error.
2. Seize opportunities to point out various men over the next few days and explain that the daddies are men with children.

3. Look at pictures in books and point out that bucks and fawns, male cats and kittens, bulls and calves all belong to the categories of animal "daddies" or "children."

4. While looking at pictures in books, help them grasp the many other ways men can be categorized: as tall, medium, and short (when categorized by height); as fat, average, thin, or skinny (when categorized by weight); as grandfathers, husbands, fathers, or sons (depending on their relationship to others); as old men, young men, and teenagers (depending on their ages).

Teaching Colors

Parents should teach toddlers the names of basic colors. Even adults may not be able to agree about whether the sofa is gray or blue, or blue or green. Muddy and mixed colors can also confuse toddlers, so parents should stick to the basic colors like red, yellow, blue, and green. Variations like chartreuse and magenta may be better left for the preschool and kindergarten crowd. Here are tips for teaching colors:

- Use the names for colors in everyday conversation. ("See the white cat?" "Hand me your red shirt." "Those yellow dandelions are so pretty.")
- Have children help sort laundry into piles of white and colored clothes.
- Provide your child with crayons and markers for coloring.
- Show them how to sort their toys into different color piles.
- When toddlers are finger-painting or coloring Easter eggs, demonstrate how some colors can be mixed to create others.
- Play the "find the color" game in the car. See how many red things the two of you can find, then how many green things, and so on. Prepare for this game by having some cards with different colors on them, so the child can be sure about which color he is to look for.
- Read *Baby's Colors* by Neil Ricklen (Little Simon, 1996), a board book for young toddlers. Another toddler favorite is *Brown Bear, Brown Bear, What Do You See?* by Eric Carle, illustrator (Henry Holt & Company, 1996).

Shapes

Toddlers need to learn to recognize basic shapes, including squares, circles, triangles, hearts, diamonds, and rectangles. (Once a child masters two shapes, you can add more.) Here are some tips for teaching shapes:

- Cut the basic shapes out of construction paper, draw them on blank note cards, or cut them out of cookie dough and bake them. They should be about 2 inches in diameter.
- Focus on two shapes at a time.
- Explain, "This one is a square. Here's another square. But this one is a circle." Holding a toddler's index finger while tracing the shapes can aid comprehension and help some youngsters remember them.
- Ask the toddler to point to the square, hand you the card with the square on it, or hand you the cookie shaped like a square. Or, if the child can talk, hold up a card or cookie and ask the child to say the name of the shape.
- As you go through the day, point out other objects shaped like circles and squares, such as doorknobs, wheels, boxes, windows, tabletops, etc.
- Have older toddlers try to draw shapes. Don't expect much success.

Locations

Learning words like *up, above, down, under, over, inside, next to, near, far,* and so on, is very hard for toddlers. Use them in your everyday expressions. Take some time for concentrated teaching, too:

Comment about locations often. ("The milk is in the refrigerator." "The milk is on top of the counter." "The milk is all over the floor!")

Present two concepts. Pick up an object (such as a book) and a container (such as a box). "The book is *in* the box. The apple is *on top* *of* the box." Then ask, "Where is the book?" If the child responds by going over to retrieve the book, simply say, "Yes, the book was *in* the box. Can you put it *on top of* the box?" Keep these games fun! Stop when your toddler loses interest.

Point out location relationships in picture books. ("The dog is in the house." "The dog is on top of his house." "The dog is next to the boy.")

Focus your child's attention on location relationships. When reading books, maintain a chatty narrative. "Where is the dog? Is he in the house? Yes, he's inside the house." "Where is the boy? There he is. Is he on top of the house? No, he's inside the house."

Read *The Foot Book* by Dr. Seuss. (Random House, 1996).

FACTS

Toddlers cannot comprehend that some quantities are the same even though they look different. For instance, an adult can pour liquid from a tall narrow glass into a short fat one to show that both glasses hold the same quantity. Still, toddlers will still say that the tall narrow glass holds more than the short fat one.

Organizing

Organizing household possessions teaches children to categorize, so having them assist with many routine household chores gives them a lot of practice. As soon as they are old enough, ask them to help you with tasks such as matching socks, putting toys into the correct containers before putting them into the toy box, putting clean silverware into the correct compartment in the drawer, sorting cans and bottles and putting them into the correct recycling bin, and putting vegetables into the refrigerator when you return from grocery shopping.

Memory Bank Deposits

Being able to store and retrieve information keeps people from having to constantly relearn everything by enabling them to build on previous knowledge. Therefore, memory is related to intelligence. Remembering is a skill toddlers develop with maturity and practice. Remembering is a two-step process: storing information in the brain, then plucking it back out of storage.

There are two types of memory: short term and long term. Most everyday information goes into the short-term memory bank, where it remains briefly before disappearing. If information is repeated often enough, it gets moved from short-term memory into long-term memory, although a single, very intense experience sometimes creates an enduring memory.

The average adult can store about seven bits of information in short-term memory at a time—the length of a phone number. Because they have spent years encountering the same information again and again, adults have transferred massive amounts of data from short-term memory into their long-term memory. Therefore, they can readily recall amazing amounts of information, such as which bureau drawer holds the socks or that the plates are kept in a particular cabinet.

Toddlers can have trouble retaining more than two bits of data. All of the thousands of bits of information toddlers encounter each day are still very new to them. Until any given piece of information is repeated often enough to be transferred to long-term memory, toddlers will continue to forget many things that parents consider very basic. Because they will find some objects and experiences particularly impressive, they will also remember small details that may surprise parents.

Fragile Memories

Although toddlers are able to remember more with each passing month, their memories remain fragile. "But you must remember Jonah. You played with him just last week," a parent tells her daughter. But no, she doesn't seem to remember. And when she sees Jonah again, she is as shy as if she were meeting him for the first time. Yet this same child remembers seeing the big green truck in the grocery store parking lot for ten seconds two weeks ago. Moreover, the ghouls and monsters that flitted across the TV screen when she was two suddenly come back to haunt her at age three, even though she didn't seem to be affected by them at the time and hasn't seen them for months.

By twelve months of age, an area of the brain called the hippocampus enables toddlers to remember events that occurred a few hours or a day before. And between twelve and eighteen months, children can engage in deferred imitation; that is, repeating someone's behavior hours, days, or weeks later.

False Memories

Memories not only slip away from toddlers with amazing ease, but it is easy to implant false ones in their highly impressionable minds, according to research reported in the journal of *Consciousness and Cognition* (1994) and the *American Journal of Psychology* (1998). For instance, when researchers told three- and four-year olds that an alligator had been eating an apple on an airplane, and later asked the children if they'd ever seen such a thing, they not only insisted that they had, they filled in the details: "He was under my bed and he was a pet and then when we was on the airplane he licked me right here[gesturing to a spot on his thigh]."

QUESTIONS?

What are false memories?
Toddlers have a hard time separating fantasy from reality. Children's inner imaginings mix with things they have heard or seen in the real world to create "false memories," or remembrances that bear little or no resemblance to anything that actually transpired.

Toddlers are easily manipulated. If parents falsely accuse their youngster of having done something wrong, the toddler may believe she in fact is guilty and end up apologizing! In conducting interrogations, ask your toddler a question once and live with whatever answers you get. If you ask a second time, you may get the answer you expect, but it's not likely to be more reliable.

Familiar Comforts

Since toddlers' poor memories make even things they've been exposed to many times seem new and different, their love of rituals and predictable routines is understandable, as is the tenacity with which they cling to familiar blankets, toys, and pacifiers. Just as adult travelers long for the comfort of familiar food after spending a few days surrounded by the heady stimulation of strange environments, recognized objects and routines offer toddlers a welcome respite by serving as comforting anchors.

Further, repetition helps toddlers move information into long-term memory. Hearing the same story night after night can be very trying for parents, but the continued exposure to the same words, phrases, and ideas increases the toddler's ability to remember them.

Rhyme and Reason

Research shows that toddlers who hear the same nursery rhymes so often that they memorize them do better in school later on. The repetition is believed to help them to develop better memories—not just for the familiar rhymes, but also for remembering things in general. Break out the Mother Goose book and start reading! Nursery rhymes are invaluable teaching devices for several reasons:

- Rhythms appeal to toddlers.
- Hearing the same short poems over and over helps youngsters focus on individual words so they can eventually sort out their meanings.
- The rhymes help them notice how small changes in sound create completely different meanings (like between "hot" and "pot" in "Pease Porridge Hot").
- Children who can recite nursery rhymes by heart do better in reading at school than toddlers with less exposure.

Nursery rhymes that involve pairing movements and words, such as in "This Little Piggy" and "Itsy Bitsy Spider" are called "finger play." The movements help children decipher the meanings of the words while teaching them concepts, such as *up* and *down* (as when children move their fingers to show the spider going up the waterspout before swooping their arms down to show what happens when rain washes the spider out).

Here are a couple of classic finger-play poems your child will love:

♪ This Little Piggy

This little piggy went to market (wiggle your child's big toe)
This little piggy stayed home (wiggle the second toe)
This little piggy ate roast beef (wiggle the third toe)
This little piggy ate none (wiggle the fourth toe)
This little piggy cried "wee, wee, wee" all the way home! (wiggle the little
     toe, then tickle up your child's leg) ♫

♪ Pat-a-Cake

Pat-a-cake, pat-a-cake, baker's man (holding your child on your lap, clap
     her hands together in the rhythm of the verse)
Bake me a cake as fast as you can
Pat it, and roll it . . . (roll her arms)
And mark it with a B (hold her hand and use it like a pen to draw
     a B on her tummy)
And throw it in the oven for Baby and me! (throw your arms open) ♫

When you need someone else to take over, put on a top kiddie hit,
like *Time to Sing* (Center for Creative Play)—it's got everything from
"One, Two, Buckle My Shoe" to "The Wheels on the Bus."

Memory Gaps

A toddler walks into the day care center he attends two days a week,
takes one look at the teacher he's known for a year, and begins
screaming as if he's never seen this stranger before. He hugs his blanket
for comfort, then settles down as soon as he is handed a toy he
recognizes or begins a familiar activity.

Because toddlers attending day care part-time don't experience the
people and routines frequently cnough to bc able to retain many
memories from week to week, they may find each new encounter almost
as overwhelming as the first. Attending day care for a half day four times
a week can be easier for them than attending for two full days.

The fragility of toddler memories has its benefits, too. If a child spits
out a new food today, try it again in a week or two. There's a good
chance she won't remember she didn't like it!

FACTS

Programs like Head Start help children by providing lots of opportunity to interact with objects and people. The educational boost helps graduates to hold their own academically throughout their school career! Since 1965, Head Start has served millions of children, including those with mental retardation, physical handicaps, emotional disturbances, speech and language impairments, and learning disabilities. For information, see *ww2.acf.dhhs.gov/programs/hsb* or call (202) 205-8572.

Boosting IQ

Psychologists have long known that depressed parents interact with and talk to their children less, which can slow the development of communication skills. Research has shown that maternal depression also adversely affects toddlers' IQs. *The National Institute of Child Health and Human Development's News Alert* (September 1999) warns that children of depressed mothers perform more poorly on a range of intellectual measures, including school readiness and communication skills. Depressed parents should definitely see a therapist!

CHAPTER 5

The Road to Independence

The toddler years are a time of great emotional intensity. At no other age are the smiles quite so pure, the sadness so heartfelt, the rage so total, or the delight so genuine. Each small disappointment, fear, and frustration can produce tears of sadness or anger; then in the twinkling of an eye those frowns can turn to smiles once again!

The Roller Coaster Years

After experiencing the ready smiles and relatively easygoing attitudes of baby days, many parents are shocked when behavior markedly deteriorates as tots begin to walk. It is common for them suddenly to resist their parents' requests and directives at every turn. It's not just the newfound freedom that drives the sudden bouts of stubbornness. It's that walking turns the toddlers' world upside down—or vertical, as the case may be. Change, even change for the better, taxes the emotional reserves of human beings of all ages and is therefore stressful.

Shortly after learning to walk, toddlers are likely to:

- Repeatedly dissolve into tears over small frustrations
- Strike out when they are angry
- Be stubborn and uncooperative
- Have a hard time falling asleep
- Wake up crying during the night
- Show other signs of stress, such as more frequent infections

Don't worry that you've created a monster. You can expect the sunnier personality to reappear when the novelty of walking wears off and toddlers have adjusted to the many changes mobility has introduced into their life. Then during the "terrible twos" (or "terrific twos," depending on your point of view), conflict heats up in earnest as struggles over autonomy take center stage.

But when the terrible twos are successfully negotiated, toddlers trust themselves as well as their parents. At that point, youngsters will still dislike many of their parents' limits and rules. They may fuss some and try to get them to change their minds. But even if they're at a loss to understand the reasons for many of their parents' more disappointing decisions, they comply more often than not.

Experience as Teacher

Between ages one and three toddlers make great strides in mastering their careening emotions. In this case, "familiarity breeds content," so toddlers encounter fewer new things that inspire fear. They know what to expect and how to behave in many situations, and they have learned to follow most of the family routines and rules. Still, even older toddlers may become upset when confronting events they find especially distressing—for instance, when Mom and Dad leave them with a sitter and walk out the door. If the toddlers have been raised in a secure and stable environment, experience will have taught them that they are not being abandoned. Although youngsters nearing their third birthday still break lots of household rules and resist routines at times, they bump into fewer unexpected no-no's while toddling through the house each day. That alone makes parenting far easier.

Growing Bodies

The increased maturity of the frontal lobes of the brain plays a role in children's ever-improving emotional control, too. These physical changes render older toddlers less impulsive and more able to plan ahead, tolerate frustration, and delay gratification. Further, as youngsters develop physically, their skin becomes somewhat less sensitive, their digestive system works better, and their sleep patterns stabilize. Perhaps hunger pangs don't strike with such intensity at age three as at age one, so a minute spent waiting seems less like a year . . . and more like only half a year!

FACTS

Emotional development during the toddler years means that as they approach age three, they shouldn't routinely dissolve into tears while having to wait to have their needs and desires satisfied. Although waiting is still hard for them, they react less intensely to small stresses but still frequently become overwhelmed and remain overly emotional by adult standards.

A Growing Trust

Being able to trust caregivers enough to accept their comfort, help, rules, and guidance is critical for toddlers' overall emotional well-being. This foundation of trust should have been established during infancy through the unwavering love and nurturing devotion of parents and other caregivers. Toddlers' growing trust in themselves complicates their trust in parents, which wanes as toddlers put more trust in their own feelings, thoughts, and ideas. Emotional swings intensify as youngsters try to balance their trust in themselves and in their parents.

The "Cookie God" or primary caregiver who rules the household tumbles from grace as toddlers realize that the cookie they wanted still exists and the parent with the power to produce it is refusing to hand it over on cue. Because toddlers can't tell the difference between their wants and their needs, they become frustrated when they want a cookie and their path is blocked by a parent's determination that they don't need one. Further, the "Cookie God" is the same adult who deprives them in lots of other horrid ways: forbidding them to eat the newspaper, write on the walls, stop up the sink, and turn on the water faucet—all of which bring so much joy to toddlers.

In order to maintain a strong relationship when trust wanes during the toddler years:

- Be true to your word.
- Invite toddlers to participate in decisions that affect them by giving them choices.
- Soothe upsets by cuddling, kissing, and speaking kindly.
- Communicate your understanding that some rules and limits are upsetting.
- Let your child's upset be her own. Don't let the situation escalate by becoming upset yourself.
- Let your child know you love him even if you dislike some of the things he does (criticize the behavior not the child).
- Show with your actions that your love and respect for her continue even when you are angry with her.
- Apologize if you become harsh and critical—this will help your child learn it is okay to make mistakes and to apologize for them.
- Understand that if you are the recipient of your child's worst scenes, it is because you are the person she trusts most.

The Parenting Challenge

Toddlers need to flex their psychic muscles in order to become more autonomous, or more able to direct their own behavior. Nevertheless, the toddler power surges that occur after learning to walk, and again during the third year of life, definitely complicate parenting. Virtually overnight, they can transform child rearing from a joy to a highly demanding endeavor.

Adults who have trouble with self-assertion, feel overwhelmed by conflict, or look to their youngster to affirm their sense of self-worth may find parenting a toddler a special burden. It is draining to tangle with a power-tripping youngster several times a day—not to mention every hour. It's hard for parents not to take the struggles personally when they are the targets of toddler wrath. It's important for parents to remember that the stage of development is driving the behavior—children are not "choosing" to create problems—and that their toddler is not railing against them but against the injustices of life itself.

Just when a youngster is feeling oh-so-powerful, he finds he can't do a simple task like put his shoes on by himself. He can't float his toy car in the toilet without a big person appearing at the door to stop him. Life keeps reminding him he's not powerful at all.

FACTS

Developmental psychologists agree that a nurturing parent-child relationship is critical for toddlers. This single relationship influences youngsters' relationships with other authority figures from today's teachers to tomorrow's bosses. It also impacts how they get along with siblings, peers, friends, and future mates.

A parent may feel her youngster doesn't trust her to know what's best, given that the tot works hard to reverse so many of her decisions. In a sense, that's true. Toddlers often trust their own knowledge about what is in their best interest more than their parents'. Realizing they are still dependent on others to make decisions and handle even the most basic aspects of their care delivers continuing blows to a budding ego.

At the same time the fear that "If I can do it myself, Mommy might stop taking care of me" looms large. Thus, failure highlights their inabilities while success threatens their relationship with parents. Accepting the disappointing reality that their newfound power to walk hasn't transformed them into an all-knowing god, and that being able to do more for themselves doesn't mean they will lose their parents' love, takes time.

Bonding

Some parents worry that lots of arguing and defiance from their toddlers reflects weak emotional attachment or insufficient bonding. In most cases the truth lies elsewhere. It is their abiding *trust* in parents that enables toddlers to pit their will against their parents' one minute and relax in their arms the next.

When children can make a parent a target of their bad moods, then turn to that same parent for comfort, it usually means that they trust the parent not to retaliate. In the past, parenting experts were adamant that caretakers should avoid being too solicitous or indulgent. With the recognition of the importance of trust the advice has changed. Rather than spoiling infants and toddlers by giving them too much time and attention, it is now believed that lots of attention makes children more emotionally secure, enabling them to tolerate more independence sooner. Experts also believe that toddlers more readily cope with rules, disappointments, and frustrations from a trusted caregiver who is loving and kind when enforcing limits.

Parents as Safe Havens

Psychologist Harry Harlow (1906–1981) conducted groundbreaking research that demonstrated how critical a nurturing parent is for children's emotional development. His studies on young monkeys have important implications for child rearing. Harlow separated newborn monkeys from their parents and raised them in cages that were barren except for a wire mesh structure. When the little orphans nursed from a baby bottle, they would cling to the wire mesh as if it were a mother.

Despite adequate nutrition it soon became evident that the emotional development of the little ones was seriously distorted. When Harlow placed something frightening in a cage, such as a noisy wind-up toy, each orphan would flee to a corner, hide its face, and tremble in terror, unable to summon the courage to approach the object for a closer look. Later, when other baby monkeys were placed in the cage of a little orphan, it didn't know how to play or interact with them. When the deprived orphans grew up, their emotional development was so stunted they couldn't even figure out how to mate.

Young monkeys raised with their mothers were much more able to cope with the wind-up toy trauma. They fled to their mothers for comfort when the frightening toy first appeared but soon became brave enough to approach it. Each time they lost courage, they ran back to their mothers for support and to regroup. Within moments they were happily playing with the new toy.

The parent-child dynamics of these monkeys, Harlow realized, mirrors what happens in the human world. A caregiver to whom the toddler is attached serves as the child's island of safety when a stranger comes into the house or when she feels frightened for any reason. Once a frightened child has spent a few moments with her human security blanket, she ventures forth with renewed courage.

Stranger Anxiety

Shy, fearful behavior around strangers (meaning anyone other than the immediate family and trusted caregivers) intensifies around twelve months of age. It gradually lessens and disappears by age three except in the shiest youngsters. Negative reactions during this period tend to be more pronounced toward men than women, and least pronounced toward other children.

When a child is distressed about a "stranger" (who can actually be a relative or neighbor the child has met many times before), hold her on your lap to help her feel safe and don't pressure her to interact. Once out of the limelight and given time to observe, most toddlers grow bolder about approaching household guests. Tell Aunt Emily and Uncle Bob not to take the rejection personally.

ESSENTIALS

Support your child's desire not to be touched by saying, "He doesn't want to be touched right now. He'll let you know when he's ready." Give your child the words to hold others at bay by instructing him, "Can you say, 'I don't like that. Please stop.' Can you say, 'Stop'?"

This is not the time to teach toddlers about "dangerous" strangers, or "good" versus "bad" touching. They're too young to understand these concepts, and emphasizing the issue may make them more afraid of people than they already are. Instead, begin teaching limits by helping children ward off *any* intrusive actions, including hugs and kisses from "strangers," like Aunt Tanya and Great-grandpa David, and either kisses or blows from a toddler friend.

Contact Comfort

Harlow's studies on young monkeys yielded another important finding: Little orphans deprived of the warmth of a live mother monkey were less healthy than their peers. Researchers have found that this, too, has parallels in the world of humans. Youngsters in orphanages often have poor weight gain. Some sicken and die if they are not held and cuddled regularly, even if they are otherwise cared for. This medical condition is called "failure to thrive."

Experts now agree that loving human touch, "contact comfort," is a basic need, as important as food and water for physical and emotional development. Contact comfort has important health benefits for people of all ages. By learning to reach out for a hug, toddlers learn a skill that will help them stay healthy!

Soothing Touches

When young toddlers are upset, words alone aren't enough to comfort them because of their limited comprehension of speech. They need:

- A shoulder to cry on when they are sad
- A lap to bury their faces in when they are afraid
- Arms to hug them and provide comfort and reassurance
- Back rubs to soothe them when they are ill
- Tickles to cheer them up

Hugging, kissing, rocking, rubbing, and cuddling have relaxing and soothing physical effects. A toddler's pulse rate slows and respiration becomes more even. Endorphins released into the bloodstream provide a sense of well-being. Soothing touches are also important for building trust and strengthening the child's emotional attachment to the primary caregiver. Studies show that youngsters in intensive care recover more rapidly if they are regularly massaged, stroked, held, or otherwise able to reap the benefits of human touch.

Holding It Together

The last thing enraged toddlers may want is to be held and comforted, especially if they are furious with the person who is trying to do the comforting. Even if out-of-control youngsters attempt to pull away, it can help them to be physically held. They are relieved that someone can contain the anger that feels so huge and overwhelming to them. It is as frightening to a toddler to be out of control as it is to an adult.

 **SSENTIALS**

To help your toddler feel better about the wildness within her, read *Where the Wild Things Are* by Maurice Sendak (HarperCollins Juvenile Books, 1988). It can comfort her to know she's not alone. She may also enjoy hearing *Alexander and the Terrible, Horrible, No Good, Very Bad Day* by Judith Viorst (Aladdin Paperbacks, 1987).

Since human touch is critical for both physical health and emotional development, parents should try to help standoffish toddlers overcome their resistance to being cuddled. Even if youngsters resist loving hugs and affectionate cuddles, they may respond enthusiastically to playing tickling games, having their back rubbed, having their hair tousled, or having their shoulders patted. As they become more comfortable with these less emotionally intense kinds of physical contact that give them a greater sense of control, they may be open to more direct and prolonged affectionate contact.

Caregivers must be sensitive and responsive to toddlers' moods. Besides noting when they are calmer and more relaxed, which may mean they are more receptive to being touched, parents should back off when the toddler expresses an inclination to retreat. Hugging by force is a no-no. Like infants, toddlers signal their desire for emotional distance by looking away. For instance, when being bounced on a hip, toddlers break eye contact when they want the bouncing to end. Next, they try to escape. They may go limp (since the dead weight makes them harder to carry), then try to slide to the ground. And if that doesn't work, they whimper, cry, scream, stiffen, and arch their backs in an effort to free themselves.

These kinds of physical struggles make toddlers more wary of being held, as well they should. Imagine if someone five times your size, even if it were someone you loved, had you locked in an embrace against your will and wouldn't let go, no matter how much you begged or pleaded! It's not surprising that toddlers with overbearing parents or relatives become increasingly standoffish.

On the other hand, physically containing an out-of-control toddler by holding her firmly can reassure her immensely. It helps to know that a big person can safely contain those scary emotions that have taken her over.

Comfort Objects

Harlow also found that if an orphan monkey was raised with two wire structures in the cage, a plain one and one that was wrapped in a soft blanket, the baby monkey chose to cling to the soft one when nursing.

Then, when a frightening toy or a group of baby monkeys was placed in the cage, the orphan again went to the soft "surrogate mother" for comfort. The blanket didn't make up for a live mom, but these little monkeys weren't nearly so impaired as those raised with only a plain wire structure. The comfort they were able to derive from the soft blanket made the difference.

In the human world, it's common for toddlers to become so attached to a particular object they can't bear to be separated from it. The object doesn't have to be something soft, like a blanket. Some youngsters develop affection for a toy truck or flashlight. What matters is the bond the child has formed with it. These special objects help toddlers cope with situations that require a separation from their parent, such as going to day care or to bed.

QUESTIONS?

What is a comfort object?
A comfort or transitional object is the popular term for a blanket, piece of clothing, toy, or other object that serves as a child's "surrogate mother." If your child derives comfort from one, respect this important relationship!

Parents may be frustrated if their toddler insists on having the same toy at his side every moment of the day and sleeps with it at night. As the months go by and their child's grip on Mr. Teddy or his "blankie" remains as tight as ever, they begin to picture their toddler walking up to the podium at high school graduation clutching the bedraggled toy under his arm.

Fortunately, no such incident has ever been recorded, and there's no reason to believe your darling will be the first! The social pressures of kindergarten can be counted on to bring a quick end to the love affair with an inanimate object—at least in public. Lots of teens still cuddle their teddy at night, so don't worry about your child's need for a comfort object, and don't push your child to relinquish it. If your child seems overly attached to a comfort object, try to give more hugs and spend more time cuddling.

Feelings 101

Much of the improvement in emotional control that takes place during the toddler years is due to youngsters' enhanced ability to communicate. As toddlers become more adept at labeling their feelings and communicating their needs, they react less impulsively. Youngsters who cannot talk out their feelings can only act them out. As they become more able to express their feelings in words, they don't have to rely on crying to signal their hunger, thirst, need for a diaper change, desire to be held, or wish to play with a particular toy. Toddlers are not able to identify their feelings with much accuracy. They simply experience a physical or psychological discomfort and they react.

Parents and other caregivers need to teach toddlers to recognize their emotional and physical states and to use the vocabulary of feelings to express discomfort. What is obvious to an adult is not at all obvious to a little person. Parents need to make it a habit to tell toddlers what they are feeling before attempting to help with whatever is upsetting them:

- "You're sad that I'm leaving." ("But I'll be back soon.")
- "You're frustrated with that puzzle." ("Do you want some help?")
- "You're happy that Daddy is home." ("Stay inside. He'll come inside in a minute.")
- "You're afraid of that clown." ("But he's just a man with makeup and paint on his face.")
- "You're angry because I won't let you play in the sandbox." ("We need to think of some other fun thing for you to do.")

Unhappy Feelings

Unhappy feelings serve a useful purpose. They let human beings know that something is wrong or that something needs to be changed. These feelings help people determine the source of their distress with greater precision. Once they know exactly what is wrong, they are in a better position to figure out how to get their needs met and desires fulfilled.

Unhappy feelings indicate that something is wrong, but toddlers may not know what that something is. They may be bored but think they are hungry.

They may be tired but think they are angry at a toy. They may be feeling ill and think they are sad because their parent is talking on the telephone.

Parents must constantly provide corrections:

- "I don't think it's your brother that's upsetting you. I think you're tired."
- "Instead of a snack, I bet a diaper change will help you feel better."
- "Your new tooth is coming in. That's why so many things are bothering you today."

Once they are able to correctly identify their feelings, toddlers will be more able to figure out what to do to feel better.

Words of Comfort

As toddlers' language skills improve, words alone are often enough to help them feel better. Whether words are combined with hugs, parents should apply regular doses of soothing words when calming upset children. Children eventually learn to comfort themselves by being soothed and comforted by parents. With time and repetition the comforting words parents say become so much a part of their toddler, he will use them to comfort himself.

Tapes of crib monologues made after toddlers have been put in bed for the night show that, to comfort themselves, they repeat the words they've heard from parents, such as "It's okay" and "Go nigh-nigh now." Other soothing phrases parents can say to their child include the following:

- "We're going home soon."
- "You'll feel better after you eat something."
- "You'll see her again tomorrow."
- "You're more scared than hurt right now."
- "It may taste bad, but this medicine will help make you well."

Trusting others to provide verbal comfort will enable children to reach out to day care teachers, sitters, and other caregivers for help and solace. During their teenage years, a phone call to share troubles with a friend or a talk with an understanding teacher will provide emotional support. By sharing feelings with trusted family members and friends, adults have access to a lifelong source of important moral support. People never outgrow their need to be nurtured!

Words That Hurt

Normal children will try to fend off criticism to maintain a sense of dignity and self-worth. The problems are likely to escalate if parents shame them for being upset. If a parent routinely heaps criticism on an upset toddler to try to settle her down, the harsh words will eventually begin to echo in the child's mind in an effort to ward off unhappy feelings whenever she is upset.

Always respect your child's feelings—even the unpleasant ones. Since the words you say will echo in your child's mind for the rest of her life, be kind so your child can learn to be kind to herself!

Needless to say, that doesn't work very well. Toddlers' turmoil increases as they battle the belief that they are bad for feeling unhappy in the first place. Harsh comments made in an attempt to contain upset youngsters too often have the effect of compounding their distress. Critical comments may teach children not to verbalize their unhappiness, but that doesn't make the distress go away. The unhappiness lingers. Derogatory statements erode self-esteem. Statements that deny the reality of children's distress increase their confusion about what they are actually feeling. Instead of learning to use their feelings as a guide to getting their needs met, they end up feeling worse and don't know what to do to make things better.

Developing Initiative

Young toddlers may experience innate urges to explore and grow and master their environment, but some youngsters become so discouraged by the difficulties they encounter they begin to back away from hard tasks. When the many things toddlers do that anger their parents are added to all the things that frustrate toddlers because they can't do them well, failure can begin to seem like the inevitable outcome of anything they try. Some youngsters become so overwhelmed by their own inadequacies that, instead of continuing to try to please their parents and develop their skills and abilities, they give up.

How toddlers view themselves—their self-concept and self-esteem—depends in large part on what their caregivers tell them about themselves. Toddlers need help to understand that most of their inadequacies stem from their age and lack of maturity and practice. If toddlers believe their incompetence stems from a basic deficiency or defect, they will lose confidence and give up readily when things are difficult for them, backing away from challenges instead of trying to overcome them.

Psychologists consider the need to develop initiative the central emotional task of the toddler years. "Failure" at this task means that shame and guilt swamp initiative. Children who feel ashamed and guilty respond to difficult tasks by raging, becoming destructive, crying, quickly giving up, and blaming others for their failings.

To help toddlers take initiative, parents need to be supportive of little ones' efforts to do things by themselves. Parents should focus on teaching, refrain from criticizing, and respond with kindness and compassion to their child's frustrations. **TABLE 5-1** shows some example actions, negative (and positive) responses, and how the negative response makes the child feel about himself.

TABLE 5-1

Child's Action: Trying to insert a straw into a box of juice

Responses That Develop Shame and Guilt: "Here, let me do it. It's too hard for you. Now look at the mess you've made. Why do you always have to be so stubborn?"
Child's View of Self: "I'm no good at this. I keep trying to do things because I'm stubborn."

Responses That Develop Initiative: "When you're older, your hands will be stronger and it will be easier for you. Do you want some help? We need to clean this mess up."
Child's View of Self: "Someday I'll be strong enough to do it by myself. Now I can ask for help if it's too hard. When I make a mess we clean it up."

Child's Action: Hits his sister because she has a toy he wants

Responses That Develop Shame and Guilt: "She had it first! Quit being such a bully."
Child's View of Self: "She has all the fun. I'm a bully."

Responses That Develop Initiative: "I know you're angry because you want to play with that, but you aren't allowed to hit. Take a time-out until you're ready to apologize to your sister."
Child's View of Self: "I feel angry when I don't get my way. If I hit I have to go to time-out and apologize."

Child's Action: Grabs the toy from her sister

Responses That Develop Shame and Guilt: "I told you she had it first! You never listen! Now go to your room."
Child's View of Self: "I never listen. Mom takes her side and sends me away."

Responses That Develop Initiative: "You mustn't hit or grab. *Ask* if you can play with her toy. Say, 'May I please play with that?' (Child says, "Play dat?") Very good. But it looks like her answer is 'no,' so you need to find something else to play with or wait in your room. I'll let you know when she's through with it."
Child's View of Self: "I'm getting good at asking for what I want. I don't always get it, though. Then I have to play with something else or go to my room."

Child's Action: Tries to help mother make the bed

Responses That Develop Shame and Guilt: "You're not helping, and you're in my way. Go find something else to do."
Child's View of Self: "When I try to help, I'm just in the way."

Responses That Develop Initiative: "You got part of the pillow in the case! If I just push it in farther and plump it up, it will be perfect. You're Mommy's little helper!"
Child's View of Self: "I'm learning to make beds. I'm a good helper!"

Child's Action: Has been told to pick up his toys

Responses That Develop Shame and Guilt: "I told you to pick those up! Why can't you just cooperate for once? If you don't do it by the time I count to ten, you're in trouble!"
Child's View of Self: "I'm uncooperative. I'm always in trouble."

Responses That Develop Initiative: "Let's have a race. Can you pick up your toys before I count to ten? Ready . . . set . . . go! (The parent drops one toy in the basket and begins counting while the child laughs and scurries to win the race.)
Child's View of Self: "I can pick up toys faster than my mom can count to ten!"

Delaying Gratification

It isn't easy for toddlers to put off until tomorrow what they want right this minute! From age twelve to thirty-six months, toddlers should get much better at managing the tension born of wanting something *now* and not being able to have it. Being able to delay gratification at the end of the toddler years means:

- Not grabbing a cookie from the counter when Mom steps out of the kitchen even though the chocolate calls to her insistently
- Protesting but not falling apart when a parent says he can't have a ride on the mechanical pony in the department store lobby
- Confining herself to some whining and foot-dragging when her father says it's time to leave the park
- Handling his anger over being forbidden to play with a toy by pleading and pouting

Being able to delay gratification means that toddlers may whimper some, whine a bit, cry a few tears, argue, and drag their feet before forging ahead. It does not mean that they continue whining until parents want to smack them, wail to the point that they have to be carried kicking and screaming from the store, argue until parents give up and give in, or fall to the floor in a tantrum. (At least, children close to age three should not be doing these things *often.*)

The Lesson of the Marshmallow

In a series of studies that shook the nation in the 1960s (as reported in Daniel Goleman's *Emotional Intelligence),* researcher Walter Michael ushered a group of four-year-olds into his office one at a time, placed a marshmallow on the table, and then announced he had to leave for a minute. He told each child not to eat the marshmallow until he got back and said that he would bring a second marshmallow. If the first marshmallow was still on the table when he returned, the child could have both. If the marshmallow was gone when he returned, the child wouldn't get a second one.

Video cameras captured the children's reactions, which ranged from gobbling the marshmallow the instant the door closed to trying to resist the sugary temptation. Some caved in despite commanding themselves aloud not to touch it, covering their eyes or turning around so as not to see it, hopping on one leg or reciting nursery rhymes in an effort to distract themselves. Clearly, this was a big challenge for them.

Most children were able to control themselves. They got the kind of reward that so often comes to those who can wait: something even better. The eventual conclusion from these studies was that being able to handle emotions constitutes "emotional intelligence." On evaluating this research, some psychologists concluded that the ability to manage emotions is even more important than IQ for success in school and in life. The idea that children's grip on their emotions could be more important than their ability to handle intellectual tasks came as a shock, and a heated national debate ensued.

FACTS

There is some evidence that emotional IQ is a critical ingredient in long-term success and happiness. Studies show that when it comes to delaying gratification and controlling impulses, children who wait their turn are more popular with peers, students who refrain from talking and getting out of their seats without permission do better in school, and young adults who go to work although they'd rather not are better able to hold down jobs.

Learning to Wait

How do you teach a toddler to hold it together and wait? Here are some tips:

Be calm, not angry. Parental anger triggers more emotional upset in tots, making difficult situations all the more taxing for them. Remember that there is nothing wrong with a child *wanting* something. When guilt and shame are added to toddlers' frustration over not having their desires fulfilled, their stress increases and that makes it more difficult for them to wait.

Don't anticipate trouble! When parents anticipate a scene and react to what they *think* will happen next, they become tense and may then overreact to a simple request. They may precipitate the very scene they want to avoid.

Be a role model. Let your child know when *you* are frustrated because you want something and don't want to wait. Let your toddler see how you handle yourself: "Oh, doesn't that cake look good! I'd really love a piece right now. But no, that will spoil my appetite. I need to wait until after supper. Darn." Soon your toddler will be able to discharge some of the tension of having to wait by talking, too.

Give reasons. Explain why your toddler must wait. It is all too easy for toddlers to conclude that their parent is withholding things and privileges capriciously. That compounds their frustration.

Furthermore, reasonable explanations enable toddlers to apply what they learn in one situation to another. Tots in church may not understand when a parent says, "You must be quiet now. People are talking to God with their hearts and you're disturbing them. You can talk later." But as their language skills improve and they continue to hear explanations, they will eventually understand. Then they can use their knowledge to figure out how to act in other situations where people are concentrating, such as at a live performance, instead of needing an adult to tell them what to do at every moment.

Sometimes parents can't give explanations because they aren't clear about the reasons for certain rules themselves. They only know they must be observed. If you can't supply a reason at the moment, think about it later. When you come up with a reason, share it with your toddler: "Remember yesterday when I said you couldn't watch TV until later? That's because too much TV isn't good for kids. Kids need to play to exercise their bodies and minds." There is sometimes a benefit to sharing reasons later rather than during a contentious moment. Children are more able to listen and consider the parents' words more objectively.

Here are some other things to consider:

- If after thinking about a conflict, you can't come up with a reason that your toddler needed to wait, it's time to hold the mirror up to yourself and consider whether you actually needed to deny your child's request.
- Hold bullying to a minimum. Every parent will have to use the "No, because I said so" line from time to time. Still, it is a power play. Children who are regularly bullied learn to bully others—including their parents when they get big enough. No one likes a bully. Toddlers who bully others at age three are at greater risk for a lifetime of home, school, social, and work problems.
- When you promise your toddler she can do it "later," "tomorrow," or "next week," be as good as your word! It's true that if you don't remind your toddler of your promise to let him finger-paint later in the afternoon, he may forget. Toddlers have short-term memories and a poor concept of time, so it's easy to trick them. But trusting that when the parent says "later," that time will actually arrive makes waiting more tolerable.
- Help your child manage the time spent waiting. When children are excitedly anticipating something, their play may become unfocused and their concentration may deteriorate. Suggest an alternate activity.

ESSENTIALS Explaining "why" may be one way to give toddlers the tools they need to work out conflicts without resorting to a blowup. One study found that 75 percent of toddlers age twenty-one to twenty-four months tried to negotiate to get parents to alter their demands. By thirty months this figure increased to 93 percent.

If children are admonished when they have difficulty waiting and hear nothing when they do wait patiently, they won't recognize that they are capable of delaying gratification of their wants and desires. When your toddler finally calms down after a scene over wanting something *now*, remember to point out her accomplishment. An hour after calm is restored, say, "I'm proud you were able to stop crying when I told you that you couldn't paint until after lunch. I'll make sure you get to do it after we eat."

Maybe your child's tantrum was so violent you were still trembling an hour later. Maybe complimenting your toddler for waiting seems like complimenting Dracula for having such a charming effect on women. But toddlers need to know they are in fact capable of waiting. They prove it every time their wish isn't gratified and they live to tell the tale!

When pointing out a child's success at delaying gratification, focus on his achievement. Save the "thank yous" for when your child has done *you* a favor. Children aren't doing their parents a favor by developing patience. This is a hard-won gift they are giving to themselves!

Building Frustration Tolerance

When a toddler learns that if at first he doesn't succeed he can try, try again and eventually get it right, he has accomplished another important emotional victory.

Temperament has a hand in dictating how toddlers react to frustration. Some concentrate long and hard on that tiny button as they struggle to fit it into the little buttonhole on their shirt, watching carefully to move all those little fingers just so in order to get the button lined up and in. Others have far less patience with these nerve-wracking situations. Their feelings of frustration overwhelm them, and when they are upset, they can't think clearly enough to work effectively. Work with your toddler to break the cycle of difficulty, frustration, upset, and giving up.

To help a toddler learn to tolerate frustration, keep the following tips in mind:

- Don't over-praise a job well done. It doesn't take toddlers long to decide that the opposite of all those "Good job!" comments is "Bad job!"
- Give lots of encouragement and moral support: "You're getting it . . . almost . . . you're close . . . by George, I think she's about to get it!"

- Express your feelings aloud so your child can hear you actively dealing with a difficult task: "This seat belt is stuck again! I've tried it a dozen times and I still can't get it to extend properly. If I pull hard, the belt comes out too far. If I don't pull hard, it's too short to buckle. I need to calm down. I know I can do this, but it's tricky. There! I got it! Hurray!"
- Always respectfully *ask* whether your toddler wants help before leaping in. Otherwise, you may inadvertently communicate, "You're obviously too incompetent to handle this yourself."
- Teach your toddler to break large and/or difficult tasks into a series of small steps. Complex tasks viewed in their entirety become overwhelming. Help your child tackle one small piece of a task at a time, and pause to help him appreciate his accomplishment before he moves on to the next step.

The Road to Independence

While some toddlers never go through the "terrible twos" stage of headstrong negativity, most pass through a period during which they become determined about handling their personal affairs themselves and making their own decisions. As independence struggles intensify, it may become readily apparent that a toddler doesn't care what she does as long as it is the opposite of what her parent wants!

What seems to be mindless toddler negativity is actually the innate impetus to become independent working within them. Without a strong inner force to propel toddlers to pit their will against their environment, why would they tackle the challenges of walking and feeding and bathing and dressing themselves? Certainly it's much easier to sit back and let older, more experienced people carry them around and do everything for them.

"Me Do It"

The inner force that compels toddlers to do things for themselves is often a hardship for parents. The drive for independence can create a crisis when parents are in a rush to be out the door while their youngster is doggedly engaged in the laborious project of eating his corn flakes one flake at a time as he learns to manage his silverware by himself. The hectic schedules of modern life certainly weren't designed with toddlers in mind!

If coping with the "me do it" drive is hard for parents, remember that it's even harder for toddlers. Mother Nature can be capricious. She pushes youngsters to be independent even when they lack the skills needed to do things by themselves. The same child who is determined to put a puzzle together by himself may lack the fine motor coordination needed to do it. One minute he is raging at the parent who dares to try to help; the next minute he recognizes his inadequacy and rages at the parent for *not* helping. Then, when the parent once again tries to show the toddler how to do it, Mother Nature whispers in the toddler's ear that he must do it himself, and he is again raging at the parent for having touched her puzzle. Now that the parent has defiled it, the youngster wants nothing to do with it.

Allow more time for getting ready in the morning and before going out in case your toddler suddenly decides she must handle some of the preparations herself, but don't allow your child to become a little dictator. Seize control when your child's attempts to be independent are inappropriate.

Children in the throes of an independence struggle put their parents in no-win situations because toddlers are caught in a series of no-win situations themselves. Their emotions vacillate wildly and their behavior becomes erratic as they insist on being independent one minute and regress to helpless dependency the next.

Toddlers in this stage may revert to the familiar comforts of thumb sucking and demand their long-discarded baby bottles back, but then treat parents' attempts to help them cut their meat as a major affront to their dignity. Long-resolved issues such as the need to wear a seat belt and hold Mommy's hand while crossing the street may become battlegrounds once again. At such moments, toddlers are too immersed in their own turmoil to consider others' feelings. If youngsters at this stage demand everything and give nothing, it's because they are in such emotional turmoil they have nothing to give. When deciding how to handle independence struggles, remember that just as toddlers must be allowed to try to do more for themselves, having too much power frightens them. They are not ready to be independent, and they know it.

The Pot of Gold

Independence struggles can be expected to resolve themselves in a matter of months. At that point, youngsters will be comfortable practicing independence when they can and accepting help when they need it. Then the clouds that cast such deep shadows over the household will part and the sunshine will return once again.

If parents feel as though they have survived a hurricane when the toddler years draw to a close, it's because they have! However, if they look to the distant horizon, they will see that the end result of this stormy period holds promise. It is so far off that parents may have to squint to see the glow. Still, the rainbow is there.

The beauty of the rainbow, the promise, will become apparent during adolescence when children's hard-won victory of balancing autonomy and dependence during the toddler years finally yields its pot of gold. As teenagers, they will be able to be close to others without sacrificing personal independence. They'll be capable of forming intimate relationships without relinquishing control of their own life. That's when parents will know the struggles during the tumultuous toddler years were worth every tear.

CHAPTER 6
Potty Proud

Today's toddlers tend to complete potty training much later than prior generations. Twenty-five years ago, 90 percent of toddlers were trained by age $2\frac{1}{2}$. Now, one third of children are still in diapers after their third birthday. Parents who wish to pursue a more lenient approach should prepare themselves for later completion of toilet training (or "toilet learning"), as well as questions and an occasional raised eyebrow from older friends and relatives.

Early Learning

By providing a potty before age twelve months, noting children's schedule of elimination, and having them sit on it several times a day (perhaps while you read a story to encourage them to stay put), toddlers may accept the potty as a part of life. With lots of praise for an occasional success and compensation for the loss of the pleasurable time having their diapers changed, some youngsters can be trained very young—*if* they are physically capable of stopping and starting the flow of urine.

Few children have this ability before age one, however. In some cases, parents who claim their youngsters were trained at a very young age may in fact have trained *themselves* to predict their toddler's need to use the potty and get them there at the right time. Most children will be in diapers throughout most or all of their toddler years, so parents should consider all the diapering options.

The Lowdown on Diapering

Today's toddlers will call the earth their home for many decades to come, and the only way to protect it is for each family to do its part. When the environmental toll of disposable diapers is considered, the cost is much greater than even their price tags suggest. With 432,000 new babies added each *day* to the 6 billion people who inhabit the world, more than a million diapers a day will be added to the landfills if just a quarter of them wear disposables! It's not just the environment that's at stake, either. Do you really want your baby to spend three years soaking in the chemicals that leach from disposable diapers?

The Cotton Advantage

Cloth diapers can aid potty training by making it easier for youngsters to feel wetness, which enhances awareness. If toddlers dislike the sensation of a cold wet diaper, cloth can increase their motivation to use the potty. Cloth diapers and plastic pants won't leak if they're 100 percent cotton and don't contain synthetic batting to give them that thick and fluffy feel. Unfortunately, polyester-filled discount brands fool lots of parents into believing that cloth doesn't work well. To ensure that the nap doesn't end up lining the dryer, avoid flannel and terry cloth. Choose cotton with long fibers.

Old-fashioned diaper pins take practice but can ensure the kind of excellent fit babies got in days gone by. Top them with a waterproof nylon or wool pants cover, and voilà! You've got a dry baby in softer, more environmentally sound garb. You might try cotton diapers and a diaper cover with Velcro tabs to eliminate the need for pins.

Easing Diaper Cleanup

Contrary to popular belief, there's no need to dunk dirty diapers in the toilet or lug water-filled pails to the washer. Drop the stool into the toilet (it's easier with diaper liners), and then toss the diaper directly into a covered pail. Store wet diapers in a separate covered pail.

Professional laundry services put diapers through as many as sixteen wash cycles, but they can be laundered at home with fewer cycles. Here's how:

1. Besides your regular dose of laundry detergent and bleach, for extra help neutralizing the uric acid, add ½ cup of baking soda to each cycle.
2. Run the dirty diapers through the cold cycle of the washing machine to prevent the stains from setting.
3. Add the wet diapers and put them both through a warm-water cycle.
4. Run them through a third cycle of very hot water.
5. Give them an extra rinse.

FACTS

If you hate the toilet-dunking routine for messy diapers, there is an alternative. A product called Little Squirt functions like a high-powered sprayer. It attaches to the water supply of the toilet—and it's *outside* the wall so no you don't have to cut through Sheetrock and plaster to install it.

Spray the contents of the diaper or reusable liner into the toilet; then toss the diaper into the diaper pail without ringing it out. The valve contains a safeguard to keep youngsters from rinsing down the entire bathroom.

Down with Diapering!

If changing time is turning into a battle of wills, check for diaper rash. If you discover a chronic or acute rash, check with your pediatrician. If nothing is physically wrong, it's probably just toddler independence asserting itself. Here are some tips to ease diapering struggles:

- Let your toddler be the official helper, handing you each item as you ask for it.
- Change the location. Spread a towel on the floor or on a bed instead of using the changing table—which may also be safer if your child is thrashing about.
- Have everything ready and laid out so you can finish fast.
- Choose easy-to-put-on diapers—cloth with Velcro tabs or disposables.
- Provide a novel toy that can only be played with during diaper changes.
- Play the "Where is Daddy's nose?/Where is your hair?" game.
- Sing a song or recite a familiar nursery rhyme. But instead of delivering it at normal speed, vary the cadence from very fast to very slow and provide a surprise burst of tickles.
- Tell your child that when he is old enough to use the potty by himself, life will be oh-so-much better!

ESSENTIALS

If your child hates having her diapers changed, play "magic tickles." Bet your child that you can make her laugh without touching her. Slowly move your hands over her bare tummy, getting as close as possible without touching her, and wiggle your fingers while telling her not to laugh. Most toddlers will soon explode into giggles!

Fearless Potty Training

It's not surprising that many parents approach potty training with such trepidation. Psychologists once thought that the methods they used had a major hand in children's personality development. Sigmund Freud went so far as to state that parents' toilet-training methods dictated a child's eventual career choice! The good doctor believed that overly lax methods would result in the kind of sloppiness that would prompt adults to enter careers like painting. Harsh training methods would lead to controlled youngsters who would enter fields emphasizing the traits of frugality, obstinacy, and orderliness, which Freud considered typical of bookkeepers and accountants.

There is absolutely no evidence that a parent's approach to potty training has anything to do with forming personality, much less career choices! Yet people still refer to exacting, overcontrolling adults as having "anal personalities," and many believe these traits stem from their potty training experiences. Indulge their fantasy if you wish, but know that the research suggests that they're wrong.

Who's in Charge?

In potty training toddlers, parents can do absolutely everything "right," but youngsters won't be successful until they are physically ready, are intellectually capable, have mastered the complex mechanics involved, and decide to refrain from wetting and soiling. In many families, the last point is the stickler. Since readiness tends to occur at the time toddlers are entering a particularly oppositional stage, the foundation for difficulties is laid if parents are very anxious to say good-bye to diapers. Starting potty training very early can be a way to lessen conflict—assuming the child is physically ready. The time to begin is before the actively oppositional period begins. On the other hand, starting potty training very late also lessens conflict—assuming parents can resign themselves to dealing with diapers.

Even if parents are very strict and insistent, potty learning offers parents potent lessons in accepting their fundamental helplessness. When it comes to deciding when and where to go to the bathroom, all the punishments and praise and presents you offer may not make much of a difference. For once, toddlers are in control. All parents and caregivers can do is teach children what they need to know to be able to use the potty, help them acquire the specific skills, try to increase their motivation, and remain confident that if nothing else, the social pressures of kindergarten (if not preschool and day care) will provide an incentive powerful enough to zap the thorniest resistance.

Physical Readiness

In order to be potty trained, children must be physically capable of controlling bladder and bowel, which means their central nervous system must have matured to the point that they can control the sphincter muscles that stop and start the flow of urine and expulsion and retention of stool. To achieve nighttime control, the child must be awakened by the sensation of a full bladder, so staying dry at night typically comes later.

It's not possible to be certain whether a youngster's muscles are still automatically giving way when the bladder fills to a certain point. A toddler may have enough physical control for successful potty training if he:

- Remains dry for three to four hours at a time
- Awakens from a nap with a dry diaper
- Passes a substantial quantity of urine at one time
- Has bowel movements that occur at predictable times
- Has well-formed stools
- Routinely goes to a specific place to urinate or have a bowel movement (e.g., a corner of the living room)
- Is able to stop the flow after urination has begun

ALERT

There is no way to be certain that after experiencing the urge to urinate, the child has the physical control of the sphincter to stop the flow. Punitive methods can cause youngsters who cannot comply with demands to feel incompetent, ashamed, and humiliated. Parental kindness and patience are in order.

The bladder is the most reactive organ when it comes to stress, and people of all ages can and do respond to emotional upset by literally "peeing in their pants." By applying pressure to perform, parents can cause youngsters to feel anxious. This undermines bladder control. Accidents in kindergarten are common, and often happen in first grade classrooms, too. Be kind! Be patient!

Cognitive Readiness

Using the potty is a complicated affair. In addition to being able to recognize and communicate the need to go to the bathroom, and follow instructions on where and how to use the toilet, children must be able to:

- Understand how urinating and passing stool happens (that it comes from them)
- Understand the purpose of the toilet (that they are to go to the bathroom there)
- Discern when their bladder is full (recognize the physical sensation of the urge to urinate)
- Recognize the urge to have a bowel movement (recognize the physical sensation of the urge to pass stool)
- Consciously contract the muscles of the abdomen to push out urine and stool while simultaneously relaxing the sphincter muscles

Psychological Readiness

Youngsters must also be emotionally up to the challenge. Psychological readiness includes:

- Being proud of their accomplishments
- Enjoying independence
- Wanting to wear underwear
- Disliking wet or soiled diapers
- Being able to sit quietly for five minutes
- *Not* being in the midst of a phase of toddler negativism
- *Not* being distracted by other major stresses

Learning to use the potty requires a lot of effort on the toddlers' part. Don't begin when they are coping with other major adjustments, such as the birth of a new sister, an older brother starting school, a change in a parent's work schedule, or an illness.

Parent Readiness

Parent readiness matters, too! Choose a time when you aren't under a lot of stress so you can be patient. You should feel very comfortable with your baby taking yet another giant leap toward independence, and have the time to be on call for at least two days. Children need far more than two days to learn, but working parents can at least help toddlers have some concentrated practice to get them started. Then the methods being used at home need to be discussed with day care center staff and baby sitters so potty training can continue during the week.

Seeing Is Believing

Before toilet training can begin, toddlers must be aware that their urine and stool come from them, and that elimination is an act on their part. If they are always in diapers, they may think all those wet and soiled clothes happen by magic. They may have better luck making the connection by:

- Having the opportunity to watch others use the bathroom. Some parents aren't comfortable with this, but it can really speed things along! Sometimes an older sibling is willing to demonstrate. Many children have opportunities to witness peers using the potty at day care.
- Being repeatedly told that they are having a bowel movement when they are grunting or straining. If you can tell when your child is going in his diaper, be sure to point it out!
- Observing themselves in the act. Letting them go around the house without clothes is messy, but toddlers simply must be able to observe that urine comes from their own body. Letting them be naked in the backyard in summer is a solution for some families.
- Watching the contents of their diaper being put into the toilet. This doesn't guarantee they'll make the connection, but may help some youngsters make sense of what is supposed to happen.

ESSENTIALS Reading can facilitate potty training in several ways. Read toddlers a story to prepare them. Then, after buying a potty, read to them daily while they sit on it. Check out *Everyone Poops* by Taro Gomi (Kane/Miller Book Pub., 1993) or the *Once upon a Potty* series by Alona Frankel (HarperCollins Juvenile Books, 1999).

What's in a Name?

The answer to that question is: Far more than some parents might anticipate. Toddlers need to learn the vocabulary of the bathroom: potty or toilet, clean and messy, wet and dry. They need words for urine and stool, too. Parents may think it's cute when their toddler refers to bowel movements as "shit" or "crap" and to urine as "piss." But professionals from pediatricians to teachers will find such language unpleasant, and most other parents will be appalled. Older children can learn that certain words are too offensive to be used in school and other social situations, but for toddlers it's an all-or-nothing proposition.

Alternative acceptable words for "number 1" are variations on *pee, pee-pee, tinkle,* and *wee-wee.* For "number 2," it's things like *BM, poop, poopy,* and *do-do.*

Some child development professionals urge parents to avoid words like "stinky." They point out that negative terms can make youngsters feel ashamed of what is a normal bodily function. And if they feel ashamed, they might not want to admit when they need to use the potty. That makes toilet training difficult indeed!

On Your Mark . . .

Buying a potty seat can be an opportunity to begin generating enthusiasm for training, but no matter how excited toddlers seem, parents shouldn't expect miracles. Once it's out of the box, they may be more interested in wearing the seat on their heads than in sitting on it.

It's better to start toilet training with a self-contained potty unit that sits on the floor. Sitting on a toilet so far from the ground can be scary for toddlers. Later, parents can provide a stepping stool and a specially designed toilet seat insert. The insert offers additional security by ensuring they don't fall in.

When buying inserts, parents should beware of brands that have a raised splashguard. Eventually most toddlers bump into it, and that can be painful enough that they refuse to use the toilet again. Some potties can be moved onto the toilet when the child is ready, and the continuity can make the transition easier.

Parents will need to explain what the potty is for: "This is where people put their poop and pee so they don't have to wear diapers. I'm going to teach you how." Having a teddy bear sit on it and discussing the bear's pride in being a big boy with a potty all his own can give a toddler a chance to observe and become comfortable with the situation before he tries it. Here are some other tips:

- Unless a child wants to remove her clothing, it's a good idea to suggest she remain dressed so the feel of the cold, hard plastic doesn't alarm her. The goal should be to get the child to sit on it every day for a week with clothes on. (But of course, if she wants to remove her pants and/or diapers, so much the better!)
- Some children are more amenable to sitting on their potty while their parent uses the toilet or while being read a story, singing songs, or reciting nursery rhymes. Forcing them to spend time sitting on the potty can lead to power struggles, so parents should decide in advance whether they're going to adopt the firm "you need to do this now" approach or let the child proceed at his own pace, although later they may decide to switch tactics.
- Whether or not their youngster sits on it, parents should be sure their toddler understands that he can use it whenever he wants, and should ask if he wants help. Take your toddler with you to the bathroom after each diaper change, and reinforce the message: "Your pee goes here" (point out the potty). "Your poop goes here" (scrape it into his potty so he can see it).

Put down the potty lid, but don't transfer stool to the toilet for flushing until the toddler has left the room. Children may enjoy flushing, and the chance to pull the handle on the tank may serve as a big incentive to use the potty. But unless parents are certain that their youngster isn't afraid of the sound and motion, it's better not to let them do it. Flushing can take on a whole new meaning when youngsters realize that it causes something of theirs to disappear—a fact they may not have grasped when parents cleaned or discarded their disposables.

Get Set . . .

After toddlers have become comfortable sitting on the potty fully clothed, the next step is for them to become accustomed to the feel on bare skin. This is a good time to introduce training pants that can be pulled on and off.

Disposable training pants may prevent children from feeling the wetness. Since they need to be able to distinguish the difference between wet and dry, cloth may be a better choice while they're awake. However, disposable training pants may be more convenient at night while children are still bed-wetting.

Parents can explain, "Kids wear training pants when they're learning to use the potty. I'll help you pull them down, or you can do it yourself." Being sensitive and responsive to toddlers' desires to handle all or portions of the chore themselves is important for keeping them motivated! During the week that the child practices sitting on the potty seat without clothes, continue to reinforce the idea that bowel movements are supposed to go into the potty. The toddler should accompany them into the bathroom to watch the contents of their messy diapers being emptied into the potty bowl.

Go!

Lots of concentrated practice in a few days is better than practice spread out over a period of weeks. Provide salty foods to increase thirst, and encourage youngsters to drink lots of liquids. If the toddler agrees, have her spend the day without clothing so you can catch her in the act and take her to the potty when nature calls.

FACTS

Praise for being a "big boy" or "big girl" can backfire when toddlers are vacillating between "me do it" and "Mommy do it." Saying "Mommy doesn't want her baby to have to wear wet diapers anymore" may provide more incentive than saying "Big kids use the potty instead of going in their diapers." Applying some cornstarch or cream after youngsters have used the potty and exchanging tickles and kisses can reassure them that mastering this skill won't turn their world upside-down.

Teaching Hygiene

Using the potty will be messy for little boys who insist on standing to urinate. Learning to aim takes practice, and splashing is inevitable. If they won't sit, have them climb onto a stool to urinate into the toilet. Make sure the stool is stable and doesn't slide. Teach children basic hygiene.

- Show them how much toilet paper to use.
- Teach girls to wipe from front to back so they don't introduce bacteria into the vagina.
- Consult your pediatrician for ways to care for an uncircumcised penis as your son goes through the potty training process.
- Provide a stepping stool so they can reach the sink.
- Help them turn on the cold water, apply soap, rub their hands together, rinse, and dry them with a towel.
- Explain the danger of turning on the hot water.

Many stomach and intestinal upsets that parents believe to be a mild case of flu are actually bacteria from poor bathroom hygiene. Toddlers spend a lot of time with their hands in their mouths; they must be taught to wash carefully every time they go to the bathroom.

Rewards and Praise

Lots of parents recognize that their personal interest in potty training is much greater than their youngster's, so they happily invest in a quantity of Hot Wheels, stickers, cookies, or other items to make the potty experience worthwhile. At first, rewards can be given for simply sitting on the potty for five minutes. Later, the parent can up the ante. To be effective, keep these tips in mind:

- The child must understand exactly what to do to earn the reward, whether it is just sitting on the potty for a specified period or urinating in or having a bowel movement in the toilet.
- Don't require the child to go for a whole day without an accident in order to earn a prize.
- Give rewards immediately; they should *not* consist of a promise of good things to come later unless the child is unusually good at planning ahead.
- Don't give the reward if the child doesn't complete the required task. You can, however, reassure the child that he'll have another chance to earn one later.
- Change the type of reward if the toddler loses interest.

When you give rewards for desired behavior, accompany them with verbal praise, since the ultimate goal is for the child to progress beyond the need for tangible goodies. However, if a toddler is in an oppositional stage, it may work better to refrain from verbal praise and simply say, "Here is your prize for having used the potty" or "You should be proud of yourself." Effusive comments like "I am so proud of you!" can trigger the rebellious impulses that make so many two-year-olds want to do the opposite of whatever they sense their parents want. Instead, try, "Aren't you proud of yourself?" This is a bit less confrontational.

ALERT

Many toddlers are content to wet their diapers, but try to avoid piddling on the floor. Many also love to run around the house naked. Allowing them to go without clothes can serve as an incentive for them to use the toilet, but you must be willing to clean up accidents patiently.

Target Practice

When parents turn potty time into a game, most kids can't wait for the chance to play. The standard procedure is to draw a bull's eye with a magic marker on a circle of tissue paper. Drop it into the potty, and see if your toddler can take aim, fire, and score a hit. Alternatively, drop a Cheerio or a square of marked toilet paper into the potty and see if the child can hit it. (This is easier for boys, but fun for all.) Boys can also try to roll a Ping-Pong ball around the bowl. (Disinfect both the ball and the hand that retrieves it afterward.)

But if parents lose interest in the games before their toddler and decline to participate, the child may decide diapers are preferable. As much as toddlers are determined to prove their independence by opposing every parental suggestion, they need all the attention of a little baby. If forced to choose, most toddlers would probably decline to grow up.

ESSENTIALS

Tinkle Toonz musical potties, available at many stores, have a moisture-activated sensor, so that when children tinkle, they receive instant positive reinforcement: a chorus of "Old MacDonald." No tinkle, no tune. It provides toddlers with that all-important sense of personal control—only they can make it work.

Tracking Progress

With a large piece of paper and a box of stars or stickers, parents can make a chart to help their toddler track her progress. After each successful use of the potty, the child gets to add a sticker to a chart under the correct day. (Instead of a chart, one mother let the child place stickers directly on the potty. He was thrilled!)

After each wet or soiled diaper, the parent may wish to note the time and day. This information can be used to determine the times of day when the child needs more help. Sometimes toddlers consider stickers a great incentive; sometimes an additional motivator in the form of a prize after the child has earned five stickers boosts enthusiasm. So you don't start the troublesome battle of "if I do what you want, what will you buy me?" consider bestowing the gift you can feel good about giving and the present toddlers love most of all: spending time with *you*. For instance, try an extra bedtime story, ten minutes longer in the bathtub, a leisurely walk around the block to study the dandelions and worms, a trip to the park, or extra time to finger-paint. Just remember that rewards work best when they're immediate!

Up with Undies, Down with Diapers!

Have your child help select underwear that can be worn as her reward for sustained continence. Let her break out her new attire when she's made it through a full day without an accident.

To increase interest in using the potty for toddlers who are intently working on independence and autonomy issues (that is, going through a very oppositional stage), parents can try making a studied show of having lost interest in it themselves. Employing a bit of reverse psychology works best if a youngster has demonstrated some enthusiasm for learning, but the pattern has been for enthusiasm to quickly fade. Some of these strategies are a bit harsh; parents need to beware, since by using them they risk creating still more control struggles:

- Suggest your tot relinquish Pull-Ups and return to diapers.
- Allow the youngster to experience the discomfort of wet and soiled diapers by being less responsive to changing them. (Delaying a few minutes is enough—the point isn't to torture little ones or to cause diaper rash!)
- Pick her up for a diaper check or change when she's engrossed in a fun activity.
- Eliminate the fun and games when changing him.
- Be less solicitous and more businesslike.

FACTS

Although the interruption of usual family routines during a trip or vacation can set potty training back, it may be better not to worry about it until returning home. Otherwise, it's a good idea to pack up the potty since strange bathrooms, which many toddlers find scary, can cause a setback. For a truly portable potty you can use in the car, try a plastic ice-cream bucket for girls and a plastic jar for boys. Don't forget a waterproof pad to put over the mattress.

Bed-Wetting

At age three, an estimated 50 percent of three-year-olds still wet the bed. Within six months, the figure drops to 25 percent; at age four, it's down to 20 percent. Bed-wetting is considered normal until age six, but the figures remain high for young adolescents, too: 8 percent of boys and 4 percent of girls. The reasons for bed-wetting are not well understood. Genetics may play a role, since studies show children who achieve nighttime continence late often have a parent who had a similar problem. Sleep patterns of hyperactive and depressed children are such that they may not awaken when they need to use the bathroom.

To help eliminate bed-wetting, try the following:

- Limit fluid intake before bedtime.
- Have youngsters use the bathroom right before going to bed.
- Try to determine the time at which the bed-wetting usually occurs, set an alarm, and walk your toddler to the bathroom during the night.

Children who wet the bed need to be handled with compassion. Parents need to trust that children don't like to wake up in a cold damp bed, and should avoid using shame, humiliation, and punishment. Instead, parents should use a plastic sheet and involve older toddlers in the cleanup. They should be able to help with removing the sheets and putting them into the laundry basket.

Bed-wetting problems should be discussed with the child's pediatrician to rule out the possibility of a medical problem and to see about exercises to help increase bladder control. Older children can sometimes overcome the problem by using a moisture-activated device that awakens them.

Bowel Problems

Many toddlers continue to have a bowel movement everywhere and anywhere, except the potty. Some are trained for a time and then regress. Is this yet another sign of the uncanny affection toddlers have for their poop? Is it a reaction to the discomfort or embarrassment of sitting naked on a potty for an extended time? Could it be a last-ditch effort to hang onto babyhood? Or perhaps it's an assertion of toddler autonomy?

Most parents never do decipher this puzzle. One thing is certain: If it's a struggle for control, parents are probably doomed to lose. Those who become angry and punitive may find themselves dealing with chronic soiling, known as encopresis (explained later). To enhance children's motivation, here is a hodgepodge of things parents have tried, with varying degrees of success:

- Have toddlers sit on the toilet for five minutes every day at the time they are likely to have a bowel movement. As soon as the time is up, reward their success for having remained seated.
- Immediately offer more desirable treats and toys when toddlers get their stool in the right place.
- If you've already tried the enthusiastic "hip-hip-hurrah" approach to drumming up pride of accomplishment, switch to being matter-of-fact when toddlers get it right, as if going to the potty were nothing unusual.
- If your approach all along has been matter-of-fact, try staging victory celebrations.
- Put them back in diapers. However, know that some youngsters then regress to wetting in them, too.
- Ask your child why he doesn't like to use the potty. You probably won't get an answer. Tell him if there's anything that bothers him about it, to let you know. Maybe at some point he will. Maybe it will be a problem you can fix.

- Have your toddler tell you when he needs to go, hand him a diaper, and let him retreat to wherever to do his own thing.
- See if spending time in an environment where other children use the potty, like a preschool, makes a difference.
- Wait for kindergarten peer pressure to solve the problem.

FACTS

How would you feel if your insides fell out and disappeared forever? This simple misunderstanding is what causes so many toddlers to work overtime to prevent disaster by becoming constipated or secreting their stool around the house. Many potty-resistant toddlers have made a dramatic turnaround after hearing the simple explanation: "When people eat food, their body uses what it needs. Then it gets rid of the part it doesn't need, which is the poop."

So why do some children insist on having bowel movements anywhere *but* the toilet? In the absence of an underlying medical problem, resistance that develops into full-blown encopresis—constant soiling—often develops from a predictable chain of events:

1. The child is slightly constipated, so her stool is a bit harder than normal. Because passing hard stool is painful, she tries not to have a bowel movement, worsening the constipation and pain.
2. If she uses the toilet, the hard stool causes the cold water to splash, hitting the child's bottom.
3. The combination of pain from passing stool, and the surprise and discomfort of being splashed makes the child nervous—even a bit afraid—about pooping in the toilet again.
4. A vicious cycle is created wherein the child's reluctance to use the toilet causes her to become increasingly constipated. Bowel movements become increasingly hard and painful, which further increases reluctance.

The situation can escalate to the point that a mass too large and hard to pass through the rectum forms in the bowel. Liquid that can't be absorbed leaks around the mass. The child cannot inhibit the flow, and continuous involuntary soiling occurs.

To break the cycle, increase his intake of fruits, vegetables, and fruit juice, and keep him well hydrated with water. If that doesn't help, check with the child's pediatrician about administering a stool softener such as mineral oil. A good stool softener will make it impossible for children to contain bowel movements once it takes effect. Since mineral oil can interfere with vitamin absorption, it may be necessary to add a multivitamin; mixing it in juice can make it more palatable.

Once the child has been having regular soft bowel movements for ten days, rectal soreness should be completely healed. At that point, it is time to work on having bowel movements on the potty. Because children in this situation have come to associate the potty with physical pain and discomfort and the whole situation may have become traumatic, breaking the negative associations and creating new, more positive ones may take some time and a lot of patience. The goal is to help toddlers recover from trauma so they can have a fresh start.

For starters, have the child sit on the potty or toilet for five minutes every day at the time she usually goes, wearing Pull-Ups while seated. Wearing Pull-Ups should add to her feelings of safety and ensure no splashing occurs if she is on the toilet and does have a bowel movement. If her resistance is too strong to be overcome by reassurance and pep talks alone, offer stickers, toys, or special privileges. Set a timer and engage in a quiet activity she enjoys, such as reading a book, playing with an Etch-A-Sketch, or reciting nursery rhymes. Reassure her that the point isn't for her to have a bowel movement; it's to learn to relax while sitting on the toilet.

Once she's sat for five minutes without a struggle for at least three days in a row, it's time to up the ante. Make rewards contingent on having a bowel movement there. Leave on her Pull-Ups to add to a feeling of comfort and to prevent splashing, if she's on the toilet. If she doesn't go during her daily five-minute regime of sitting on the potty, provide verbal praise and tell her she can still earn the reward if she goes while sitting on the potty later. Ask her to tell you when she needs to go.

After a week of having regular bowel movements on the potty, her memories of the trauma are fading (Let's hope!). At that point, have her remove her training pants and try having a bowel movement in the potty or toilet. Continue to set a timer to ensure that she sits for five minutes, but only provide a reward after she actually uses the potty, which may be later in the day.

Bathroom Explorers

No sooner have the struggles to get toddlers into the bathroom finally ended than the struggles to keep them out are likely to heat up. They want to use every commode in every store, gas station, park, zoo, church, and museum they enter! Since getting to a public facility takes longer, toddlers quickly learn they must announce their need to use the toilet further in advance, well before the urge becomes intense. That, combined with their keen interest in exploring the bathrooms of the world, makes it hard for them to decipher whether their faint urge to "go" stems from physical need or emotional desire. In time, they'll learn to more accurately predict their needs and understand their sensations and feelings. Until then, happy exploring!

CHAPTER 7
Safety First

W hat can toddlers get into? The obvious answer is, everything within reach. But how far, exactly, can they reach? Much farther than you might think possible! Consider everything that can be climbed on, fallen off of, pulled open (or over!), and used to extend their reach. The list of hazards is endless. Use common sense and watch carefully to see the kinds of danger your child might get into.

Instant Trouble

Faster than a parent can dash to the next room to answer the phone, run to the kitchen to remove burning food from the stove, or hurry to open the front door, a toddler can get into serious trouble. After an accident, the common parental refrain is, "But I only turned my back for a moment." Parents never dream their child would eat Grandpa's medication lying on the table, or that their toddler, in the midst of having a bath, would turn on the hot water.

If you suspect your child has ingested something he shouldn't have, call Poison Control immediately. Keep the phone number posted by every phone in your home: ☎(800) 722-7112. For area code 215, dial ☎(215) 386-2100. For serious injuries, call ☎911.

Safety at Home

Some basic safety precautions should be obvious to every parent. In fact, child welfare departments consider them so basic and obvious that if parents don't adhere to them, they could be charged with "child endangerment" or "failure to protect," which means that their toddler could be placed in foster care while the parents attend court-ordered counseling sessions and parenting classes. So parents simply must avoid the following:

- Keeping a gun at home to which a toddler could have access (Guns and ammunition must be stored separately, locked up, and out of reach.)
- Driving under the influence of alcohol or any illicit drug
- Giving alcohol to a toddler
- Leaving drugs—illicit or otherwise—within reach of a toddler
- Putting toddlers under forty pounds in a car without a safety seat
- Putting children over forty pounds in a car without a safety belt
- Exposing youngsters to domestic violence
- Injuring a child in any way, including hitting hard enough to leave a bruise or welt

- Shaking an infant or toddler (which can cause brain damage serious enough to result in death!)
- Dragging a youngster by the arm (the combination of a pull and a twist causes spiral fractures)

Of course you should not *deliberately* hurt your child, but there is more to it than that. Special care needs to be taken to avoid hazardous or unhealthy situations. The best introduction to creating a safe and healthy environment for children throughout their lives is the very exciting event known as "childproofing."

Here are some basic ways to reduce potential danger zones in your home:

- Cover unused electrical outlets with plastic guards or heavy furniture.
- Replace frayed electrical cords.
- Install safety latches on cabinet and appliance doors and toilets.
- Keep plastic bags out of reach. (Use cloth bags or boxes for storing toys; store food in waxed paper.)
- Place small items that could be swallowed out of reach, including buttons, coin collections, and marbles. (Don't forget to hide the dish containing hard candies, too.)
- Lock up knives and other sharp or pointed objects.
- Unplug small appliances such as hair dryers, blenders, and toasters; and don't let the cords dangle from countertops or dressers.
- Beware of rugs that slip and uneven carpeting. (Put skidproof mats on tile and hardwood floors.)
- Lower the thermostat on the water heater to prevent scalding.
- Keep garage door openers out of reach.
- Check and clean furnaces, flues, and chimneys annually.

Firearms

Parents must keep guns and ammunition locked, and they must store them separately. Hiding them isn't enough, and here's why: An investigative news reporter interviewed youngsters in their homes about where the family's gun was located. As the cameras rolled, the common response was, "I'll show you, but you have to promise not to tell. I'm not supposed to know." One youngster after the next then lead the reporter to a suitcase stored under the parent's bed, to the bottom of the stack of clothes at the back of a dresser drawer, or to some other "secret" location.

In one case, the reporter examined the gun and said, "But there aren't any bullets in here."

"Up there," the little one said, opening the closet door and pointing to a shelf high above his head. He indicated he'd need a chair to reach the box.

Teaching preschoolers (and teens!) about the dangers of guns made no difference. Immediately following the talk, the children were placed in a playroom with a box that held toy guns and a real one. They didn't even pause before going straight for the steel. The moral for their astounded parents was clear: Hiding firearms isn't enough. They must be locked up! (And if you have youngsters, consider not keeping any firearms in your home at all.)

FACTS

In some states, parents engaged in domestic violence can be charged with child endangerment, even when the abuse or violence is not directed toward the toddler. Professionals know that the emotional damage resulting from such scenes can have lifelong repercussions. If you think your child is safe because your partner only hits you, think again.

Bathtub Seats

About 1 million bathtub seats are sold in the United States each year. But if you think these handy devices mean you can sneak out of the bathroom for even a minute, you're wrong! An analysis of U.S. Consumer Product Safety Commission data revealed that bathtub seats were involved in the deaths of thirty-two children age five to fifteen months between 1983 and 1995. In twenty-nine of these deaths, the drowning occurred when the child was left in the seat unattended. Several toddlers managed to crawl out, then slipped and fell. So if you use them, keep these points in mind:

- Collect everything you need—towels, shampoo, soap—*before* filling the tub.
- Don't trust an older sibling to supervise. According to the study, eleven deaths occurred when a big brother or sister was left in charge.
- Ignore the doorbell, the telephone, your pager, and the soup boiling over on the stove.
- Ignore your other child's call, too. The study showed that 24 percent of the deaths occurred while a parent ran to check on the other child.
- If you leave the bathroom for even a second, take your dripping baby with you!

Some deaths occurred in the presence of a caregiver who couldn't get the straps off fast enough when the child ended up facedown in the water. It may be better to forget bathtub seats altogether!

Toy Chests

When the toddler reaches inside a toy chest and the lid falls on his hand or head, the result can be serious injury or even death. When a child climbs inside and lowers the lid, the result can be asphyxiation. The safety standards for a toy chest include the following:

- A hinged lid that will stay open rather than falling shut
- NO latch, so a child who has crawled inside and lowered the lid can push it open
- Air holes for ventilation

When shopping for a toy chest, check for all three safety features, especially check the lid's hinge or select a box with a lightweight top. If you're using a metal trunk or another box to store toys, remove the lid.

According to the American Academy of Pediatrics, trampolines are too dangerous for toddlers. There is a serious risk of spinal cord injury from the jolt of landing, but other nasty accidents are all too common. Toddlers don't have the coordination to control their jumping or their landing.

Safe Strollers and Playpens

While in a stroller, toddlers are apt to lean out to look, rock from side to side when excited, and hurl themselves about when angry. To guard against tips and spills, choose a stroller with wheels set far enough apart to provide a wide base and with rear wheels positioned behind the weight of the toddler. Before making the purchase, check to make sure the stroller doesn't become unstable when the toddler is in a reclining position. The latches should also be secure enough not to open by accident.

When your toddler is in the stroller, keep his seat belt on, even when he is sleeping. And be careful when opening and closing strollers. This is a prime time for parents and toddlers to pinch their fingers.

When purchasing a playpen, check to be sure that the holes in the mesh are small enough so toddlers can't step into them and climb up the side. Don't leave toddlers unattended in mesh playpens with a side down. Tots can become caught and strangle in the loose mesh. The bars on wooden pens should be no more than $2\frac{1}{2}$ inches apart so toddlers can't get their heads caught. For both types of playpens, avoid placing large toys inside that children could stand on to gain enough height to crawl over the top. Double check the latches to be sure they are secure enough so the playpen doesn't collapse, and so they don't catch a toddler's fingers.

ESSENTIALS   For questions about the safety of any product, call the U.S. Consumer Product Safety Commission hotline at ☎(800) 638-2772.

Be Prepared!

In the event of chemical poisoning, have the container by your side when you call poison control so you can answer questions by reading the label. If the poisoning is from a plant and you don't know its name, take a piece with you to the phone so you can describe it, or to the emergency room so you can show it. Be ready to provide the following information:

- The brand name and ingredients (for medicines and chemicals)
- The species name (if you know it)—the shape, size, and color (if you don't)—for a plant the child ingested or the insect or animal (such as a snake) that bit him
- An estimate of how much material was ingested
- How much time has elapsed since the poisoning
- The child's condition
- Any medical problems or allergies the child has

In the event of a poisoning emergency:

1. Call 911 if your child has collapsed, is having convulsions, has stopped breathing, or you feel that the amount or kind of the ingested poison is going to require a trip to the emergency room.
2. Don't wait to see if accidentally ingested medication actually has an effect before calling poison control. It's better to be safe than sorry!
3. Keep a one-ounce bottle of syrup of ipecac for inducing vomiting on hand for each child in the home, but DO NOT induce vomiting unless a medical professional says to do so. You can double the problem if the ingested poison is the kind that burns the throat.
4. Call a neighbor for help while waiting for an ambulance so you'll have a cooler head on hand, and someone to help with your other children.

Chemical Potpourri

Modern households are filled with substances that parents may never have thought of as being particularly dangerous . . . but that's because they never considered eating them!

- One of the more dangerous substances for toddlers is lead, which has been linked with lower IQ, aggression, and antisocial behavior. Since lead is commonly used in paint, especially in older homes, parents should be especially careful about sweeping up chips and flakes from walls and window frames. Check your blinds, too; some newer models have lead-based paint. If you discover lead in your home, alert your pediatrician and see about having your child tested.
- In 1998 alone, 17,000 children required treatment after drinking either rubbing alcohol or liquor.
- Also in 1998, 980 children under age six were treated for injuries relating to glue.

When parents are childproofing the house, they should be careful that all of the following potentially hazardous substances are beyond children's reach:

✖Ammonia	✖Fabric finishers and softeners	✖Matches and lighters
✖Antistatic products	✖Fertilizers	✖Mothballs
✖Batteries	✖Fire extinguishers	✖Oven cleaners
✖Bleaches	✖Fireworks	✖Paints (including watercolors)
✖Boric acid	✖Floor cleaners and polishes	✖Pencil lead
✖Caulk	✖Gasoline	✖Pesticides
✖Cigarettes and nicotine	✖Herbicides	✖Photographic chemicals
✖Cleansers	✖Incense	✖Polishes and waxes
✖Dishwasher detergents and rinses	✖Indoor plant foods	✖Room deodorizers and air fresheners
✖Disinfectants	✖Ink	✖Rust removers
✖Drain cleaners	✖Insect repellants	✖Soldering flux
✖Dyes for fabrics and foods (And unless that Easter egg dye says "nontoxic," watch those eggs like a hawk!)	✖Insulation	✖Stain removers
	✖Kerosene	✖Starch
	✖Laundry detergents and additives	✖Stripping agents
	✖Lighter fluid	✖Toilet bowl cleaners
		✖Typewriter correction fluid

Poisons via the Eye

If a child gets a dangerous substance in her eye, call 911 or poison control to see if there is a need for professional medical attention. Recommendations typically include the following:

1. Fill a pitcher with tepid (not hot!) water.
2. Keep the child from rubbing his eyes by wrapping him in a blanket, sheet, or towel that is large enough to keep his arms at his sides.
3. Do not force the eyelid open.
4. Pour the water into the eye from a distance of 2 to 3 inches.
5. Repeat for a full fifteen minutes.
6. Encourage the child to blink as much as possible.

Cosmetics

It's one thing to put dye on your hair, quite another to put it in a stomach! Products whose safety you never thought to question should be kept well out of reach of little hands:

- Creams, lotions, and makeup
- Douches
- Eye products
- Hair-coloring agents (dyes, bleaches, rinses)
- Hairsprays, gels, and relaxers
- Hair removers
- Lipsticks
- Nail polishes and removers
- Perfumes and aftershaves
- Shampoos and conditioners
- Suntan and sunscreen products
- Toothpaste, mouthwashes, and rinses

FACTS

Dangerous Plants

With a toddler in the house, parents should give serious thought to sacrificing their plants. Besides the safety issue that arises if little ones actually eat some, they will most probably pull off the leaves, dump out the dirt, and rip them to shreds. Since it's a safe bet that at least a piece or two will end up in his mouth, which may mean he swallows some, it makes sense to resign yourself to doing without much indoor greenery for the foreseeable future. An amazing range of flowers and plants are toxic, including common ones like foxglove, mistletoe, philodendron, poinsettia, oleander, and tulips. Check with a local nursery to be sure any greenery you keep in or around your house isn't toxic to toddlers.

Poisonous Insects

Exposed roots, rough stones, and sharp sticks are a potential danger in their own right, but they are also perfect tools for digging, poking, and exploring the great outdoors. While a toddler is outside, she can also be exposed to a variety of nasty bugs. The following list will tell you what to look for, both during and after the encounter.

Fire ants. These very aggressive pests derive their name from the firelike pain of their stings. A white pustule appears after twenty-four to forty-eight hours at the site of the sting of some species. Pustules must be kept clean, as they readily become infected and can leave permanent scarring. Some toddlers are hypersensitive to the venom and can develop chest pains, nausea, dizziness, shock, or lapse into coma.

Bees, wasps, and hornets. Swelling can occur immediately but may not manifest for five to six hours. Either way, it can be dramatic, last for three to four days, and be accompanied by bruising and itching. Apply ice for five to fifteen minutes, but be careful not to freeze tender toddler skin. Swelling at the sting site doesn't signal an allergic reaction. A child who is allergic to a sting will begin reacting within a few minutes or hours. Allergy symptoms include flushing, anxiety, swelling in areas other than the site of the sting (especially around the mouth and eyelids), hives, difficulties breathing, dizziness, nausea, cramps, diarrhea, and unconsciousness. In the event of an allergic reaction, call 911.

Spiders. The infamous black widows don't always inject poison. Poison control can tell you how to assess the wound and determine whether a trip to the ER is necessary. More problematic is the brown recluse spider; six out of ten species are poisonous. Their color ranges from tan to brown. Most species bear a violin-shaped marking on their bodies. Symptoms include fever, malaise, rash, vomiting, and diarrhea. Call poison control.

Dangerous Gases

The following gases are hazardous: carbon dioxide, carbon monoxide, chlorine, methane, natural gas, and propane. In the event of an accident:

1. Avoid breathing the fumes yourself.
2. Get your toddler to fresh air fast.
3. Open doors or windows (if this can be done without spreading dangerous fumes).
4. Administer artificial respiration and chest compressions if the child isn't breathing and call 911.

Buckle Up . . . Carefully

The leading cause of death in children ages one to four is unintentional injuries, and the vast majority of those are incurred during automobile accidents. Don't even think of starting your car engine until your toddler is securely fastened into a car seat or, for children over forty pounds, until they are buckled into a seat belt. But first, be sure to have done your homework:

- Check with the car seat's manufacturer. There has been recall after recall since 1998; more than 10 million models have been deemed unsafe. The handles break on many that double as carriers, tumbling children to the ground.
- Install car seats in the backseat in accordance with the directions. Unless properly installed, car seats can't be counted on to protect your child.
- Check the fit of the seat belt. Standard seat belts can be dangerous for little people, so booster seats are recommended for youngsters weighing in at forty to eighty pounds.
- Consider purchasing a clip that changes the angle of the seat belt so it runs across the shoulder instead of the neck and fits securely across the lap.
- Failing to use the shoulder strap can cause the lap belt to be pulled too tight during a deceleration accident, causing abdominal injuries.
- Tucking the shoulder strap under the arm can prevent the strap from engaging properly during a sudden stop, rendering it useless.

ALERT

Beware of air bags in your car. Although they can save lives, the explosion as they inflate has resulted in massive injuries and even death for children. Many parents of young children have had them deactivated.

The dangers of drinking and driving are well known. However, when a toddler is on board, even one drink is too many. Depending on an individual's tolerance for alcohol, just one or two drinks can significantly slow reflexes, and driving with an active or cranky toddler requires optimal concentration and reflexes. A common side effect of alcohol is that it convinces people they are fine when they may not be fine at all. "Just a few beers" is not safe, either. In general, one beer = one glass of wine = one mixed drink = one shot of whiskey.

Swimming Pools

Swimming pools—and that includes kiddie pools—are lethal for unattended children, who have the highest drowning rates in the United States. In the sunny states of Arizona, California, Florida, and Texas, drowning is the leading cause of death for toddlers. The greatest danger is of a toddler gaining access to a swimming pool without the parents knowing they are capable of doing so. Even sturdy fences with tall gates and big locks are ineffective if they are left unlocked or propped open! Keep the following cautions in mind:

- Just because a swimming pool gate is locked today doesn't mean it will be locked tomorrow.
- Just because a pool gate is locked doesn't mean a child won't find a way to climb over it.
- Supervision is the primary preventative measure against drowning.
- Water safety training doesn't improve children's poolside behavior.
- Swimming lessons decrease children's fear of the water, making them more likely to enter water when no one is present to supervise.

If your child is taking swimming lessons for fun, have at it. But if you're hoping your child will learn poolside safety, forget it. Even toddlers who received careful instruction from professionals didn't improve. If toddlers overcome their fear of the water and learn to swim in a water babies class, watch out! Once they're no longer afraid, they're bolder about jumping in. If they do, instead of using the skills they've mastered in swimming class, they're likely to panic. Little fishes remain at high risk for drowning.

Fire Safety

It doesn't take a lot of smarts to know that Christmas tree lights on a dry tree are a fire hazard. It should be obvious, too, that smoking in bed is a no-no. The proof lies in the telltale hole or singed spot on a comforter, blanket, pillowcase, or sheet. What if you'd fallen asleep?

Matches and lighters must be kept from little fingers. Just because a parent has trouble igniting a safety match or operating a child-resistant lighter doesn't mean toddlers won't succeed on the first or second try. Also, don't run electrical cords under carpeting!

Few people consider what happens when the family cat hops onto the end table and its tail brushes a burning candle. Or when the cat spends a few minutes grooming itself with its tale draped over the pot of burning incense. Once Miss Kitty feels the heat of the flames, it races through the house, spreading the fire.

Given how inexpensive smoke detectors are, there's no excuse not to have them. Here are a few safety tips about smoke detectors:

- Position smoke detectors outside every bedroom (inside if the door is kept closed at night) and on each level of the home.
- Make sure the smoke detector is working by depressing the test button once a month.
- Vacuum cobwebs and dust from the alarms monthly.
- Replace batteries at least once a year.
- Replace the alarms every ten years.

In the kitchen, install knob covers on the range so toddlers can't turn the stove on. Then, when cooking, make it harder for your toddler to reach hot pans or skillets by using the back burners of the stove. Always turn the handles of pans and skillets toward the back so they are less likely to be bumped by the cook or grabbed by a little hand with a long reach.

And, since fires can and do happen despite everyone's best efforts to prevent them:

- Buy fire extinguishers that can be used against both electrical and liquid flames. Get the kind that shows the remaining pressure. When it's reading low, replace the unit.
- Create a fire escape plan by walking into each room and figuring out how you could get yourself and your child to safety if you were trapped there.

When shopping for safe pajamas, look for the brands that are flame-resistant and fit snugly. Loose-fitting cotton T-shirts catch fire easily and burn quickly. The main culprits, responsible for 200 serious sleepwear accidents each year, are candles, matches, lighters, and stove burners. Beware of dangling sleeves!

Keeping Your Cool

It's one thing to be alarmed, scared, or frightened. It's quite another to be panic-stricken. There's no way to predict how a panicked person will react. They sometimes do and say things that are so completely out of character that they don't even recognize themselves when they later ponder their behavior during the crisis. The adrenaline surge can strengthen parents' arms to the point that they accomplish feats they never could have accomplished under normal circumstances, such as lifting the front end of a car to extricate a trapped child from beneath a tire.

Some acquire a steely calm. All emotion disappears and, like a robot, they go on automatic pilot. Later, they are astounded to realize they ended up doing exactly what needed to be done. Others are overcome by emotion. Logic and reason disappear; their minds freeze; and they cannot recall the most basic information. The sayings "She was scared out of her wits," "He was frightened out of his mind," and "I was so out of it, I couldn't remember my own name" are famous for a reason. We'd like to think we'd react correctly in an emergency, but until we have actually been through one, we don't know what we would do. When tapes of parents talking to 911 dispatchers are replayed on TV, conversations frequently go like this:

How old is your child?
I don't know! Please hurry! He's bleeding!

Even if parents are sure their minds wouldn't fail in a crisis, a panicked baby sitter could certainly experience a mental lapse. The solution is to create an emergency list, duplicate it, and post a copy by each telephone in the home. Be sure to include phone numbers for:

- Emergencies in your community (such as 911)
- The emergency room of the local hospital
- Poison control: ☎(800) 722-7112 (within area code 215: ☎(215) 386-2100)
- Police and fire stations
- Your child's pediatrician
- A neighbor

Police dispatchers and other emergency personnel should be able to help callers focus so they can describe the crisis and the victim's current condition. But be sure to post the following critical information by the phone so the caller can simply read it aloud: Your address with detailed directions to your house, including the names of major intersections, readily visible landmarks, and a brief description of your dwelling (e.g., brown brick house with a red shingle roof and two-car garage facing the street).

Create a subheading for each child, and list the following information:

- Name
- Age
- Sex
- Height and weight
- Medical problems
- Allergies
- Names and doses of prescription medications
- Names and doses of over-the-counter medications

Lifesaving Skills

Basic lifesaving skills are familiar to many people, but used by few. This is the time to refresh those skills—with hope they'll never be used.

CPR

Every parent should take a basic course in CPR, cardiopulmonary resuscitation. The Red Cross and American Heart Association offer courses in communities across the country. In them, students learn to administer artificial respiration to people who have stopped breathing, chest compressions if someone's heart has stopped beating, abdominal thrusts for choking, and basic first aid. The cost of these courses is nominal; they are readily available in most communities, so there's really no excuse not to take one. Not all include the specific techniques for reviving infants and toddlers, which are different than those used for adults. Check to be sure that what you need to learn will be taught.

FACTS

To find a CPR course near you, check the American Heart Association's Web page at ✑ *www.cpr-ecc.org* or call ☎(800) AHA-USA1. Or go to the Red Cross Web site at ✑ *www.redcross.org/services/ hss/courses.* You can also contact your local parks and recreations department, hospital, chamber of commerce, school district, fire department, ambulance service, or YMCA for course descriptions and locations.

Young children account for more than half of the 7,000 drownings that occur each year, so it really is worth parent's while to acquire CPR skills. An online video demonstration can be viewed at ✑*www.heartinfo.org/cpr/cpr.html#retpulse.*

Artificial Respiration

Five minutes without oxygen is enough to cause permanent brain damage; a few more minutes and death is probable. The exception is if the body is very cold, it needs less oxygen, sometimes enabling youngsters to survive for longer periods. If a child has stopped breathing due to swelling of the air passages caused by a medical problem such as asthma, an allergic reaction, or a respiratory infection, artificial respiration should be started immediately. However, if the child has stopped breathing due to an object stuck in his windpipe, artificial respiration might force it farther into the child's windpipe or even the lungs. Before attempting artificial respiration, a rescuer should follow the instructions for choking (see the section "Treating a Choking Victim").

For artificial respiration, follow these steps:

1. Place the youngster face up on the ground, lift the chin up and tilt the head back to keep the tongue from blocking the air passages. Examine the mouth and remove any visible obstructions with a curled finger.

2. Cover the child's nose and mouth tightly with your mouth and gives two gentle breaths lasting 1 to 1½ seconds each. Be careful not to blow too much or too hard; this will cause the child's lungs to hemorrhage. When properly done, you should be able to see the child's chest rise. The child's head must remain tilted up throughout to keep the wind passages open.

3. If the child does not resume breathing on his own, administer additional breaths at the rate of about twenty per minute until a medical team arrives.

4. If vomiting occurs, as is often the case, turn the child's head to the side to prevent choking. Then quickly clear the mouth cavity before resuming assisted breathing.

Chest Compressions

The heart delivers oxygen-enriched blood to the brain. If the child has collapsed and is non-responsive—that is, he doesn't moan, cough, or move even when his shoulder is tapped and his name is called—check for a pulse at the carotid artery. The easiest way to find the carotid artery is to place your fingertips (not the thumb, which can confuse the issue because thumbs have a pulse) in the groove of the child's neck, next to the windpipe, near the jaw.

What is the carotid artery?
The carotid artery refers to either of two large arteries on each side of the neck that carry blood to the head.

If you can't find a pulse, someone trained in CPR needs to manually pump the blood via chest compressions while you call 911. Compressions can damage the heart if it is already beating, so it's important to be sure there is no pulse before beginning. Here is the procedure for carrying out chest compressions:

1. Place a flat hand on the child's chest on the lower half of the breastbone, which is located between the nipples, and push down with the heel of your hand.
2. The child's chest should depress one-third to one-half the depth of the child's chest, far less than is needed for an adult.
3. Repeat this action at the rate of 100 compressions per minute.

When you combine mouth-to-mouth breathing and chest compressions, deliver five chest compressions for each breath until help arrives, and check occasionally to see if the heart has begun beating on its own.

Treating a Choking Victim

If a child is eating or playing with a small toy and begins to choke, his air passage may be partially or completely blocked. Signs of a partially blocked air passage include choking or coughing that starts very suddenly, gagging, or breathing that is noisy and high pitched.

If a child can manage to breathe a little bit, call 911 or get her to an emergency room immediately. Trying to dislodge the object could end up making matters worse by cutting off the child's air completely. If a child's ability to breathe is almost completely cut off or if breathing has stopped altogether, the situation is desperate and the child must have immediate assistance to keep her alive until an emergency medical team arrives.

Symptoms of desperate trouble include:

- The ribs and chest are sucked in when the toddler tries to breathe
- The toddler can't get enough air to cough
- The toddler can only wheeze softly or make soft high-pitched sounds
- The toddler can't make any sound at all
- The lips and skin are bluish

If the toddler is unconscious, look in the child's throat and try t o remove the blockage. If that doesn't work, administer two rescue breaths. If the child doesn't start breathing on her own, start chest compressions. Sometimes the compressions will eject the object from the windpipe.

If a toddler can't breathe but is still conscious, the goal is to force her to cough; something she can't do on her own because she is unable to take in enough air. Begin by explaining that you will help her. Quickly position her in front of you, reach around her with both arms, make a fist, and place it so that your thumb rests just above the navel and below the breastbone. Grasp your fist with your other hand. Give five quick thrusts, pressing upward and in. The object may be expelled. If not, give five more abdominal thrusts. Keep trying until the object is ejected.

If the child loses consciousness, lay the child down, lift her chin, open her mouth to look for the object, remove it if you can, and help her breathe with artificial respiration. If her heart stops, start chest compressions until medical help arrives.

Take a class to learn how to perform CPR, chest compressions, and other emergency first aid procedures correctly. It is easy to inflict injury in the process!

Toddlers' tongues, throats, and facial muscles aren't well developed. That, combined with the fact that they lack a full set of teeth, increases the risk of choking. Here are some things you can do to help prevent your child from choking.

- Peel and cut grapes lengthwise
- Mash hot dogs
- Cut meat into very small pieces
- Forget peanuts and stick to small amounts of peanut butter
- Keep hard candies out of reach and don't ever let them have any
- Avoid popcorn

Keep small toy pieces out of reach, too, and watch out for loose buttons and snaps on clothing that could fall off and be swallowed. Coins present another hazard. Children swallow more than 3,000 coins per year, according to the American Association of Poison Control Centers. Most pass through toddlers' systems without doing any harm, although some get stuck in the esophagus (warning signs are wheezing, gagging, and excessive drooling) or at the point where the small intestine connects to the bowel. Coins may sit in the stomach for days. To have a penny minted since 1982 linger in the stomach for more than a day poses a special hazard of zinc poisoning. Stomach acid begins to dissolve the zinc within two days of ingestion.

ALERT

Lengths of yarn, ropes, or string—any dangling material longer than 16 inches—can pose a strangulation hazard. Be especially careful to keep cords of mini-blinds and curtains from dangling within a toddler's reach.

First-Aid Kit

Whether you make your own or buy one in the store, every home should have a first-aid kit, stored where toddlers' prying hands can't reach it. It's a good idea to keep one in the trunk of the car, too. The American Red Cross recommends stocking the following items:

✚ Activated charcoal*	✚ Gauze pads and
✚ Adhesive tape	roller gauze (assorted sizes)
✚ Antiseptic ointment	✚ Hand cleaner
✚ Band-Aids	✚ Plastic bags
(assorted sizes)	✚ Scissors and tweezers
✚ Blanket	✚ Small flashlight and extra batteries
✚ Cold pack	✚ Syrup of ipecac*
✚ Disposable gloves	✚ Triangular bandage

* Use only if instructed by the Poison Control Center

In addition, parents might want to add a bulb aspirator, useful for removing mucus and foreign objects from the nose. For the kit stowed in the car, consider adding an old credit card for scraping out stingers and splinters, sunscreen, and insect repellant.

Medication Safety

While it might be tempting to refer to medicine as "candy" when you're trying to get some down a reluctant toddler's throat, don't! Just think what will happen if he gets into a bottle or a box when you're not around. Many parents don't realize that overdoses of vitamins can be dangerous, too. Follow these basic safety strategies:

- Call medicine by its real name.
- Use products with child-resistant packaging.
- Don't confuse "child-resistant" with "childproof." (The name changed when it was discovered how quickly toddlers could get the covers off. Very few items are toddler-proof!)
- Keep medications in their original containers to avoid confusion down the road.
- Avoid storing liquid medicines in cups or soft-drink containers that might tempt a thirsty toddler.

- Install childproof locks on cabinets, drawers, and closets where medications are stored. (Don't depend solely on locks! Little fingers can sometimes work them open.)
- Keep track of how much medicine has been used. (If you discover his hand in the bottle and pink syrup ringing his mouth, or her hand in the pills and white powder on her tongue, you'll have an idea how much has been ingested.)
- Treat vitamins containing iron like the medicine it is; an overdose can be fatal.
- Check the dosages and use a proper spoon or vial for measuring before each administration. (A teaspoon from your set of measuring spoons is NOT the same as a teaspoon from your silverware drawer.)
- Don't mix medications without your pediatrician's approval.
- If the phone rings while you're administering medication, take it with you. (Don't leave unattended drugs around a toddler!)

Don't take your own medication around a toddler—you don't want her to mimic you. Children need to learn that when it comes to prescriptions and over-the-counter medications, they are to take *only* what a caretaker administers. That includes vitamins! Even when you think a toddler understands, he probably doesn't!

Older Is *Not* Better

Parents should check the medicine cabinet from time to time and dispose of expired medications and those more than two years old. Flush them down the toilet and rinse bottles before discarding in the trash. The chemical changes that occur over time can render some ineffective. Others can become poisonous! Always discard aspirin that smells like vinegar; it has lost its effectiveness. Likewise, throw away any liquids that have separated or changed colors. And finally, dispose of old eye drops and eye washes; fungus can grow in them.

FACTS

In 1998, an astounding 70,242 children under age six were treated in health care facilities after accidentally ingesting medication, ranging from acetaminophen to nitroglycerin. That included more than 6,000 youngsters who ingested diaper products.

When it comes to toddlers and medication, you can't be "too careful." Keep prescription and over-the-counter medications locked up and out of reach at all times!

Herbal Safety

There's no guarantee that an herb is safe, and some homeopathic remedies can pack a big punch. Before administering alternative remedies to a toddler, check the following:

- That it has been tested on youngsters
- That its effectiveness has been established
- The kinds of side effects and adverse reactions that may occur
- That it won't interact with other prescription and over-the-counter medications your toddler is taking

CHAPTER 8
Doling Out Discipline

M any parents believe that "discipline" is the same thing as "punishment," and it is unfortunate that the two concepts have become synonymous in so many people's minds. Really, the word *discipline* means "teaching" or "learning," and comes from the word *discipulus,* which means "pupil." Disciplining toddlers involves teaching young pupils. It falls to the most important teachers in their lives, their parents, to serve as their principal instructors.

Little Disciples

Teaching little disciples is a long, slow process. They have little experience on which to build, and their language skills prevent them from understanding much of what is said to them. In addition, their memory skills are so poor that they forget much of what they've been taught from moment to moment and from day to day. Finally, they lack the intellectual skills to use what they learn in one situation to guide their behavior in another.

When it comes to disciplining toddlers, patience and repetition are the teacher's most important attributes!

Teaching about No-No's

When parents say "no-no," it is clear to *them* exactly what they want the toddler to stop doing or to stay away from. But what is obvious to them may not be at all clear to the toddler. How do you teach what "no-no" means? Here are a few ideas:

- Change your tone of voice when you say it.
- Accompany your words with a frown and shake of the head.
- Try to get your child to repeat your words, or at least your gestures.
- If your child mimics your words or gestures, smile and gush, "That's right!"

Toddlers may still not associate the phrase and gesture with an expected behavior, but at least they are being helped to focus on those two important words.

Don't Just Say No

The problem with "just saying no" is that toddlers don't learn what they *can* do. A child may not be *trying* to create chaos and ill will as she goes from one forbidden activity to the next. He doesn't know what is off limits and what is permissible. Follow up "no-no" and "don't" with an "it's all right to" or "you can" when appropriate.

Offering alternatives may not prevent toddlers from becoming upset if they're very taken with something. Still, offering alternatives provides an important lesson: When the road we want to go down is blocked, we need to find another one.

Too Many No-No's

The easiest way for parents to reduce the number of "no-no's" and "don't touches" is to childproof the home by putting away and securing as many dangerous and fragile objects as possible, and to provide lots of objects for them to manipulate.

ESSENTIALS

Instead of saying "no-no," some parents prefer "That's not okay." Either way, it takes many repetitions for youngsters to decipher the meaning and longer still to relate the words to their behavior.

Ultimately, the goal is for toddlers to learn to control themselves instead of relying on adults to control them. But developing self-control won't be accomplished in a matter of days, weeks, or even months or years. Until then, you may be better off putting more energy into controlling the environment. That way, you can spend less time struggling to control your youngsters and more time enjoying them.

The Problem with "No"

As anyone who has studied a foreign language knows, learning to understand and use negative words is no small task. In English, things get particularly confusing. Even adults aren't always sure what answering "yes" to a question means; for example, "You're not going to touch the stove, are you?" When addressing toddlers, keep things simple!

Since negatives like *don't* occur at the beginning of sentences, toddlers often miss them. They don't even realize they're being spoken to until the parent has made it halfway through the sentence. So when you say, "Don't touch the stove," the toddler may only hear ". . . touch the stove" or ". . . the stove." It's no wonder toddlers so often do exactly the opposite of what their parents are telling them!

Make it a habit to tell toddlers what *to do* rather than what *not* to do. Instead of "Don't touch the stove," you might say instead, "Keep your hands at your sides!"

INSTEAD OF THE NEGATIVE . . .	TRY THE POSITIVE . . .
"Don't go in the street."	"Stay on the grass."
"Quit yelling."	"Use your soft voice."
"Don't hit your sister."	"Ask her for the truck. Can you say 'truck, please'?"
"Don't touch the flowers."	"Put your hands behind your back and put your nose up close so you can sniff—like this."
"Don't bang the cup on the table."	"Put your cup down until you want a drink."

Why Not?

It's not always necessary to provide reasons for "no." Sometimes "no" can simply be "because I said so." But as children become increasingly independent, an adult won't be present at every moment to supervise. They need to be able to assess objects—and eventually situations and people—to determine what and who is safe. For example, if youngsters understand that they can't play with the lamp because it has an electric cord and a glass bulb, by middle childhood they will better be able to protect themselves when they come upon other interesting appliances and objects containing glass.

Show-and-Tell

Often parents can satisfy toddler's curiosity about forbidden objects by taking a moment for show-and-tell. Using the example of the lamp, a parent might do the following:

- Help the child look under the shade.
- Point out the glass.
- Hold the child's finger and help her touch the glass so she can feel it.
- Explain the importance of touching glass gently.
- Explain that light bulbs get hot if the lamp is turned on.
- Point out the cord and say that it's a no-no, too.

Young toddlers won't understand much of what is said. Still, parents' serious tone and hands-on demonstration can help satisfy their curiosity while communicating that lamps are to be handled with care.

Distraction

To keep very young toddlers away from things they're not to touch and dissuade them from forbidden pastimes, distraction is the simplest, most straightforward, least confrontational way to achieve compliance. With this technique, simply remove the forbidden object or move the toddler away from it, and say, "No, don't play with that." Frown, and shake your head, and then offer an alternate toy or activity.

If the tears don't stop quickly, the new toy or activity probably isn't very appealing, or the upset is about something else entirely. A big reaction to a small deprivation can be a sign that they are tired, hungry, ill or coming down with something, going through a stressful period, or going through a spurt of independence.

Redirection

When toddlers have matured to the point that they can remember the item their parent took away (which they demonstrate by trying to search for an object that has been removed), a teaching device known as "redirection" works well. Redirection simply involves the following:

- Setting a limit ("No, don't play with the lamp.")
- Giving a reason ("It's dangerous. The bulb could break. And you mustn't play with anything that has a cord.")

- Enticing toddlers into a different activity ("Let's find something else for you to play with. How about your flashlight?")

Like distraction, redirection is a simple, straightforward way to minimize or avoid confrontations. The challenge in redirecting a child is to find an activity as enticing as the one they've chosen. Here are some common no-no's and possible alternatives:

Jumping on the furniture. Slip old cases over pillows, place them on the carpet (or on blankets folded to make a pad), clear the area of end tables and other hard objects that could hurt them, and let them jump! Or purchase a beanbag chair children can jump on.

Throwing toys. Give them a dishtowel tied in string, two socks rolled together, a foam rubber ball, a sponge, and let them toss. If they need the sound of the *thunk,* consider letting them hurl a plastic bottle onto a linoleum floor or into a large metal pot.

Playing in the toilet bowl. Fill a plastic dish tub half full of water, set it on towels on the laundry room floor (or, on wash day, empty the dirty clothes hamper onto the floor), and let them play.

Sometimes parents come up with great alternatives, but toddlers feel compelled to say "no" because they are practicing independence. This can set the scene for many conflicts. Prime times for resistant behavior are shortly after learning to walk and during the second year.

Offering Choices

When simple redirection fails, try a different approach. Let's say that Jenny wants to paint. Her mother declines and offers her an alternative, "How about playing in your sandbox?" Jenny loves the sandbox, but her upset over her mother's refusal to let her paint quickly escalates into loud wails and roars. What's going on? It could be that she wants an indoor activity, so the sandbox fails to appeal. It could be that she is working on autonomy issues and needs to have a hand in deciding what she does next instead of always being told what to do.

ESSENTIALS Distraction works especially well before youngsters have achieved object constancy. Until then, they don't understand that objects still exist even if they can't see them at the moment. To them, out of sight really does mean out of mind.

Offering choices gives toddlers an opportunity to practice making decisions and to have more control over their lives.

Jenny's mother could say, "Painting is messy, and we have company coming over soon. You can play in your sandbox or read a book. Which would you prefer?" Jenny may need to finish wailing her disappointment over not being allowed to paint before she'll be ready to move on, in which case her mother can say, "When you decide whether you want the sandbox or a story, let me know."

When offering choices:

Keep them limited. Toddlers can become confused and overwhelmed when considering too many options. Until age three, they may have trouble with more than two.

Don't insist on an immediate decision. Crying is a toddler's way of expressing disappointment. The victory comes when they're able to recover and forge ahead.

Hold firm. This can be difficult in the face of intense toddler opposition.

Dangerous Situations

The time for parents to step out of the teaching role into that of policing is when their toddler is approaching danger. That way, they can stage an immediate rescue.

For instance, sooner or later most youngsters will want to explore electrical cords. When a young toddler reaches for one and suddenly hears his parent's loud voice, he is likely to pause, smile, and reach for the cord again. The parent may believe the child's pause means he understood the "No, don't touch!" warning. From the child's ensuing smile and renewed attempt to reach for the cord, adults may assume the kind of defiance that makes them want to tear their hair out by the roots.

However, the pause may simply be a response to the parent's voice; it doesn't mean that he understood the warning. Even if he does surmise from the parent's tone that he is being warned about *something*, he may not realize he is being warned away from the cord. How can toddlers comprehend that a cord is dangerous when they don't know about either cords or danger, and haven't even touched one yet?

When a toddler is approaching danger, follow these steps:

1. Say, "No! Don't touch!" or "Stop!" in a firm, authoritative tone.
2. If the child pauses, be sure to smile, nod, and provide positive reinforcement by saying, "Thank you" to let him know he responded correctly: he paused.
3. Don't wait to see what will happen next; grab him fast.
4. Explain, "That's *dangerous*, honey. It will hurt you."
5. Say "No-no," shake your head, and frown to convey your message nonverbally.
6. Try to get him to say "No-no" and shake his head.
7. Move him away from the danger.

If the child toddles back to the cord, you will need to either repeat the process as often as needed, distract him by providing something different to do, or offer him choices for alternate toys or activities.

ESSENTIALS
To make sure your toddler listens to you and not the voice propelling her to touch anything and everything, it is imperative to establish and maintain a good relationship. To this end, pick your battles, focusing on only one or two issues at a time; praise more often than you chastise; and spend more time enjoying each other's company than you spend praising *or* chastising.

If you physically move him away from the cord, he may conclude that you are playing a wonderful chasing game. He may head back in that direction the moment he is released, hoping for more. Once again, you may see his actions as defiant. It's important to consider that by this point the cord may be the farthest thing from his mind.

Would it be easier just to issue a warning and then slap the child to drive home the message that he must stay away from a dangerous object? Although it might seem easier in the short-run, there are a number of problems with slapping a toddler to convey the no-no message:

- Toddlers may lose trust in the parent. Slaps that are delivered "out of the blue" can make youngsters chronically tense and uncomfortable around anyone they have learned may hit them unexpectedly. If a child thinks he and his parent were playing a chasing game and didn't realize touching the cord was the issue, the slap will certainly take him by surprise. This can seriously undermine the parent-child relationship.
- Toddlers may learn that when their parent uses that particular tone of voice, they had better run fast to avoid being hit. This is *not* a lesson that will serve them well when the danger is approaching a busy street, hot stove, swimming pool, or a big dog!
- Toddlers may learn that they must not do certain things when their parent is around. The sooner children can move from needing parents to control them to controlling themselves, the better for everyone.

Even after toddlers understand that they're not supposed to touch particular items, they may still be driven to engage in forbidden activities, because they have two voices inside of them issuing very different directives. Mother Nature pushes them to explore and become independent. Their parents insist that many interesting activities and objects are off limits, and oppose their desire to make up their own minds.

The Problem with Praise

Brian was contentedly munching his cereal when his mother breezed by the table and gave him the thumbs-up sign. "Good job," she said. Brian's smile faded as he bleakly surveyed his brimming cereal bowl. He was already full, and he'd barely dented it. He wanted to please his mother, but knew he was going to have to let her down.

Just as parents use expressions like "No-no" or "That's not okay" to mean "Stop" or "Don't," they use expressions like "Good job!" or "Way to go" to mean "Yes, that's what I want you to do." If Brian's mother had said, "It looks like you're enjoying that cereal," he could have said "yes" without feeling obligated to eat more.

Contrary to popular opinion, praising youngsters doesn't necessarily improve their self-esteem. Praise encourages them to focus on their success at pleasing adults and at measuring up to other people's expectations, rather than the achievement itself.

Children with good self-esteem feel pleased with themselves. When evaluating their own behavior, they feel they measure up to their personal expectations. But praise can actually serve to undermine self-esteem. First-born children, whose parents are apt to applaud each small gurgle and goo and record each new accomplishment in their bulging baby book, tend to be the least emotionally secure and suffer more problems with self-esteem than the rest of the brood whose successes receive far less attention. Meanwhile, the middle child, typically lost in a no-man's land between the accomplished older sibling and the darling baby, has a harder time finding ways to impress. Yet youngsters sandwiched in the middle of the pack tend to be more self-confident.

The following parent comments point out some of the pitfalls of praise:

- "I like the bright colors in your drawing" suggests to the child that to please the parent, he should use bright colors. Expressing interest and asking a neutral question such as, "What did you draw?" or "Tell me about your picture" enables the child to share his drawing and his feelings about it without having his choice of crayons judged.
- If the parent exclaims, "Good catch!" when the ball lands in their toddler's arms, it's understandable why she becomes upset when it

lands on the floor on subsequent tries: the youngster assumes they are "bad" catches.

- "Good boy!" the parent says when the toddler uses the potty by himself. This kind of evaluation—"You're good because you did what I wanted"—can cause toddlers who are in the throws of a struggle over independence to respond by refusing to use the potty thereafter. Instead, try, "You should be proud of yourself." Although that still conveys your opinion, it encourages the child to evaluate *himself* in a positive light rather than to focus exclusively on your opinion.

There's nothing wrong with saying "Good" to teach a child to do things in a certain way. Certainly there are "right" and "wrong" ways to do many things. However, giving positive feedback in situations that are meant to be fun can cause toddlers to turn play sessions into grim tests of their competence.

Praising Accomplishments

After an hour or so has gone by without a repetition of a particular behavior problem, parents should make it a point to praise their child's accomplishment. Because toddlers get into so many things and break so many rules, it's easy to spend more time focusing on what they do wrong than on what they do right.

If, when you say, "I'm so glad you've left the TV off," the child runs toward it, hurry on over but try to give her the benefit of the doubt. There's a good chance she'll look at the controls without touching them and announce that it's a no-no, or wait for you to frown and shake your head and discuss this no-no with her once again. If so, she's making fabulous progress! Give her a hug and try to let her know you share the delight in her accomplishment. It's important for toddlers to realize that they really are capable of learning self-control and pleasing their parents. And parents will feel much better knowing that the child is making strides in learning to keep herself safe.

Time-Out

Providing time-outs is an excellent teaching device to help toddlers learn to adhere to important rules and regain control when they are unable to contain themselves. Simply tell your toddler to sit down until she can settle down and observe the limit you have set or behave in accordance with the rules you have established.

FACTS

Many parents send toddlers to their rooms for time-out, but this isn't an option for youngsters who need to be watched at every moment, and being sent away can make toddlers feel rejected. The point of time-out is to teach, not to punish, although until children learn the advantages of being contained, they may certainly *feel* punished.

The rule of thumb is to assign one minute of time out per year of age, so a two-year-old should be required to sit for two minutes at most. If toddlers weren't upset to begin with, they may become very angry about being prevented from engaging in the activity they have chosen. You may not wish to start the clock until the child has settled down.

When the child has regained control, discuss the event that precipitated the time-out to help him learn from the experience so he knows what to do if the same situation arises in the future. It helps to begin the discussion by praising the toddler for having regained control. Besides starting the discussion on a positive note, praise helps little ones focus on their important accomplishment, and keeps both the parent and child from being overly focused on the misdeeds.

Reviewing what transpired and figuring out what to do differently is beyond younger toddlers and will be too hard for older toddlers until they are familiar with the process. In the beginning, you may have to do most or all of the talking for your toddler:

Do you know why I sent you to time-out? *Blank stare*

Because you turned on the TV after I told you not to. *Blank stare*

You can't watch any more TV today. Too much TV watching isn't good for kids, remember? *Blank stare*

The TV needs to stay off, okay? *Nods*

There's still no guarantee that the toddler understood the question. If he turns on the TV again, the parent will need to assign another minute or two in time-out. The point of time-out is to teach several important lessons children can use throughout their lives:

1. Important rules must be followed.
2. If people disregard rules, there are consequences, which may be unpleasant.
3. If people don't control themselves, someone else will control them.
4. When people are upset and out of control, taking a brief time-out can help them calm down.

Most children learn the value of time-outs in short order. In fact, once they have become accustomed to the procedure, toddlers will begin sitting down or running off to their rooms when they are upset over a parental demand or prohibition. During their self-imposed time-out, they will finish crying and re-emerge, settled, a few minutes later.

Spanking

While spankings may more quickly control a child who is repeatedly engaging in forbidden behavior, the fatal flaw is that the parent is controlling the child's behavior. Children need to learn to control their own behavior. Corporal punishment is controversial, but even some social worker champions of abused youngsters consider spanking to be a reasonable course of action in situations involving imminent danger, such as running into the street, reaching for a hot stove, provoking an animal, or running around a swimming pool. They recommend an on-the-spot administration of three swats on the bottom with the open hand (never an object) accompanied by an explanation such as, "Running into the street is a no-no! It's dangerous!" Like hitting a puppy with a newspaper, the goal is for the sound of the swat and the parent's angry voice (not pain) to evoke the correct response to danger—fear.

Parents should not remove the child's clothes, since a hard hand against a soft bottom can cause bruising, which is considered abuse. Also, grabbing a toddler by the arm and jerking, or even holding on tightly while swatting, can cause spiral fractures if the child twists.

Parents who don't spank can usually elicit the same reaction by swooping the child away from danger while shouting, "Stay out of the street! It's dangerous!" and then refusing to comfort the crying child for a few minutes, saying, "No, I'm not giving you a hug right now. I'm upset. You're not supposed to run into the street!"

Relying on corporal punishment is a known risk factor for child abuse, perhaps because parents of strong-willed children find they must hit harder and harder to have an impact. Even if parents are not abusive, a common result is that children mimic their parents and relieve their frustrations by hitting others. If you think that hellion in the grocery store is spoiled rotten and needs a good spanking, you've probably got it backward, because being frequent spanking is associated with poorer behavior, not better.

Although toddlers may appear to be learning self-control from lots of hard spankings, they may only be learning to be subservient to the parental thumb. As soon as children find themselves in a situation where the parent doesn't spank—for example, in public—toddlers' lack of self-control becomes evident. So there's a good chance that the parent with the out-of-control toddler in the grocery store is the most frustrated shopper on the scene and will spank the toddler as soon as they get to the car or arrive home.

Delayed punishments may relieve the parent's frustration, but a toddler's poor memory won't allow him to understand the reason he was hit. By the time the toddler is punished, breaking the pickle jar, refusing to stay in the cart, throwing a tantrum at the candy counter, and swinging on the metal rail in the check-out line will probably be just a blur for the parent, too. Even if the parent could recite the list of broken rules, the child wouldn't be able to remember all these no-no's the next time she's at the store.

Handling Tantrums

Not every toddler has tantrums, but most do. They are most common between ages two and three, when there can be as many as one to two daily for several weeks, and others intermittently. Not all tantrums were created equal. Telling them apart can be tricky.

Stress Tantrums

The toddler is stressed (tired; hungry; ill; or cranky due to a number of small disappointments, changes, and/or defeats), when some unpleasant thing happens. Perhaps he hates to have his diaper changed, and Dad insisted on it. Or Mom kept her hands on the grocery cart when he wanted to push it himself. Or his toy broke. That one small incident becomes the straw that broke the camel's back, and suddenly the toddler loses control. The screaming and carrying-on is out of proportion to the problem at hand because the upset isn't about a single event. It's the result of an accumulation of stress that has taken its toll on a tyke who, because of his age, doesn't have a lot of emotional control to begin with.

Trying to sidestep a stress tantrum may merely be postponing the inevitable. As things heat up, it becomes increasingly clear that the toddler is trying to provoke a struggle.

To manage stress tantrums:

1. Hold the child firmly but lovingly and provide reassurance that she'll be okay in a bit. This assumes you *can* hold her. Children may thrash too wildly to be safely held.
2. If she's endangering himself, other people, or property as she rolls about the floor, clear the area if you can. Otherwise, move her to a safe place, like a carpeted floor.

3. Let her cry it out. Tears are a great tension reliever.
4. Empathize with the fact that she's having a hard day.
5. When the tantrum ends, ask if she'd like to sit on your lap and have you rock her, or lie down and have you rub her back.
6. Provide reassurance that things will get easier for her when her new tooth comes through, she's rested, she's adjusted to her new day care center, or the stressful situation has passed.

When it comes to stress tantrums, the best cure lies in prevention. Consider them a signal that your toddler is under more pressure than she can manage and see if there's a way to help lessen it. Remember that toddlers are already under a lot of stress because they are struggling with their personal sense of inadequacy that comes from wanting to do things and being unable to do them, having lots to communicate and being unable to say much, and wanting to be independent while being emotionally needy.

FACTS

In a stress tantrum, the child isn't trying to get something; instead, she is trying to get rid of the unpleasant feelings that have accumulated. Having a momentary whim gratified helps a stressed toddler feel better, but not for long. The next small crisis produces another upset of similar or even greater intensity because the *real* problem—feeling generally overwhelmed—remains.

Manipulative Tantrums

Some children learn to tantrum to get something. Their manipulative tantrums are their way of saying "I want something and I want it *now*!" Once their end is achieved—freedom to run around the store, liberation from the car seat, permission to eat the cookie or to have a toy—they settle down. Tantrums in public are common because many children have learned if they stage a big one, they will immediately be taken home, which is exactly what they want.

ALERT

If the tantrum is causing a public, and disruptive, scene in a store, movie theater, or restaurant, remove the child, if you can. You can deal with the tantrum, and the issue behind it, once you're in a calm and private area.

It can be hard to hold firm in the face of manipulative tantrums. Their fearsome intensity can quickly melt parental resolve. But of course, every time you appease the child by giving in, you drive home the lesson that screaming, hitting, kicking, thrashing, breath-holding, fainting, and even head-banging and vomiting are workable ways to achieve goals.

If the behaviors during manipulative tantrums are particularly dramatic, discuss the problem with your pediatrician to satisfy yourself that the quickest, most effective way to end this kind of tantrum—ignoring it—is a safe option. Behaviors that warrant a professional opinion include banging his head or other self-injurious behavior, or holding her breath to the point of turning purple, passing out, precipitating an asthma attack, or vomiting.

To end manipulative tantrums:

- If she's a raging puddle on the floor, tell her you'll talk to her when she's settled down.
- Carry her to an open space where she can't harm herself or something else, preferably with carpet to soften the blows, if she's flinging herself around.
- Step over her and busy yourself nearby (but out of kicking range) by studiously ignoring her.
- Remain alert to what is happening so you can intervene if she tries to hurt herself or something else.

The challenge is not to take manipulative tantrums personally. See them for what they are: a child's rage at rules and limits. By failing to give in and not paying attention to her, you're showing what happens when people are assailed by crushing disappointments: life goes on. When a tantrum ends and the child has settled down:

- See it as the victory it is—the child regained control on her own.
- Don't attempt to discuss what transpired before or during the tantrum—let the subject drop.
- Be warm enough to show her you're not angry with her—respond to her desire to be held, hear a story, or have you participate in another quiet activity once she's settled down.
- Don't try to compensate for having held firm by being overly solicitous.

If throwing a tantrum has worked in the past, the predictable short-term result when parents don't give in is an *increase* in both the intensity and frequency of tantrums. Confused youngsters work harder to employ the strategy that has worked so well in the past to get their way. It may take a number of scenes before they grasp that tantrums are no longer a useful method for getting what they want.

Communication Tantrums

Sometimes toddlers throw tantrums out of sheer frustration over their inability to communicate their needs. For instance, it's very clear that your toddler wants something. It's clear to your toddler that you have it. Try as you might, you can't figure out what your child is asking for. He tries every way he can think of to get the message across, and then dissolves.

Or it is all too clear what your toddler wants: ice cream. He is sure it is in the freezer, because that's where it's kept. Except that there isn't any ice cream there or anywhere else because you're fresh out. He's sure you're withholding it, and you can't find a way to explain it to him. Maybe she wants to watch a particular video, but the tape is broken. Or he wants his pacifier, but it's lost. The only recourse is to provide reassurance that you would give him what he wanted if you could and let him rage at the injustice of it.

It's not easy being any age, but it can be particularly hard to be a toddler. Parents who remain sympathetic as children struggle through these trying moments may also feel helpless. Remember that by demonstrating your love for your youngster when she is at her very worst, you are in fact helping a lot.

CHAPTER 9
Food Fiesta

Filling a toddler tummy with food is easy. Filling it nutritiously to meet the needs of a growing dynamo, and instilling healthy habits that last a lifetime can pose major challenges. Although this is a prime time for power struggles as parents begin begging, bribing, pressuring, and punishing to get youngsters to open up and swallow, the fact is toddlers actually need very few calories.

The Toddler Appetite

During the first twelve months of life, children triple their birth weight, gaining about 1½ pounds per month. But between twelve and twenty-four months, toddlers typically gain only 4 to 6 pounds—less than ½ pound per month. Between twenty-four and thirty-six months, they only gain 3½ to 5½ pounds—just over ⅓ pound per month! And those are averages, so some months they'll gain even less!

Since the beginning of the toddler years is also when parents try to get them to eat a greater variety of foods, it is easy to assume that resistance is due to being finicky. But consider the following:

- When toddlers consume very little food, it's probably because they just aren't hungry or haven't become accustomed to a new flavor!
- Unless your child's pediatrician suggests a need to spur weight gain, don't focus on *how much* a child is eating, but rather ensure that the *quality* of the little food consumed is excellent.
- If your child is losing weight or you're concerned about an overly dainty appetite, discuss the matter with your pediatrician.

When to Wean

It is unusual to see toddlers nursing, because most parents struggle in earnest to wean them from the bottle or breast early in the second year of life. This is unfortunate. Children continue to receive protection against illness as long as they nurse. In societies where nature is allowed to take its course, self-weaning occurs between ages 3 and 4; the *minimum* age is 2½. When they are ready to stop nursing, they simply taper off and lose interest.

FACTS

The American Association of Pediatrics now recommends that breast feeding continue for at least twelve months, and "thereafter for as long as mutually desired." The World Health Organization recommends "two years of age or beyond." Weaning at eighteen to twenty-four months is associated with higher IQ; virtually no research is available on youngsters weaned at older ages.

If you need to wean a toddler before he's ready, it will probably be difficult. Remember that they are severing a powerful emotional attachment. You can soften the blow by trying the following:

- Choose a time when the youngster isn't coping with other major stresses.
- Tell your child you are going to wean him.
- Provide milk in a cup with meals.
- Nurse after meals, when the child has less of an appetite.
- Eliminate one bottle or nursing session at a time, beginning with the one the child is least attached to—typically in the middle of the day.
- Avoid the cues that trigger the desire to be nursed by staying busy and sitting in a different chair.
- Spend the time you would have devoted to nursing reading a story, reciting nursery rhymes, or playing together.
- Offer bottle-fed babies a bottle of water.
- Wait five days before eliminating a second bottle or nursing session.
- Eliminate bedtime feedings last. (Provide other kinds of comfort until the child learns to fall asleep without being nursed. If possible, have Dad handle bedtime.)

Introducing Solids

If your child is not well into solid foods by his first birthday, keep in mind that breastmilk alone does not meet the nutritional requirements of a one-year-old. If you plan on breastfeeding exclusively past six months, consult your pediatrician for information on how to supplement your baby's diet.

Toddlers need solid food, too. Introduce new foods gradually, at least two to three days apart, so there is time to assess food allergies. Common symptoms of food allergy include itchy, watery eyes; repeated sneezing attacks; itchy skin; clear mucus running from the nose; rash; hives; "slapped," or very red, cheeks; or behavioral changes.

Five Squares a Day

Because toddler tummies are small, offer them five small meals a day rather than three big ones. An easy way to keep youngsters nutritionally well primed is to serve between-meal snacks that emphasize finger foods. That way, toddlers can more readily manage the mechanics of eating themselves, and there's less cooking and cleanup for the chef. (Remember not to let them wander as they munch!)

Popular Finger Foods:

Cheese sandwiches (cut in quarters)	Hard-boiled egg slices
	Luncheon meat in a pita
Fish-shaped crackers	Mozzarella cheese sticks
Fortified cereal	Vegetable sticks
Fruit wedges	Whole-wheat crackers

From Table to Tummy

For a decade, parents were told to let youngsters decide what to eat. Adults were instructed to put the food on the table, and then sit back, relax, and let nature take its course. According to a widely publicized study, when little ones were offered a selection of nutritious foods and allowed to eat whatever they wished without parental interference—although they might fill up on potatoes for a meal or two—over the course of a week they consumed a diet that would make a nutritionist smile. The media urged parents to stop worrying and back off, reassuring them that if tots were allowed to follow their instincts, they would consume what their bodies needed.

But there was a catch, and few reporters bothered to mention it: Everything that the scientists had placed before their little research subjects was a healthy choice. Coca-Cola and M&Ms were *not* on the menu! If parents want to trust Mother Nature to guide their toddler in the right direction, every dish they serve would have to be something she made herself. And that wise woman of the cosmos doesn't bake Ding Dongs, stir up batches of Jell-O Pudding, or make trips to McDonald's.

ALERT

Toddlers are supposed to be roly-poly. They'll lose the round belly after turning three. Until then, serve whole milk to ensure they get enough fat (after age two, 2 percent is sufficient). Don't put them on a diet except under doctor's orders, and avoid fat-free foods.

Minimal Diets

Since most American adults were pushed to "clean their plates" and eat more than needed while growing up, they automatically do the same with their children. Even those who don't use heavy-handed tactics to pass on their poor eating habits routinely provide not-so-subtle nudges, crooning, "This broccoli is so delicious," hoping their youngster will get the hint and eat, never mind that he's not hungry.

What about all that mashing and banging and tossing and rolling to experience food in all its most disgusting forms? Pediatrician and bestselling author T. Berry Brazelton believes that allowing toddlers to linger and play with their food in hopes a random bite will end up in their tummies should be a no-no, too. There are less messy ways, he contends, for kids to enhance their motor skills.

Alarmed by the appalling height/weight statistics (a majority are now decidedly overweight), the rise in kiddie cholesterol, the obsession with dieting (one-third of nine-year-old girls claim they're trying to shed pounds), and the exponential growth of eating disorders among teens and young adults, Dr. Brazelton presents a minimum daily diet in his book, *Touchpoints: The Essential Reference* (Perseus Press, 1994):

- 16 ounces of milk (or the equivalent in cheese, yogurt, or ice cream)
- 2 ounces of protein or complex carbohydrates high in iron (meat, an egg, or fortified cereal)
- 1 ounce of orange juice or fresh fruit
- One multivitamin (but only if absolutely necessary to eliminate the vegetable wars)

Of course, toddlers shouldn't be allowed to supplement this fare with foods that are essentially nutrition-free! If this meager menu isn't sufficient, offer them healthy food choices.

Good for You

When it comes to menu planning, variety is important for more than making toddler taste buds tingle. No single food is perfect, so children need to eat many different foods for optimal nutrition. For instance, oranges are rich in vitamin C but lack vitamin B_{12}. Apricots are high in beta-carotene. Scientists have only just begun to unravel the exact components of plants and animals that are good for humankind, and they continue to add to the list.

FACTS

Calorie counting gets tricky, especially when half of everything that goes onto toddlers' plates ends up in their clothes or on the floor. Parents may find it easier to think in terms of the number of servings instead.

Only a few generalities are certain: fresh foods are better than processed; pesticide-free food is healthier. So take up cooking and go organic! The typical American diet consists of so much poor-quality food; parents need to learn to separate the wheat from the chaff so they can identify the good stuff. Fortunately, labeling has improved, which makes it easier to figure out which packaged goods are healthy choices.

The first thing chefs need to know is that besides supplying vitamins, minerals, and other ingredients needed for good health (such as fiber), foods provide energy. Energy is measured in calories. Calories, which are measured in grams, come from three sources: proteins, fats, and sugars. Children need all three kinds. Parents need to keep track of which kind of calories their youngsters consume to be sure they are serving enough of each.

SOURCES OF CALORIES

SOURCE	AMOUNT	APPROXIMATE NUMBER OF CALORIES
Protein	1 gram	4
Carbohydrate	1 gram	4
Fat	1 gram	9

The number of calories needed depends on a toddler's individual metabolism, growth rate, and activity level, so the average number of calories a child needs at any particular time will vary. Large, active toddlers need more calories; small, sedentary toddlers need fewer. Foods that are low in fat can still be high in calories if they contain a lot of sugar. You must read the labels to determine how many calories a food actually contains. Here are some *general* guidelines:

RECOMMENDED DAILY CALORIES

AGE	FROM PROTEIN	FROM CARBOHYDRATES	FROM FAT	TOTAL
	(15%)	(55%)	(30%)	(100%)
1	165	605	330	1,100
2	180	660	360	1,200
3	195	715	390	1,300

Nutritional Pyramid

What started as the Four Food Groups is now the Nutritional Pyramid. The following sections provide details on specific serving sizes, but the pyramid is a handy visual reference. The habits formed now will help keep your child healthy as he grows.

FIGURE 9-1:
Nutritional
Pyramid

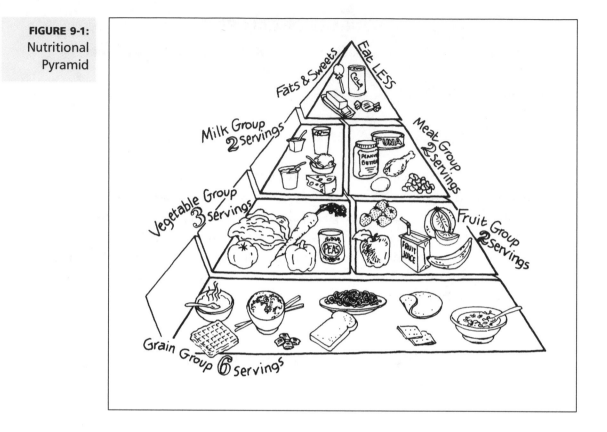

Servings of Protein

Protein, which is essential for good nutrition, comes from meats, poultry, fish, eggs, nuts, and beans. It's the extras—the skin and fat or addition of oil for frying, butter for baking, and cream sauces for smothering—that quickly add to the calories from fat. Milk, cheese, and yogurt are also high in protein and are rich sources of another essential nutrient, calcium. Low-fat products are preferable for children over age two because they have fewer calories from fat. Provide two to four toddler servings of meat and high-protein alternatives daily, and three to four servings of milk, yogurt, and cheese. One toddler serving equals:

- 1 whole egg or 2 whites
- ³⁄₄ cup milk
- ¹⁄₄ cup nonfat dry milk

- ¹⁄₄ cup baked beans
- 3 slices turkey luncheon meat
- ³⁄₄ ounce hard cheese

- ¹/₂ cup yogurt
- 3 tablespoons cottage cheese
- ³/₄ ounce poultry, meat, or fish
- 1¹/₂ tablespoons peanut butter

Contrary to what people often think, grains are healthy foods and are not fattening. It's when you add butter, cheese, whole milk, and assorted fat-rich sauces that the calories from fat quickly add up.

Servings of Complex Carbohydrates

Bread, rice, cereal, and pasta, which are made primarily or wholly from grains, provide energy from complex carbohydrates. Parents should provide six to eleven servings per day. One toddler serving equals:

- ¹/₂ slice whole-grain bread
- ¹/₄ English muffin
- ¹/₄ whole-grain bagel
- 2 to 3 whole-wheat crackers
- ¹/₃ cup cold cereal
- ¹/₄ cup cooked pasta or rice (brown or wild is best)
- ¹/₄ cup hot cereal

Servings of Fat

When it comes to calories from fat, the problem is usually keeping children from getting too much, especially after age two—processed foods tend to be loaded with it. But don't let round tummies and folds of baby fat fool you. Toddlers don't need low-fat diets unless there's a special reason! Parents should provide five to eight servings per day from ages twelve to twenty-four months, and add a half serving to each end of the range from ages twenty-four to thirty-six months. One toddler serving equals:

- ³/₄ cup whole milk or yogurt
- 1¹/₂ cups 2 percent milk
- 1 tablespoon peanut butter
- 1 egg
- ¹/₂ tablespoon oil, butter, margarine, or mayonnaise
- 9 French fries
- 2 chicken nuggets
- 1¹/₂ ounces beef, lamb, or pork
- 2¹/₂ ounces poultry
- ¹/₂ cup ice cream

The World Health Organization has recommended adding DHA (docosahexaenoic acid), a fatty acid found in mother's milk, to formula for bottle-fed tots. Studies show it can make a significant difference in mental and physical development. European formula manufacturers now include it in their recipes. Check with your pediatrician.

Servings of Vegetables

Vegetables contain small amounts of protein. What makes vegetables so important are the vitamins and fiber they also contain. Most of the vitamins are lost in the canning process. The recommended daily allowance (RDA) charts on packaged foods list how much of needed vitamins and other nutrients foods contain. If you're using a lot of preprocessed foods, learn to read the labels! Keep these points in mind:

1. Frozen vegetables are better than canned since fewer vitamins are lost in processing. Vegetables lightly steamed in cookware with a tight-fitting lid are better still. Raw vegetables are best of all.
2. Starchy vegetables like potatoes and yams are especially rich in nutrients, but they become a less-than-great choice when fat—butter, cheese, gravy, sour cream, or oil—is added.
3. Beans, which are rich in vitamins and fiber as well as protein, can meet vegetable or protein requirements.

Servings of Fruit

Fruit—including fresh, dried, frozen, and home-squeezed into juice—is rich in vitamins, especially vitamin C. Beware of fruit canned in sugary syrup, and juices that contain mostly sugar and only a squirt of real fruit juice. A few drops can result in a label that proclaims in large letters, "Contains real juice!" The question is *how much* juice, and you must read the label to find out.

Offer two or more servings of fruit per day. One serving equals approximately 1 tablespoon per year of life, so two-year-olds need at least 4 tablespoons per day. The equivalent is:

- $\frac{1}{2}$ cup (4 ounces) of juice
- 3 to 4 tablespoons of fruit

Don't Forget Fiber!

Fiber is important for proper functioning of the bowels. Hefty portions serve as an antidote for chronic constipation. Offer three or more servings of vegetables per day. One serving equals approximately 1 tablespoon per year of life, so two-year-olds need at least 6 tablespoons per day. Besides raw vegetables, other high-fiber foods include whole-grain breads and cereals, beans and peas, and fruit.

Calcium Counts

Calcium is required for bone growth, so to ensure your child gets enough calcium, you will need to provide daily doses from another source. Good choices include broccoli, calcium-fortified orange juice, calcium-fortified soymilk, canned sardines or salmon (*with* the bones), goat's milk, kale, tofu, and turnip greens.

Serving Liquids

Toddlers need 4 to 6 cups of liquids daily under normal circumstances—more in hot weather or if they are ill with fever, vomiting, or diarrhea. Besides water (from the tap or bottled, plain or carbonated), good sources of liquids include soup, fruit or vegetable juices, and milk.

But note that milk provides only ⅔ cup of liquid per cup served; the rest is solids. Also, many bottled waters do not contain fluoride. Either choose a brand and get the chemical composition from the bottler, or have your child drink tap water instead.

FACTS

Children need lots of iron, and one of the best sources is iron-fortified cereal. Other iron-rich foods include beef, liver, dried peas and beans, dried fruit, blackstrap molasses, and wheat germ. To help with iron absorption, serve a food rich in vitamin C at the same meal.

Recommended Daily Allowances (RDAs)

The RDAs for children ages one through three are as follows (according to *Smart Medicine for a Healthier Child* by Janet Zand, Rachel Walton, and Bob Rountree):

✔ **Protein:** 16 g (grams)
✔ **Vitamin A:** 400 mcg (micrograms)
✔ **Vitamin D:** 10 mcg
✔ **Vitamin E:** 6 mg (milligrams)
✔ **Vitamin K:** 15 mcg
✔ **Vitamin B_1:** 0.7 mg
✔ **Vitamin B_2:** 0.8 mg
✔ **Vitamin B_3:** 9 mg
✔ **Vitamin B_5:** 3 mg

✔ **Vitamin B_6:** 1 mg
✔ **Vitamin B_{12}:** 0.7 mcg
✔ **Vitamin C:** 40 mg
✔ **Biotin:** 20 mcg
✔ **Folic Acid:** 50 mcg
✔ **Calcium:** 800 mg
✔ **Magnesium:** 80 mg
✔ **Phosphorus:** 800 mg
✔ **Potassium:**
    1,000 mg (age 1–2)
    1,400 mg (age 2–3)

✔ **Sodium:** 225 mg
   (age 1–2)
   300 mg (age 2–3)
✔ **Chromium:** 20–80 mcg
✔ **Copper:** 0.7 mg
✔ **Iron:** 10 mg
✔ **Selenium:** 20 mcg
✔ **Zinc:** 10 mg
✔ **Iodine:** 70 mcg
✔ **Fluoride:** 0.7 mg

Good Vitamins

It's important to include at least one vitamin A–rich and one vitamin C–rich food in children's diets each day.

Foods rich in vitamin A include: apricots, broccoli, Brussels sprouts, cantaloupe, carrots, green leafy vegetables, mangos, papayas, and sweet potatoes.

Foods rich in vitamin C include: bell peppers, broccoli, cantaloupe, citrus, kiwi, mangos, papayas, peaches, potatoes (with skin), strawberries, sweet potatoes, and tomatoes. As you can see, there are several foods that supply both vitamins.

Special Bodies, Special Needs

Of course, no smorgasbord can meet the nutritional requirements of every child. Some children's bodies are unable to absorb proper amounts of iron, so they need a supplement. Also, many toddlers are allergic to certain foods or ingredients, or suffer from juvenile diabetes, and must therefore avoid certain ingredients. Make sure your toddler has regular medical checkups and discuss any special nutritional needs or concerns with your pediatrician.

ESSENTIALS   When playing chef for a little vegetarian, take special precautions to mix vegetables properly so kids get enough protein, iron, zinc, and B vitamins. Little vegans should also get calcium supplements. Consult your pediatrician for recommendations.

Chewing and Chopping

Once toddlers sprout enough teeth to chop through a carrot, hard foods become more of a choking hazard, not less. Be sure to cut crunchy foods to the size of half a grape before serving. Some squishy foods can also pose problems, given the ease with which they can become lodged in youngster's throats. Foods like grapes should be cut in half, and hot dogs and other meats should be served in pieces small enough to be swallowed easily. Even very soft food can be a problem if toddlers stuff their mouths or try to talk while their mouth is full. Discourage them from doing either.

The Joy of Dipping

Some kids love sauces, salad dressings, and condiments like ketchup—either because of the taste or for the sheer joy of dipping. Many go through a phase of wanting to add ketchup to everything; they think it improves the taste of everything from turkey to cereal! To date, there are no reports of children being adversely affected by this kind of strange culinary preference.

Adding sauces can encourage toddlers to do a better job on their veggies. But if they are just as happy to eat their foods *au naturel*, why encourage them to slather on extras that are typically high in salt, chemicals, and fat? Rather than passing on unhealthy family traditions to the next generation, it's better to let them die out. So, before you resort to salad dressing, try a squeeze of lemon and pinch of herbs. Don't boil rice, pasta, or vegetables in salt. Add it after the food is on your toddler's plate, if necessary.

Leisurely Meals

If toddlers take ages to finish a meal, why rush them? The modern trend to race through life notwithstanding, nowhere is it written that food must be consumed within fifteen minutes. Toddlers need a long time to eat for several reasons. It is challenging for them to get food onto a spoon or fork and into their mouth. Furthermore, they don't have many teeth to chew with, and their poor ability to coordinate the muscles of their face and mouth makes chewing and swallowing difficult.

And of course, they must pause to enjoy the sensation of eggs sliding through their fingers and the sound of pickles being banged on a plate. Given that all that fingering and mouthing is good for their motor skills and cognitive development, they derive lots of benefit from the assorted activities they indulge in while satisfying their bird-sized appetites. Let them take their time. Otherwise, they may have difficulty consuming enough to keep them well nourished.

To end a marathon meal but still ensure they've had enough to eat, try the following tactics:

- Announce that since he's not eating, the meal is ending, and you're going to take away his plate.
- If he doesn't begin aiming the food toward his mouth on cue, he may not have understood. Demonstrate by removing the plate.
- If he fusses, assume he is still hungry and return his plate to him.
- If he resumes playing instead of eating, offer to feed him. (Until their fine motor skills develop, toddlers have trouble getting food into their mouths.)
- If he eats or allows himself to be fed, wait to remove the plate until the next time he begins playing. Then remove it for keeps.
- Offer water if he cries, and reassure him that he will be served again at snack time or the next meal.

Healthy Appetites

It is all too easy to interfere with youngsters' ability to interpret the physical cravings that guide them to satisfy bona fide nutritional needs. So you don't confuse them, follow these do's and don'ts:

DO	DON'T
Provide only healthy choices	Offer junk foods
Let children dawdle through their meals	Rush them
Offer to help feed them	Insist on helping
Serve previously refused foods early in a meal, when they're hungriest	Force them to eat things they don't like
Offer small portions, and let them know they are free to ask for more	Give large servings and coax them to eat
Make mealtime relaxed and enjoyable	Nag them about eating
Let them eat as little or as much as they want	Play "here comes the airplane" to induce them to open up and eat more

Up with Veggies

Sugar coatings work to get kids to eat cereal. Why shouldn't it work to get kids to eat veggies, too? As it turns out, it does. If you sprinkle some sugar on broccoli, peas, lettuce—or whatever—most children will gladly gobble the greens. Once they've developed a taste for the vegetables in question, reduce the amount of sugar added to subsequent servings until it is eliminated altogether.

Cute Concoctions

Kids may resist the raw carrots, celery, alfalfa sprouts, and broccoli lying on their plates in traditional arrangements, which is to say in small piles. A glob of cottage cheese and smear of peanut butter on bread may not hold much appeal for finicky eaters. But turn those same ingredients into 3-D designs, and toddlers are apt to undergo a dramatic attitude change. Who can resist a figure made of carrot legs, celery arms, cottage cheese face, raisin eyes, tomato smile, and alfalfa sprout hair lounging amid broccoli trees growing in peanut butter sand anchored in cement—er, crackers? To entice kids to eat good foods, be creative! Here are a few other ideas you can try:

- Cut bread with cookie cutters to create interesting shapes before topping with cheese or vegetables. The leftover bread can be frozen and eventually used to stuff chicken or turkey.
- Slice a banana lengthwise to make a boat; stand a piece of sliced cheese inside to make a sail; and float it in a pool of blueberry yogurt. You can even infest the water with shark fins made from salami slices. (If that combination doesn't sound appealing to you, remember that your child probably won't mind, and it all ends up in the same place, anyway!)
- Spread strips of toast with cream cheese or peanut butter and top with a row of raisins for an enticing dish of "ants on a log."

Broadening Culinary Horizons

The first and second times tots taste peas, broccoli, and any number of other foods parents consider healthy, it is common for toddlers to turn up their noses at them. After trying again and again, the best recourse, nutritionists say, is for parents to try yet again and again. It can take eight to ten exposures before a youngster develops a taste for a new food.

Offering new foods and encouraging their toddler to take a taste is one kind of "exposure" most parents have used successfully. Heavy-handed tactics like force-feeding are more likely to harden resistance than induce acceptance . . . and may propel a child toward lifelong eating problems.

However, most tots are destined to dislike certain foods. Just as many adults never develop a taste for liver or cringe at the sight of Roquefort dressing, little ones have definite preferences. Other things being equal, one way to tell that a child is in a growth spurt is an increase in appetite. While her appetite is hefty, she may be more receptive to new and previously rejected foods. Offer them early in the meal, when she is hungry and less finicky.

Little Farmers

There is one (almost) guaranteed cure for kids who spurn leafy greens and assorted vegetables that parents consider healthy. When toddlers participate in growing them, their negative attitude is apt to undergo a dramatic transformation once it's time to eat the fruits (er, vegetables) of their labors. Homegrown tomatoes, carrots, and lettuce are so much more flavorful, it's much easier to get kids hooked on the taste.

Families don't need a garden; many vegetables have been developed that do well in patio pots. Herbs, of course, can be grown at any time of year; all they require is a sunny window. Help little ones pinch off chives, basil, parsley, cilantro, oregano, or other favorites to sprinkle on their salad or cooked vegetables.

Shorty Chefs

Involving little ones in food preparation creates the kind of pride of accomplishment that can bring about a willingness to eat their creations. Toddlers are so good at shredding important papers. Put that talent to work tearing the washed lettuce leaves into pieces and dropping them into the salad bowls. Pull up a chair or step stool so youngsters can join you at the counter. Enlist their help with a variety of food preparation chores by giving very young toddlers directions for one simple task at a time and giving a hands-on demonstration.

Until youngsters master a task and are old enough to remember how things were done in the past, they will need lots of feedback and repetition: "Put this bun on this plate," "Yes, that's right." "No, like this. Put the bun on the plate." Older toddlers should be able to handle more general single-step directions: "Put the buns on the plates," although they may also need a demonstration. As they approach age three, they may be able to handle two-step directions: "Get the buns out of the refrigerator and put them on the plates."

Toddlers as young as fifteen months should be able to help with a number of chores such as:

Scrubbing fruits and vegetables. Since a brief rinse in water is all that's required, this is an easy one for toddlers.

Pouring water. Let them pour water a cup at a time into the pot that will be used for boiling pasta, rice, eggs, vegetables, or cooked cereal. Keep them away from the stove, and let them work with cold to lukewarm water only!

Spreading. Let them use a plastic knife to spread peanut butter or cream cheese on celery sticks.

Making omelets. Let them sprinkle shredded cheese onto the eggs; the eggs and pan must be cool.

Cutting cookies. Put each ingredient for the cookie recipe into a separate bowl. Help toddlers pour them all into one bowl, stir, roll out the dough, and cut it with cookie cutters.

Stirring juices. After you pour the thawed juice into the pitcher of water, have your toddler stir. Teach her to stir gently, but use a big pitcher so there's room to slosh!

Cleaning the counter. Toddlers can wipe down the counter with a damp dishrag or sponge. (Not that you'll end up with a clean counter for the first year or two or even three. Focus on the participation, not the result.)

Setting the table. Keep the directions simple! First instruct them to put a fork by each plate. When they are finished, they can do the spoons, and then the bread knives. They can also put out the butter, ketchup, salt and pepper, napkins, too, if they're given one item to do at a time.

Include toddlers in the decision-making, too. For instance, "Do you want to put green or black olives on the salads?" and let them dip their (washed) fingers into the jar to add some to the plates. At mealtime, be sure you gush your compliments to the chef! It may take an eighteen-month-old ten minutes to extricate a slice of cheese from its cellophane wrapper, and it may be pretty mangled by that point. Still, the parent can place a piece of bread on the child's plate, hand him the remaining cheese, and tell him to put it on his bread to finish making his sandwich.

It only takes a few minutes spent together in the kitchen each day—by the time youngsters are three, they will be able to make a substantial contribution. In the long run, parents will be paid back with interest for the time and extra work kiddie "help" costs them now. In the short term, the benefits include:

- The entertainment value of a fun activity
- The boosts to self-esteem that come from actively participating in family life
- The time spent interacting with parents and other family members
- Increased interest in eating what they've prepared
- A sense of accomplishment
- Increased autonomy
- A recognition of their worth as a contributing family member

Food Struggles

It's easy for mealtimes to degenerate into food struggles when parents obsess about each pea on their child's plate, so it's not a good policy to spend mealtimes counting them. If you pay too much attention to exactly what children consume, it's easy for food struggles to develop—and they are notoriously difficult to win. Parents can lead toddlers to vegetables, but even if they tried to force them down their throats, they can't keep them in their stomachs. Overall, the biggest impediment to a well balanced diet is that bane of modern households: snacking.

"I'm Hungry"

It's not time for dinner, but your toddler is hungry. Should she have to wait? If the answer is "yes," you risk sending the message that the clock is more important in determining her need to eat than the signals her tummy is sending. The goal, some nutritionists suggest, should be for toddlers to learn to tune in to their internal hunger cues, not ignore them.

Offer part of the regular meal in advance, like the salad or vegetables, so the child gets a nutritious snack and a head start on dinner. A child may turn up his nose at the chance to start on his soup before the rest of the family. But if he's hungry, he'll eat it. The trouble begins when the cook prepares special between-meal snacks to satisfy kiddie culinary whims.

Eating Jags

The predictability of an unvarying menu can help anxious youngsters feel more secure. Refusing to eat anything except a few special dishes can also be a way of establishing personal control. There are two distinctly opposite, but equally valid, ways of approaching this problem.

ESSENTIALS

Lots of books for toddlers deal with the issue of food. *The Very Hungry Caterpillar* by Eric Carle (Putnam Publishing Group Juvenile, 1984) is an award-winning book they'll love learning from. *Cloudy with a Chance of Meatballs* by Judi Barrett (Aladdin Paperbacks, 1982) will tickle their funny bones.

The first way is to eliminate all food struggles by serving what your child wants. If a war for control is driving the resistance, catering to toddler demands eliminates the toddler's need to battle over food. Supplement his diet with vitamin tablets, milk, and fruit juice to maintain nutrition. Continue to make other foods available by placing them on his plate if he'll allow them to be there, or place them on a separate plate nearby. If both of those create upset, simply follow your normal serving procedures for the rest of the family. If your toddler does request something additional, dish out a serving. Studiously avoid questions about whether he likes it and comments about being glad that he's eaten something besides the usual. The goal is to not draw attention to his eating or make an issue of it, thereby preventing a basis for renewed resistance.

The second way is to ignore the child's demands, serve what you will, and wait until hunger motivates her to eat. The refusal to eat a well-balanced meal often stems from snacking. Some toddlers constrict their diets to the point that it seems that if it were up to them, they'd only eat one or two things—such as grilled cheese sandwiches, hamburgers, or a particular type of cereal—three meals a day, everyday. "If I don't fix what she wants, she wouldn't eat anything," their parents claim.

But how true is that, really? The bottom line is that many youngsters consume far more between meals than during them, so when breakfast, lunch, and dinner arrive, they can afford to be choosy. The surefire way to end eating jags and get the vast majority of toddlers to eat what they're served at meals is to stop fulfilling their desire for off-the-menu items and junk-food snacks.

Test of Wills

Many parents find that eliminating unscheduled snacking is easier said than done, however. Children's refusal to eat dinner means that they will be hungry soon after. If parents hold firm on their nothing-until-the-next-regularly-scheduled-meal-or-snack policy, they soon have a very cranky youngster on their hands. If they hold firm through the crankiness, they have a truly hungry child on their hands, and the "I hungry" wails can be wrenching enough to thaw the firmest parental resolve.

Children will not die of hunger from being put to bed without their dinner. Unless they are suffering from diabetes or another disorder, they won't end up nutritionally deficient, either. So if parents don't back down, the problem will be solved when the child sits down to breakfast with bona fide hunger pangs.

Autistic children often have very persistent food obsessions, but although this is rare, it is possible for any exceptionally strong-willed toddler to dig in his heels and reject food despite intense hunger. More often, it is the parents' fear that the child will die of malnutrition before deigning to eat a well-balanced meal that drives them to allow continuing between-meal snacks.

Passing on the Problems

A 2001 study in *Journal of the American Academy of Child and Adolescent Psychiatry* (March 2001) found that mothers with eating disorders were more intrusive with their infants during mealtimes (and during play, too). Toddler weight was found to be related to both the amount of conflict during mealtimes and the mother's preoccupation with her own weight—with lower toddler poundage associated with more conflict and more personal maternal weight worries.

FACTS

Toddlers, like adults, will eat out of boredom. If the parent responds to requests for a snack by offering several healthy alternatives but the child refuses anything but a cookie, she's probably not hungry. An appealing activity or nap may do a better job of eliminating the crankiness.

Further, toddlers must be simultaneously nurtured (by being fed) and given firm limits (by restraining them in a high chair and keeping them from throwing food). Balancing the two is a heady emotional experience, and research shows that parents who had highly conflicted relationships with their own parents have a harder time filling both roles.

All the emphasis on food can make the toddler years particularly trying for adults with eating disorders. This is a good time to enter counseling, therapy, or join an Eaters Anonymous support group to get some real culinary help.

No Sweets!

Some parents are determined never to allow candy to pass their children's lips so they won't develop a taste for sweets. Unfortunately, this strategy can backfire by imbuing creamy, crunchy, gooey, sugary foods with the heady mystique of the forbidden.

Although palates differ, anthropologists believe that the human love of sweets is inborn. Apparently our taste buds were designed to guide primitive humans toward edible, calorie-rich plants (typically sweet) and away from poisonous ones (generally bitter). Unless children are being raised on a desert island, sooner or later they will discover the wonders of cakes, candy bars, cookies, and pies. And if they have a normal set of taste buds, they will probably love them.

If a bank teller or doctor's receptionist offers your toddler a lollipop, jumping in to forbid the gift in the absence of a compelling reason may be exerting the kind of control that causes youngsters to work overtime to satisfy their in-born sweet tooth. (A compelling reason to step in would be if the child has a medical problem, such as diabetes or an allergy.) Certainly it is reasonable to insist toddlers wait to consume their gift until later. In doing so, parents may teach the most important lesson: it's okay to eat sweets at certain times. It's when they're consumed just "whenever" that they become a problem.

At least, that is the generally accepted wisdom from experts in the toddler nutrition field: monitor the consumption of "junk foods" at home and accept that standards will be lower outside of it. However, there may be merit to a stricter approach, given the exceptionally poor diets of most Americans, the rise in obesity and cholesterol in children, and the omnipresence of less-than-optimal food that subjects youngsters to continuing temptation.

Strange Cravings

Rather than satisfying the normal toddler urge to explore anything and everything with their mouths, some youngsters actually consume materials not meant to be ingested. Pica is a craving for unnatural foods or items such as soil, paint, string, cloth, hair—even feces and animal droppings. It is a desire for items that aren't food at all and have no nutritional value. Pica does not usually signal a deficiency of vitamins and minerals. It is most prevalent among mentally retarded youngsters, but can develop among otherwise normal youngsters, too. It typically occurs in children age eighteen months to two years, and parents must monitor these youngsters carefully to prevent them from satisfying their strange cravings. Pica usually only lasts a few months before disappearing on its own.

Children with rumination disorder vomit their food into their mouths without signs of nausea or retching or stomach upset. They may eject it from their mouths, or proceed to chew it again and swallow it without signs of disgust. It occurs most commonly among children with Sandifer's syndrome, esophageal reflux, and mental retardation, typically beginning between three and twelve months. Consult your pediatrician if your child shows signs of these disorders.

High Chairs and Booster Seats

When purchasing high chairs, choose one with a wide base, since that adds stability. To keep toddlers safe:

- Position high chairs away from hazards, such as stoves, windows, and drapery cords.
- Don't allow the child to stand in the chair unsupervised. (If the chair tips or the child loses his balance and falls, it's a long way to the ground head first.)
- Use the safety belt rather than relying on the tray to hold the child in.
- Be sure the tray is properly latched on both sides, as babies tend to push against the tray when seated.
- Periodically check for loose screws and a wobbly base.

ESSENTIALS

Applesauce, milk, and tomatoes dribbling down your toddler's legs will eventually land on your floor. Until her aim improves to the point where most of the food ends up in her mouth, spread a few newspapers or a drop cloth under her high chair to cut down on cleanup.

Magazines or old telephone books wrapped in contact paper make adequate booster seats, although their lack of a safety belt makes them useless for youngsters who refuse to remain seated. Buying one for everyday use so that older toddlers can sit at the table has some advantages. Tending to toddlers can be easier when they are sitting at the same level, then adults can eat with fewer distractions. Putting the child's plate and cup on a tray can help contain the mess, and being on the same level with everyone else makes her feel more like part of the family. As she mimics those around her, her behavior, manners, and even food choices may improve.

Restaurant Survival

Toddlers can make very unpleasant dining companions in restaurants because dining out requires two skills they haven't yet mastered: sitting and waiting. Taking them to places designed for adults is apt to be a miserable experience for the parents, the child, and other patrons as well. The rule of thumb is not to look to restaurants as a place to relax and enjoy yourself.

You can minimize upsets, however, by arriving prepared. In general, the fancier the restaurant, the longer the wait; so if the cupboard in your diaper bag is bare, don't even wait for the waiter— as you're being seated, ask the host to bring bread or crackers posthaste. It's a good idea to arrive with entertainment, too. Try to bring something new and different; otherwise, the novelty of items on the table will hold much more appeal. Rather than beginning the litany of no-no's the minute a small hand gravitates toward a coffee cup, scan the table for items your toddler can safely play with. Trying to prevent youngsters from touching anything guarantees a series of noisy scenes. Toddlers simply must have something to do, so be realistic. Allow them to bang a spoon if there's a tablecloth to dampen the sound or to shred a napkin.

ALERT

Be careful to keep your voice down when chastising your toddler. Parental nagging is often louder and more incessant than an occasional whine from a toddler, and hence more disruptive to other patrons.

Given the challenge of coping with toddlers in standard establishments, it's better to stick to kid-friendly restaurants. Many places have been specially designed for families with tots. Unfortunately, they often come up short in the nutrition department, but areas for climbing and crawling offer some compensation by offering opportunities to practice their physical skills. Parents shouldn't expect to relax while toddlers entertain themselves, however. Most structures are overly challenging for tots, and if bigger kids are roughhousing, play areas can be outright dangerous. Close monitoring is imperative. If a sign forbids children under a certain height from entering an area, believe it! On the other hand, ignore the signs prohibiting big people from entering if your toddler is in a potentially dangerous situation. Climb on in and stage a rescue!

CHAPTER 10
Sleepy Time

Minding a toddler is an every-waking-moment job. It's no wonder that caregivers look forward to toddlers' sleep time like thirsty desert wanderers crawling toward an oasis. Many parents can recover and regroup, work on a personal project for more than ten minutes, or have an adult conversation only when their youngster's eyelids drift closed.

Counting the ZZZs

Like everything else about the diaper-and-training pants crowd, the need for sleep varies dramatically from child to child. Survey any group of toddler caretakers, and they report tremendous variations. Some twelve-month-olds subsist on only nine hours of sleep in any twenty-four-hour period, rarely napping for more than an hour. Meanwhile, some three-year-olds are still sawing enough logs each night to raze a forest and supplement their nighttime slumber with a long afternoon snooze, too, for a total daily sleep time of thirteen hours or more.

	SHUT-EYE AVERAGES			
AGE	TOTAL SLEEP	NIGHTTIME SLEEP	NAPPING SLEEP	NUMBER OF NAPS
12 months	13¾ hours	11¼ hours	2½ hours	2
18 months	13½ hours	11¼ hours	2¼ hours	1
24 months	13 hours	11 hours	2 hours	1
36 months	12 hours	10½ hours	1½ hours	1

FACTS

The journal *Sleep* reported that nine- to twelve-month-olds averaged two naps per day. At fifteen to twenty-five months, the average dropped to one afternoon nap. Most children continue afternoon naps until age four.

How are parents to decide how much sleep their toddler needs? If a child is relaxed and content, it's doubtful that he's sleep deprived, no matter that parents have deep circles under their eyes from entertaining him eighteen hours a day. But since fussier toddlers tend to have more difficulties sleeping, it can be hard to sort out whether the fussiness is caused by a lack of sleep or if their high-strung personalities keep them from getting concentrated, restful shut-eye.

Your toddler may be sleep-deprived if he or she is:

- Routinely falling asleep in the car
- Hard to awaken in the morning and from naps

- Cranky and irritable during the day
- Hyperactive before bedtime
- Likely to fall asleep before bedtime

Sleepy Face

As any adult insomniac knows, being sleepy and being tired are very different. Being overly tired makes falling asleep difficult because in response to the achiness that often accompanies being overtired, the muscles tense. It's impossible to relax mentally to the point of drifting off when the body is physically primed for action. It is much easier to get sleepy children to close their eyes than it is tired ones!

Parents should make an effort to notice the subtle changes in their toddler's appearance so they can more readily discern whether he's rested, sleepy, or tired. When toddlers are very sleepy:

- Their faces look softer, even puffy
- The muscles around the lips and chin may droop
- Their movements slow
- They become less animated
- They may yawn

If they are tired, on the other hand, they are apt to show signs of tension and increased physical strain:

- Their faces show signs of strain
- The muscles around the eyes tense
- The eyes may appear sunken
- Activity level may increase
- Play becomes less focused
- Crankiness is common

To facilitate getting a toddler to sleep, try getting her into bed when she's sleepy. This means she's physically more relaxed. It's harder when she's physically and emotionally tense from being tired.

Reading the Signals

A common reason that children of all ages don't want to sleep is because life is so grand. They want to live every moment to the fullest. They don't want to be shut up alone in a room while other family members are out in the living room having fun. Even if everyone else is in bed, some youngsters would rather be out in the living room having fun all by themselves than lying awake in a darkened room.

Toddlers don't connect crankiness to a need for sleep. They have to be taught to recognize these bodily sensations and emotional reactions. Then they will eventually recognize the signals. If they actively fight going to bed, they may become upset by the mere comment, "You look sleepy now" or "I think you're unhappy because you're tired" because they suspect those fateful words, "Time for bed" will soon follow. Nevertheless, parents should continue to share their observations.

ESSENTIALS

Just as toddlers need to tune into the internal signals that let them know when and how much they need to eat, it is essential that toddlers learn to interpret the internal cues that indicate a need for sleep so that one day they can take care of themselves.

Schedules Help!

Whether parents put balky toddlers down for the night and let the tantrums run their course or let them stay up until they collapse from exhaustion in the wee hours, conduct "rise and shine" at the same time each morning and prevent longer-than-usual naps that compensate for missed sleep. Studies on insomnia demonstrate that establishing a schedule is crucial. Being extra tired ups the odds that children will be ready to sleep at the next nap or bedtime.

The invariable routine of a rigid bedtime and nap schedule can go a long way toward regulating toddlers' sleep patterns. The human body operates in circadian rhythms—a predictable cycle that causes people to fall a sleep at night and awaken in the morning at about the same time each day. These rhythms change over the life span. If left to their own devices, teenagers would stay up half the night and sleep half the day; on the other hand, senior citizens naturally fall asleep early and awaken shortly after dawn.

A sudden increase in need to sleep in the absence of extra exercise or stress is often a signal that a virus or another illness is brewing. Keep your eyes open!

Not all toddlers run on the same clock, however, and it is difficult when theirs doesn't adhere to the rest of the family. Some night owls have a hard time sleeping at night no matter how early they get up; early birds may awaken long before the rest of the family despite having gone to bed late the night before. Instead of their biological clocks being reset by a consistent schedule that conforms to the rest of the family, they lie awake in bed and are chronically sleep deprived.

Resetting the Alarm

There are no guarantees, but many parents can sometimes reset their toddlers' internal clocks by following a rigid schedule that will bring them more in line with the rest of the family. To do this:

- Awaken young toddlers at the same time each morning.
- Put them down for naps at the same time each day.
- Awaken them from naps at the same time.
- Awaken them from afternoon naps by 4 P.M. to ensure sleepiness at bedtime.
- Keep bedtimes consistent.
- Coordinate with other caregivers to be sure the daily routines are the same.

The Battle of the Bed

So many American parents struggle with getting children to take naps and go to bed at night that, when surveyed, sleep problems routinely appear near the top of the list of the child-rearing problems. The bedtime battles being waged across America are by no means universal. In cultures where families bed down together—and that includes most of the world—sleep problems are virtually unheard of.

When foreign parents hear about the accepted American practice of isolating little children in darkened rooms and placing them in beds that have bars like cages, they are shocked. To them, this sounds unspeakably cruel. "Put children to bed by themselves?" they exclaim. "But aren't they frightened and lonely?"

Certainly the continuing after-lights-out attention seeking from toddlers, and the ongoing worries about monsters and burglars among older children suggest that fear and loneliness are exactly what they experience. In many cultures, parents get toddlers ready for bed, then allow them to rejoin the family until they express an interest in sleeping. If they don't ask to go to bed, parents wait until they fall asleep on the couch or wherever, then carry them into a shared sleep area.

When American parents wait for youngsters to conk out on their own before carrying them to bed, some find the problems persist. That's because they are taken to their own bedroom. So as not to end up alone, toddlers may fight their feelings of sleepiness and become overly tired. That can end up with them being chronically sleep deprived.

The Family Bed

American taboos are quickly falling by the wayside as more parents find that the age-old solution of letting toddlers sleep with them virtually eliminates bedtime scenes and helps everyone get better rest. But although this practice appears more kid-friendly on the surface, there's no guarantee that it will enhance a toddler's life. The loss of the parent's alone time can make it harder for them to remain patient with their youngster during the day, which is clearly not in a toddler's best interest. Additionally, the loss of private time with their partner can jeopardize marital relationships, which, given the stress of rearing a toddler, may already be strained.

Big Bed Safety

Toddlers are probably in greater jeopardy from sleeping alone in cribs than from bunking with parents, given the risk that they'll climb over the bars and fall to the floor, become trapped between the mattress and the bars, or that another emergency will arise that a parent asleep in another room won't hear. Still, accidents in big beds do occur, and there are some precautions parents should take before deciding to sleep with their little one.

FACTS

Researchers at the U.S. Consumer Product Safety Commission reported 515 deaths among children under age two between 1990 and 1997 while sleeping on adult beds. The vast majority was younger than three months and no figures for toddlers are available, but the commission recommended *against* sleeping with children under age two. Of these deaths, 121 were reported to be due to a parent or older sibling lying on top of the child, while 394 became trapped in the bed structure (for example, becoming wedged between the mattress and wall).

- If you push your toddler's bed up against yours, check to be sure he can't become wedged between the mattresses of the two beds or between his mattress and the wall.
- Don't use a slatted headboard, foot railing, or side railing that could trap a child's head.
- Don't sleep together in a waterbed.
- Check out co-sleepers, which are advertised to be a safe alternative. These three-sided cribs are designed to attach to the parent's bed.
- Keep your child's bed away from dangling cords from curtains or blinds; they are strangling hazards.
- Do not sleep together if you are under the influence of drugs or alcohol. That might keep you from being aware of having rolled on top of your child.

Co-Sleeping

In a co-sleeping arrangement, the crib or toddler bed is pushed up against the parent's bed or a specially designed co-sleeper is attached. The bars can be lowered as needed for breastfeeding and hands-on comfort, and raised to keep her within her space. When the youngster graduates to a twin bed, her sheets can be tucked in around her so she doesn't gravitate toward her parents.

ESSENTIALS

To enhance the decor of co-sleepers, buy a comforter or bedspread one size larger than your bed and use it to cover both. A double bed next to a single one will look like a queen-size, a queen will look like a king.

Bad Bedfellows

Many parents find that having the family snuggled up together in the same bed produces some of their warmest moments. Others find it far from pleasant. Some toddlers thrash, toss, elbow, wiggle, wet, and are generally difficult sleeping companions. Early risers may chatter, hum, poke, and play.

If parents don't want to share their bed, moving the crib or toddler bed into the parent's bedroom can eliminate the loneliness and enhance children's sense of safety and security. This usually translates into less resistance at bedtime. Some children can tolerate being on the opposite side of the room with a curtain or room divider to provide some privacy for the parents.

Experimenting to see whether sleeping together at night is a workable arrangement can prove costly. Once children have discovered the security, warmth, and comfort of sleeping with a human teddy bear, they are likely to be more resistant than ever to going back to a darkened bedroom with the stuffed variety. Of course every child is different, and after spending a few months in a parent's bed, some may feel sufficiently secure so that sleeping alone becomes much easier. Some toddlers relish the privilege of being "big enough" to have their very own bed and are delighted to make the switch to sleeping in their very own room.

If parents decide to oust a small bedfellow, the best time to initiate the project is when separation and attachment issues are less of a factor—typically around age three. Otherwise, aim for a period when the child isn't going through a lot of other difficult adjustments, separation anxiety isn't a major issue, the child wants to grow up rather than regress to baby days, and independence conflicts aren't paramount.

FACTS

Little ones love how their parents smell! Assuming a youngster won't fall off a bed that lacks bars, tucking him between the parent's sheets at naptime, if not at bedtime, can increase his sense of safety and feeling of well-being. To make sure you can tolerate his smell when you tumble into bed at night, be sure to spread out a waterproof pad before you tuck him in.

From Crib to Toddler Bed

Cribs are recalled due to safety defects and hazards from time to time, so check with the manufacturer before making your purchase. When conducting your own inspection, watch for the two common problems. First, the slats shouldn't be more than $2\,^{3}/_{8}$ inches apart so children can't get their heads caught between them. Second, make sure older models weren't painted with a lead-based paint.

Cribs are not for climbers! Be careful about putting toys into a toddler's crib; if she steps on top of them, it may give her just the boost she needs to make it up the side and over the bars. It is dangerous for toddlers to climb over the bars of the crib because a fall from such a great height poses the risk of injury. Some little monkeys surprise their parents by managing to climb out not long after their first birthday. Put some padding on the floor beneath the crib to soften it in the event of a fall. As soon as your little one begins scaling the bars, it's time to move up to a toddler bed.

Toddler beds are a great next step because they have rails to keep youngsters from falling out—and from feeling afraid they might fall out. They are also lower to the ground and pose less danger to climbers; although if a child is routinely crawling out, it may be better to keep the bars down to reduce the risk of a fall.

ESSENTIALS

Many children are in love with their toddler beds initially because they're so easy to climb out of! Parents must decide whether it's better to lower the bars, which makes climbing less dangerous or to keep the bars up to prevent a fall while sleeping. Another option is to have the child sleep on the mattress on the floor.

Since many toddler beds use the same size mattress as a crib, it's best to stick with the old one if at all possible. The familiar feel and smell of the old mattress can help smooth the transition from the crib. The quality of toddler bed frames varies dramatically from brand to brand. If you plan to lie down with your child to read stories or sleep, be sure to get a model sturdy enough to support both of you.

Making the Transition

How will your toddler handle the transition from crib to toddler bed? There's simply no way to predict it. It's smooth as silk for some, decidedly difficult for others. If a child is very resistant to change, slow to adapt to new situations, or a sentimentalist, leaving the safety and security of the crib can be trying. Given a toddler's love of predictability and routine, it's a bad idea to let him step into his room to find his beloved crib gone. He may not find his parent's idea of a great surprise to be so wonderful. Perhaps he didn't like his crib at all. Nevertheless, it was the steady friend that kept him safe night after night for as long as he can remember. If possible, provide a gradual transition.

The secret to getting youngsters to give up their crib more willingly, many parents say, is to have them participate in the process from the very beginning. If parents assume the role of enthusiastic cheerleaders trying to whip up excitement about the change, it will be infectious. Try these ideas:

- Have toddlers help pick out their very own "big boy" or "big girl" bed, or at least the sheets.
- Have them assist as you haul the bed into the room and set it up.
- Ask if they want their crib toys moved. If so, hand over the toys one by one and let them do the arranging.
- Let a doll try it out for size, or ask if you can lie on it.
- Play a pretend game of "nite-nite" so the youngster can try it out long before naptime or bedtime, when they're likely to be less frazzled and cranky.

No matter how well toddlers seem to be handling the switch up to this point, it's anybody's guess how they will react when it's time to bed down for the night. Many toddlers find the change upsetting. Here are a few more ideas to help ease this transition:

- Let your youngster choose which bed to sleep in if possible. Some youngsters take to it instantly, but months may go by before they suddenly decide they're ready.
- Raise the bars on the toddler bed so they feel more secure and aren't afraid of falling out.
- Consider leaving the bedroom door open or a night light on to lessen fearfulness.
- Put a gate across the doorway to discourage roaming.
- Avoid making the change when other major upheavals are occurring, such as a change in sitters or the birth of a sibling.
- Provide some extra bedtime TLC to help your toddler calm down so she can drift off.
- If you must remove the crib, it may help to let an upset child sleep on the mattress on the floor next to the toddler bed.

Some toddlers gladly make the move and never again express an interest in their crib. However, for many the excitement and enthusiasm about being "a big boy" suddenly disappears at naptime. Or, a youngster may be happy to nap in his new bed during the day, only to appear shocked and appalled when it's suggested that he sleep there at night.

Many children like to take naps on it for a few days before tackling it at night.

Toddlers who are initially very resistant may to continue to want their crib for a few days or weeks, then spontaneously opt for the toddler bed. Some continue to ignore it for months before deciding they're ready. Many parents find it's best not to apply any pressure, since toddlers can be so quick to dig in their heels and do the opposite of whatever their parents want. They suggest leaving the crib up and remaining indifferent as to where the child sleeps.

Sometimes a toddler can't have a choice. A new baby is coming, so parents need her to relinquish her crib and move on. Parents in this situation may worry that being ousted because of a sibling will be yet another terrible blow that adds to the toddler's feeling of being displaced.

If the transition turns out to be very hard, sometimes the only consolation is that in a matter of hours, days, or weeks, the new bed will become sufficiently familiar and the toddler will adjust. Sometimes it turns out to be surprisingly easy. The youngster is delighted to participate in the preparations for the new baby, is thrilled because the move makes the coming sibling seem more real, and enjoys her lofty status of big sister. There's just no second-guessing a toddler!

Staying Put

The toddler who won't stay put in a toddler bed poses a real dilemma for parents: What to do with a little one who scurries out of bed the minute parents have finished tucking him in? What to do with the little insomniac who rises in the middle of the night when everyone is asleep and forays into the house? The first step to getting a child to stay in bed is to discuss it.

Explain that it is dangerous for him to be up by himself, that he must stay in bed unless it's an emergency, and that he is to call Mommy or Daddy from his bedroom if he needs something. After that explanation, which a child may or may not understand, make it a policy to studiously avoid further conversation. Limit verbal exchanges to repeating in a firm tone of voice, "You're supposed to stay in bed unless it's an emergency.

Go back to bed and call if you need something." (This assumes the parent has a baby monitor or is close enough to his room to hear him call.)

ESSENTIALS As with anything you are trying to teach your toddler, bedtime procedures are established with baby steps. Be patient and consistent as you train your child to stay in bed for the night.

Walk him back to his room, help him into bed, issue another reminder to call if he needs something, and leave. Toddlers in this situation are apt to cry or call before you make it through the bedroom door. If that happens, turn around and go right back to his bedside to check on him, just as you promised.

In getting across any new idea to a toddler, you need to go one step at a time and show him how things are supposed to go. Stepping out of the room and turning right back around to go back in demonstrates what is to happen: He calls; you respond. That can provide reassurance that having to be a big boy sleeping in a big bed doesn't mean he is expected to be independent. If a toddler doesn't start climbing back out of bed the moment the parent turned to leave, that should be considered a victory.

Remain calm and matter-of-fact as you approach your child's bed, and say, "I heard you calling/crying. Is everything all right? What do you want?" Provide a drink of water if a child says he's thirsty, do the monster check if he's scared; then give him a pat and tell him he's doing fine, that it will take a while to get used to the new bed. Repeat the procedure several times, avoiding all conversation except:

I heard you call. What do you want?
No. You're fine now. It's time to get some sleep.
Good night.

Begin extending the time between visits to the child's room. Difficulty with the transition to a strange bed is understandable, too. Many adults have a hard time sleeping when they're away from home for the very same reason.

It may seem inhumane to install a door protector and close the door to contain a toddler who keeps popping out of a toddler bed after everyone else is asleep. But given the danger youngsters can get into roaming the house, it may be the only recourse. Be sure to completely safety-proof the bedroom first!

Bedrooms As Jails?

Many parents work hard to make their youngsters' bedrooms more appealing in the hope that toddlers will be less resistant to bedtime and naps, only to find that although they love the Snoopy sheets and Little Mermaid wallpaper, they continue to act as though they're being sent to the torture chamber when carried there at night. In many cases, the reason for the resistance is clear: If children are sent to the bedroom for time-outs to contain problematic behavior during the day, they may come to associate the bedroom with being punished, which worsens bedtime struggles.

Time-out is a positive teaching device. Most youngsters eventually retreat to the comforting solitude of their bedroom without being instructed because they recognize their need to separate themselves from the family and calm down. But as long as they continue to resist being exiled, they can develop negative associations to the area in which they are confined.

The logical solution is to use an alternate location for time-out. Unfortunately, what is logical may not be practical. In general, it is recommended that children sit on the floor in the same room as the parent during time-outs so they're not left unattended, but sometimes a parent needs a physical separation at these stressful moments. A playpen in another room can work for children who won't try to climb out.

Winding Down

Insisting that toddlers nap or go to bed if they aren't sleepy can provoke power struggles. Instead, have them observe quiet time. A noisy environment can certainly interfere with a child's ability to fall asleep. After entering dreamland, some can tolerate a lot of hullabaloo; others remain susceptible to being awakened by sounds, especially during lighter phases of sleep. If you can't produce a quiet environment on cue, classical music can help to mask telltale sounds that suggest interesting happenings are going on elsewhere in the house.

To create a quiet and relaxing transition, help them unwind by providing soothing entertainment, such as listening to music or looking at books. Bath time routines help, too. Discourage continued requests to get up by putting a kitchen timer in their bedroom. Tell them that, unless it's an emergency, they must wait until the alarm sounds before getting up or calling to you.

Once they do relax, sleep may not be far behind. Even if sleep doesn't follow immediately, children need to learn to relax and spend time entertaining themselves. Common strategies parents use to help their toddler fall asleep include rocking them to sleep, singing lullabies, telling stories, giving back rubs, holding their hand, and taking the child into their bed.

ALERT

Nursing and giving children a bottle to help them fall asleep is *not* a good idea, dentists say, because the milk pools in their mouth, rotting their teeth. The same problem applies to juice and other sweet beverages. Remember: only water!

Meanwhile, some desperate parents have gone so far as to childproof their little night owl's bedroom, leaving no outlet uncovered, no hard edge exposed. They empty it of all toys except board books, stuffed animals, and other toys that can be safely enjoyed without supervision, and remove all furniture but the bed. They install a gate across the doorway to contain their darling, and allow them to play until they're ready to sleep, instructing them to call Mommy and Daddy if they need anything. Then they head off to dreamland, and let their night owl entertain himself.

Stress and Exercise

Little insomniacs may not lie awake pondering their worries like their adult counterparts do, but stress definitely makes it harder for them to unwind at sleep times, or fall back asleep if they awaken. The birth of a new baby, a change in child care staff, weaning, cranky parents—anything that produces stress—can complicate sleep and result in sudden difficulties at bedtime.

Exercise relieves pent-up energy born of stress, tension, and the basic need to be on the go. Be sure your child gets lots of chances to run and jump and engage in active physical play during the day. A kiddie exercise class may encourage more sedentary types to move more and sit less. Then, spend more time engaging in quiet, pleasurable activities before naps and bedtime to soothe frazzled nerves. Try an extra-long bath, a second storybook, or a third chorus of a lullaby. Remember, however, that although stress can make it harder to relax enough to sleep, this too is something children need to learn to do. Anytime they are able to recover from an upset during the day, point it out. This skill will serve them well at night.

Rituals

Rituals that induce relaxation can help toddlers make the transition from a busy, active day to sleep. Going through an invariable progression from taking a bath, hearing a story, listening to a lullaby, and saying prayers helps toddler insomniacs, just like their adult counterparts. As people come to associate the ritual with sleep, their bodies automatically begin to relax.

Many parents don't consider instituting naptime rituals, but they can make a real difference. It's good to communicate with your baby sitters or child care workers, if possible, so that the routine never varies. Rituals should be designed to soothe, so avoid stimulating activities like roughhousing, tickling, and exciting or scary stories.

Some children engage in troublesome rituals such as repetitive rocking, which can escalate into head banging, as a way to soothe themselves. It usually stops by eighteen months. You can help by not overreacting, by padding the sides of the crib, and by beefing up other bedtime rituals to provide a more gradual transition.

Sleep Skills

The downside of all that rocking and singing and back rubbing and music playing to quiet fretful children and help them fall asleep is that they come to depend on someone or something outside of themselves—a real problem if they wake up in the middle of the night. Children need to learn eventually to handle the task of falling asleep—and of falling back asleep—unassisted.

Many parents dedicate themselves to learning how to put their child to sleep, when the goal should be for *toddlers* to learn to put *themselves* to sleep and to put themselves back to asleep after awakening. Sleep experts point out that children need to acquire a specific set of sleep skills. Surprisingly, they don't come naturally to many. Children must learn how to fall asleep, fall back asleep, and sleep through the night.

ESSENTIALS   To help toddlers wind down at bedtime, check out books like *Goodnight Moon* by Margaret Wise Brown (HarperFestival, 1991), *Dr. Seuss's Sleep Book* (Random House, 1962), *Time for Bed* by Mem Fox (Harcourt Brace, 1997), and *The Going to Bed Book* by Sandra Boynton (Little Simon, 1995).

The first step is for them to learn to spend time alone. Being comfortable spending time alone in a crib or toddler bed is a prerequisite for falling asleep and for falling back asleep. By handing toddlers a stuffed animal after they awaken in the morning or from a nap, leaving the room, and waiting five to fifteen minutes to rescue them, parents can give them time to practice being by themselves in their cribs. Some experts say this can serve them well at night.

Sleep Cycles

Children cycle in and out of different sleep phases throughout the night, entering a light sleep phase six to eight times. It is during these light sleep periods they are most likely to awaken. Adults typically awaken three to four times per night, although they may not be alert enough to remember. If toddlers awaken fully during each and every cycle, and must depend on a parent's help to get back to sleep . . . Well, there's no need to finish that sentence.

Sometimes parents can alter the sleep cycles by breaking into them. Try awakening the toddler just before you go to bed. Spend a few minutes smiling and chatting, then help her fall back asleep.

Many parents assume that hunger pangs are causing her to awaken at 10 P.M., at 2 A.M., and again at 5 A.M. More likely, she's cycling through sleep stages. If you suspect hunger is an issue, serve a hefty before-bedtime snack then set an alarm so you can awaken her at midnight for another. Scheduling a regular midnight feeding helps toddlers develop a schedule, and effectively separates food from sleep issues.

FACTS

Aromatherapy can produce short-term relief from anxiety and induce sleep. In a study of geriatric patients, lavender oil dispersed in the air enabled them to sleep as well as they did on prescription medication. The patients were less restless; plus, their rooms smelled better! Manufacturers are now concocting lavender-laced lotions and sleeping aids for toddlers. Consult your pediatrician.

Keep in mind, however, that popping a bottle into a child's mouth each time he cries at night encourages him to use food as an emotional crutch, and that the point of a bottle should be to satisfy a nutritional need. If you do decide to use bottles as soothing devices, stick to serving water to prevent the major cause of childhood cavities: sugary liquids sitting in the mouth.

Nighttime Rituals

When parents exit the bedroom, and leave a little one screaming, they don't have to feel like meanies who are abandoning helpless babes to a dangerous world. They could think of themselves as teachers who are confident that their child is safe, and that with time and practice he can discover the state of relaxation needed to fall asleep.

The problem with continued quick responses to soothe crying tots is that it perpetuates their dependency and helps them avoid the task at hand: learning to fall asleep on their own. As the sleep-teacher, the parents need to:

- Set up the conditions that are conducive for sleep.
- Check from time to time to be sure a wailing toddler is safe.
- Provide frightened youngsters with a comforting pat and reassurance that "you're okay."
- Remain confident that the child can learn.

Holding Firm

In two-parent homes, it may be best to have the adult who is less intensely connected to the child be the one to manage bedtime complaints and middle-of-the-night pleas for attention. Since bedtime brings up separation issues for adults as well as for children, the more connected parent may experience some anxiety that the child picks up on. This can intensify the distress and separation anxiety of both. The parent in charge of putting the child to bed should follow this approach:

1. Say "good night," tell the toddler she'll be fine, give her a comforting pat, and leave.
2. If crying persists, return after two to three minutes to see that she's okay.
3. Give her another pat, tell her she's fine, and leave.
4. Return after five minutes for another quick check to make sure the screaming doesn't mean she's ill or injured.

5. Provide another comforting pat, calm reassurance that she's okay, and leave.
6. Continue checking and providing reassurance at five- to ten-minute intervals.
7. Avoid checking if the intensity of the crying is abating (so as not to disturb her if she is beginning to relax or fall asleep).

The advantage to this approach is that children learn to fall asleep and to fall back asleep by themselves. By continuing to show up at the crib at regular intervals, the parent makes sure that the child is all right and provides reassurance that she has not been abandoned. Try to provide reassurance without reconnecting—hold talking to a minimum; don't pick your child up. Many parents are amazed at how quickly the youngster they thought would never settle down proceeds to do just that.

Meanwhile, others are amazed that two weeks later the child still manages to scream for an hour. With toddlers, there's no way to predict what will happen. Sometimes the parent's attitude plays a role. If the parent is distressed about the child's intense crying, the youngster will sense it. The timed parental visits to the nursery meant to reassure may have the opposite effect.

Handling Hysteria

What happens when parents refrain from running into their wailing toddler's bedroom to help him fall asleep, and he is so upset he vomits? Or he cries so hard, he can't catch his breath and begins gasping for air? This is the point at which many parents decide the "give him time to learn to settle himself down" approach is doing more harm than good. Check with your pediatrician to see whether it's okay to hold firm under these circumstances. If so, be as sympathetic as you would toward any little person who is having such a hard time mastering something difficult. Then change the sheets, clean him up, tuck him in, give him a pat, and tell him he'll be okay. Tell him it's time to sleep, wish him sweet dreams, and leave. Return a few minutes later to check on him to be sure he's not ill.

Sleep Strategies

If a child awakens crying and parents determine that she isn't ill, they can verbally reassure her that she is fine or offer a stuffed animal or other favored toy for comfort. What happens next is up to each family. Philosophies of what's best for toddlers differ. Sleep problems are among the toughest, and what is acceptable to parents in one household is definitely not workable in another. You can:

- Leave and stay away no matter how hard the child cries, so that he can eventually learn to fall asleep by himself. (Be sure the hard crying doesn't signal illness or injury.)
- Remain physically present to provide some reassurance and moral support, moving a chair a few inches farther from the crib each night until you are out the door, thereby helping the child to feel more secure while he learns to fall asleep on his own.
- Hold, rock, sing, carry, and otherwise soothe the child to help him fall asleep.
- Invite the child into your bed.

Whether you sleep together or apart; or respond to each call from the bedroom, only go in when your child is hysterical, or resolutely stay away, don't judge others negatively for doing it their way—and don't let them judge you.

ESSENTIALS Toddlers are spiritual beings, too. Like adults, they can derive comfort from prayer and from having religious objects in their rooms. Knowing that God is watching over them can help put their minds at ease.

Parental Paranoia

It's certainly normal for parents to get tired and cranky when dealing with a balky toddler. It's understandable that parents might take it personally when a youngster is so exhausted that his eyes are falling closed, yet can rise to battle when parents try to get him into bed. But it is dangerous to cross the thin but all-important line from irritation to paranoia, wherein parents conclude "My child is refusing to go to bed in order to upset me." Thoughts like that make them question their child's love and undermine their own self-confidence. Some then feel justified about evening the score with the youngster who is "trying" to get to them.

It is a serious distortion of reality to think that a child doesn't want to sleep just because he's angry with his parent, when the truth lies elsewhere: Toddlers don't want to go to bed because they don't like to go to bed. Period. And that often makes parents angry.

Independent Types

When the terrible two's negativity sets in and toddlers feel driven to disagree with every other thing the parent does or says, they may resist going to bed just because they've been told that's what they must do. Again, parents need to resist taking this personally and remain focused on the child's innate struggle for autonomy and independence.

Letting toddlers be in charge of some bedtime decisions can help satisfy their need to be in control. Let them pick which story is read, which pajamas are worn, which stuffed animals go into the crib, whether the night-light is on or off, and which music you play.

Bored to Sleep

When older toddlers refuse to stay in bed, some parents have successfully bored them to sleep. They refuse to provide any attention, announce that they themselves are going to bed, proceed with their normal bedtime preparations, and climb into bed, feigning sleep.

Ideally, children become bored enough from the lack of attention and ask to be taken to bed, or they wind down and fall asleep on their own. Then parents can climb out from under the covers, carry the youngster to his bed, and enjoy the rest of their evening undisturbed. Obviously this trick is only workable if it is safe for the toddler to be up and about the house by herself.

Monster Control

If fears of the dark are keeping your toddler awake, try dousing monsters and assorted goblins in beams from a night-light. It can stop them in their tracks. Often a fear of a nighttime visit from a wild animal or cartoon character can be overcome by outfitting the child with a special repellant guaranteed to render a beastie harmless. The repellant can be anything from a flashlight to a small magic stone (make sure it's too big to fit in the mouth!) to a designated stick they can wave like a magic wand. Since sound can banish monsters, keeping a rattle under their pillow to shake at the shadows in their closet and the branches outside their window can also hold imaginary beasts at bay. Placing a protective object in the room, such as an oversized teddy bear to stand watch, can be reassuring.

Nightmares

The brain waves of tiny babies suggest that even the youngest members of our species dream. Some say that when they smile while sleeping, they are greeting the angels who have dropped by for a visit.

Similarly, many toddlers have nightmares. Because children in this age group have such a poor ability to distinguish reality from fantasy, it can be impossible to convince them that the monsters and big bad bears weren't real. Nevertheless, provide lots of reassurance that "it was just a dream." When they're old enough, they'll understand the difference.

There are no proven ways to eliminate nightmares, but the following techniques can help:

- Reduce your child's overall stress level.
- Avoid scary bedtime stories.
- Keep bedtime rituals soothing and relaxing.
- Avoid roughhousing before bedtime.
- Avoid mentioning scary things.

Encourage your child to share the bad dreams, since this helps many toddlers feel better. If his vocabulary is limited, try to help him tell it. If he says, "Bear," ask, "Was it a scary bear?" Avoid questions like, "Was the bear trying to eat somebody?" so as not to implant more fear!

FACTS

"Good night, sleep tight, don't let the bedbugs bite" can conjure up frightening images that are later replayed in dreams. Instead, try the far gentler Spanish saying: *"Duérmate con los angelitos"* (pronounced *d'where-mah-tay cone lows ahn-hay-lee-toes*) or the English equivalent: May you sleep with the little angels.

Sleep Terrors

These sudden, unexplained bouts of screaming and wild thrashing within the first few hours of going to sleep can be terrifying to parents who find themselves unable to comfort their youngster. Although children appear to be awake, they are actually asleep during these episodes and have no memory of them on awakening. Sleep terrors are believed to occur at the transition from one phase of sleep to another. The only reported dangers are sleep walking, which can lead to injury, and some very upset parents! If sleep terrors are occurring regularly, some experts recommend re-setting the sleep cycle:

1. Rouse the toddler about fifteen minutes before the episodes typically occur.
2. Keep him fully awake for five minutes.
3. Continue nightly until the episodes stop—usually in about a week.

Recipes for Insomnia

Most everyone knows that coffee and tea deliver a hefty dose of caffeine, the ingredient of choice for increasing the heart and respiration rate and keeping people awake. But some people don't realize that:

• Most brown-colored sodas contain this same stimulant
• Some light-colored sodas now contain caffeine, too

- Some cold and headache remedies also contain caffeine
- Black and green teas contain caffeine; herbal kinds do not
- Caffeine can pass through breastmilk, although the quantities are small
- Chocolate contains a caffeine-like substance called theobromine, a weaker stimulant than caffeine
- To determine whether a manufactured product contains caffeine, read the label

Some toddlers are affected more than others, but anything containing caffeine is on the list of before bedtime no-no's—exactly *how long* before depends on the toddler. Some adults complain that drinking a cup of coffee at 3 P.M. keeps them from falling asleep when they turn in at 10. Likewise, it's a good idea to keep anything with caffeine off the list of toddler foods and beverages if getting them down for naps is a problem.

Cane sugar and artificial colorings have also been known to turn some youngsters into whirling dervishes. So do some food allergies. Exercise greater-than-normal caution about bedtime snacks for toddlers who have a hard time winding down and dozing off. Having the child undergo allergy testing may be a good idea.

ESSENTIALS

If soothing music isn't boring your toddler to tears—and to sleep—perhaps a little crib-side excitement will do the trick. Try a tape or CD like *Mother Goose from Morning until Night*, a compilation of songs, nursery rhymes, and fairy tales.

Just as there are foods that keep people awake, there are foods that promote sleep. All those feelings of heavy-lidded peace and contentment after a Thanksgiving feast aren't just from the warmth of an extended family meal. Turkey, which is rich in tryptophan, induces sleep. Stuffing, a complex carbohydrate, facilitates the absorption of tryptophan. A snack that combines a food high in tryptophan with a complex carbohydrate can help induce feelings of well-being and slow brain activity. If you're not up to roasting a bird with homemade stuffing for a toddler bedtime snack, try these ideas:

- A turkey sandwich
- An egg with cheese and toast
- Pasta with cheese
- Tuna with whole-wheat crackers
- Chicken and rice

Exhausting Work

It's not surprising that so many toddlers resist bedtime. Having to make their sleep/wake cycles conform to those of other family members isn't easy when your body is running on a different biological clock. The bad news is that lots of youngsters continue to resist bedtimes throughout their childhoods, and getting teenagers to cooperate with lights out can be even more difficult since their biological clocks begin to change, turning them into night owls.

The good news is that it's far easier to deal with the crankiness of a sleep-avoidant older child than with a sleep-deprived toddler. Parents can anticipate that even if they're not getting much rest now, once children have mastered basic sleep skills, things will get better!

CHAPTER 11
Fun and Games

Toys designed especially for kids are a relatively new invention. Just a few generations ago, toddlers spent their time with everyday household objects. Getting modern youngsters to confine themselves to items that have been especially purchased for them can be difficult. Their favorites will probably turn out to be very different from what toy manufacturers would like them to choose!

The Best Toys

Perhaps children are programmed to master the world they will one day inherit, and that is why they automatically gravitate toward the everyday household objects their parents use. In any event, until TV ads and trips to the store change their minds, it won't matter to youngsters that the house doesn't contain a single store-bought toy. Toddlers' attention spans are short, but they are easy to entertain. Since everything is new to them, every room is filled with objects they find fascinating. (That, of course, is both a blessing and a curse!)

Parents already have all they need on hand to keep their child busy for the next two years. As every toddler knows, the pots that parents only consider useful for cooking make wonderful drums, hats, dollhouses, and containers for filling and dumping. The plastic lids from juice cans are fun to stack, and the sound they make when smacked together is music to little people's ears. Before you buy lots of manufactured toys and trail your toddler around the house with long litanies of no-no's, ask yourself if the household object she's chosen to investigate must really be off limits:

- Could she actually ruin it?
- Would it be dangerous if she mouthed or chewed it?
- Does it have sharp edges or rough surfaces that could cause abrasions or cuts?
- Does it have dangling cords that could strangle?
- Could small parts be bitten off, swallowed, or cause choking?
- Could moving parts or hinges catch a hand, pinch a finger, or smash a foot?

If not, maybe it's okay for your toddler to play with it. Try not to inhibit learning! With supervised independence, your toddler will find plenty of safe items in your kitchen or bathroom to keep him entertained for hours.

Is the toy small enough to fit through the middle of a toilet paper roll? Then it's small enough to fit into a toddler's throat . . . meaning it's *not* a safe toy!

Plastic Containers

So many foods come in plastic containers and they make great toys. Just wash them and hand them over. Be sure to save the containers from cottage cheese, whipped topping, soft-spread margarine, and yogurt. The colorful plastic tops from cans of cooking spray, and other nontoxic aerosol products also make pretty toys.

Kitchen Utensils

Take a quick look around the kitchen, and you'll see lots of items a toddler would be delighted to manipulate, bang, stack, and, inevitably, taste:

- Beaters from electric mixers (kids love the shape)
- Ladles (show them how to use one to scoop up a ball)
- Tongs (useful for picking up small objects)
- Spatulas (show them how to slide them under a small object; see if they can move from squatting to standing without dropping it)
- Pie and cake tins (for filling, dumping, banging, and clanging)
- Cookie cutters (to put in and dump out of pie tins or cardboard boxes; check for sharp edges first)

Nesters and Stackers

It's not easy to stack a few metal spoons, but toddlers practice visual/motor skills when they try. And they learn important information about shape, size, and volume by fitting items inside one another. Try nesting plastic bowls, measuring cups, measuring spoons, and nesting plastic funnels.

First, give a nesting demonstration. Next, turn the cups upside-down and give a stacking demonstration. Then let them do their own thing. Just don't hover and try to dictate how toddlers play. Stacking three objects is a challenge for an eighteen-month-old. It may take days, weeks, or months to figure out how to fit nesting objects one inside the other or how to stack a group from biggest to smallest. While they might be able to create an organized pile or tidy arrangement much sooner if a parent were to guide and coach every step of the way, learning to solve problems on their own spurs intellectual development.

ESSENTIALS   Don't short-circuit learning by providing the answer. Let their brains do the work! Toddler learning (and fun!) comes from exercising mental muscles by experimenting again and again until a puzzle problem is solved.

Little Drummers

Toddlers love to drum, and for many, their high chair tray is their favorite instrument. For safety's sake, you must draw the line if they begin beating on something breakable. Drumming can also become dangerous if they create enough vibration to cause hot liquid to slosh or spill or a bowl to topple over. Say, "Don't bang the plate. It might break!" while removing it, but don't except young toddlers to understand. If you prefer the serenade of toddler banging to toddler wailing, trade a breakable plate for a sturdier item.

Boxes!

Cardboard boxes are great for kids of all ages, providing entertainment that can last for hours. Keep a supply of various sizes and shapes on hand, including empty shoe boxes, Band-Aid boxes, tea boxes, tissue boxes, gift boxes, packing boxes, and cereal boxes.

The most wondrous of all, of course, is an appliance box. If you haven't bought a refrigerator or big-screen TV lately, you're bound to find a giant box at your local recycling center or at stores that sell large appliances. Cut a door, windows, even a small escape hatch, and your toddler has a castle, fort, spaceship, cave, or anything else she can imagine.

ESSENTIALS   Give your child some ideas for creative play, but let his imagination do most of the work. You'll be surprised to realize how much he has learned from you already, and you'll have a better understanding of how his mind works.

You can go all-out with paint on the exterior, contact paper, wallpaper, and fabric scrap curtains. Outfit the playhouse with a small pillow and blanket to make a little bed. Better yet, let your child decide how he wants it decorated. But don't go too far. Even the best packing boxes don't last forever.

Use boxes to make a toy kitchen sized to your child. Cut a square in the side of a box for an oven door and draw or paint burners for a stove top, a refrigerator, and a freezer door so they'll open, just like on your kitchen appliance. Cut a small hole in the top of a box and insert a plastic whipped topping container for a sink; then cut cabinet doors in the front. Stock the kitchenette with cottage-cheese-container bowls, pots, yogurt-container cups, and a few plastic spoons. Show toddlers how plastic coffee-can lids can be platters and plates.

At-Home Favorites

Looking for ideas that will keep your kids entertained for hours? Try these time-tested kid favorites. You can create many of these toys using materials you already have around the house, and you'll probably have as much fun as your child does. Plus the assembly process is a great bonding experience for parent and child—something you can't say about many store-bought toys.

Shakes, Rattles, and Rings

Sew dried beans, rice, or peas into a sock or a piece of stocking; and put some sand or pasta into a plastic bottle (topped with a lid that stays put despite prying fingers!)—your toddler has a start on a percussion band. Stitch jingle bells onto a cloth (sew them well—if the bells come off, they're small enough to swallow!), and let the tambourine music begin! What about cymbals? Why, pie tins, of course!

Pull Toys

Tie a short cord to a box or stuffed animal to make a pull toy, or tie several boxes together with string for a train. But beware! Sixteen inches is the maximum length for cord; which reduces the chance it will create a strangling hazard. A toddler's ability to get entangled in seconds is amazing.

Homemade Blocks

Cut a clean quart or half-gallon-size cardboard milk container in half cross-wise. Push the two halves together to make a square block. A few dozen gallons later, you'll have enough blocks to keep a play group of toddlers happy for a year. To jazz the blocks up, cover them with plain paper or fabric and color the sides with different shapes (triangles, circles, and squares), capital letters, or numbers. Or glue on pictures of animals cut from magazines.

SSENTIALS Who says blocks have to be square? Show your toddler how to build a giant tower from a variety of household items, including pots, pans, books, cardboard boxes, or cardboard tubes.

Puzzles

To make a beginner's puzzle, cut a hole in the top of an oatmeal box ½ inch larger than some puzzle pieces so toddlers can drop wooden blocks, measuring spoons, or juice-can lids through the hole. Or cut several holes of different sizes into the top and sides of a shoebox so your toddler can fit small cars and other toys inside.

To make an intermediate board puzzle, cut a large circle from the center of a heavy-duty cardboard box with an X-acto knife (using every precaution around both young fingers, and your own). Glue the piece of cardboard from which the hole was cut onto another square of cardboard, which will create the backing. Show your child how to fit the circle into the puzzle. Using other pieces of cardboard, make more puzzles in the shape of a square, a diamond, an arrow, and a cone. Paint them bright colors to add to their eye-catching appeal.

To make more advanced puzzles, cut the front of a cereal box into three pieces and show your toddler how to put them together. Or glue a colorful picture from a magazine like *National Geographic* onto a piece of cardboard. Cut it into three to five pieces.

Sock Puppets and Dolls

To make a puppet, slip an old sock onto your hand to figure out where the eyes should be, and sew on buttons (sew them well—buttons are choking hazards!) or round pieces of felt. If you want to be really creative, make a whole family of puppets and add yarn for hair, felt ears, red felt tongues, bow ties, or lace collars.

To make a doll, use one stuffed sock to make the head and torso, another to make the arms, and a third to make the legs. Then add felt eyes, nose, and mouth; yarn hair; and clothes; or leave her as is.

Bubbles

Make them yourself by mixing ½ cup water, ½ cup liquid soap, and 1 tablespoon cooking oil. To add to the fun, stir in some food coloring. A straw, an egg holder from an Easter egg dye kit (for those really big bubbles), or a wire or pipe cleaner bent into the shape of a *P* make nifty bubble-blowers.

Play Dough

It takes a few gallons to get modern kids through elementary school, so why not learn how to make your own? In a saucepan, combine ½ cup salt, 1 cup flour, and 2 tablespoons cream of tartar. Then add 1 cup cold water, a few drops of food coloring, and 1 tablespoon of vegetable oil. Mix until smooth, and cook over medium heat, stirring frequently. When the mixture sticks to the pan, sticks together firmly, and is no longer slimy to the touch, it's finished. Turn it out onto waxed paper, knead it a dozen times, and let it sit. When the dough is cool, store it in a container with a tight-fitting lid or sealed plastic bags to prevent drying.

Now comes the fun. Sit down with you child and show him how to:

- Roll bits of play dough into a worm or snake
- Roll a bigger piece into a ball
- Flatten the ball into a cookie or pancake
- Pinch off little bits to make peas and put them onto a tiny play-dough plate
- Prick it with a pen or pencil
- Slice it with a cheese slicer
- Cut it with a plastic knife
- Cut it with cookie cutters

Supervise carefully to be sure your toddler doesn't try to make a "meal" of the cookies and pancakes! Remember that the fun and learning come from the doing, not the final product!

Silly Putty

Pour 1 tablespoon of liquid starch into a bowl. In a separate bowl, mix 2 tablespoons of white glue and 2 to 3 drops of food coloring. Pour the glue onto the starch and allow it to stand for five minutes, or until the glue absorbs the starch. Remove the mixture from the bowl and knead it until it reaches the desired consistency; more kneading improves the consistency. Store the mixture in a sealed plastic bag or in the traditional plastic Easter egg.

Finger Paints

Pour ½ cup cornstarch into a large bowl. Blend in 1 cup of cold water; then add 2 more cups. Microwave the liquid for eight to nine minutes, stirring every two minutes until thickened. Pour it into six separate bowls and stir in food coloring. Let it cool. Then roll up your child's sleeves, give him some paper, and let your little Picasso begin. Demonstrate how to smear a layer of a single color over a multicolored drawing, and then use a fingernail or plastic spoon to scrape through the top layer to expose the colors beneath.

For easy clean up, put paper, finger paints, and your naked toddler in an empty bathtub. Toddlers can do their Picasso number without constantly being reminded to not make a mess. You need to remain close at hand to enforce a few important no-no's: Don't turn on the water, don't dump out all the paint, and don't eat your masterpieces. Leave a few paintings in the tub to dry; then hang them on the fridge.

Science Fun

Simply stirring water into sugar or salt and watching it dissolve counts as a bona fide scientific experience for a toddler. So does seeing skin turn wrinkly during an extra-long bath, hearing a tea kettle sing, feeling the cool air inside a refrigerator, or smelling the aroma of cooking food.

Simply watching a tomato fall to the floor and roll until it bumps the cabinet teaches cause/effect, inertia versus motion. With so many fascinating things everywhere tots look, they don't need specific science training.

To really impress a youngster with science magic, though, have her put a teaspoon of baking soda in a small bowl. Then put some vinegar in a child-size pitcher and let her pour it slowly into the bowl. If you don't know what happens when you mix these two ingredients, you're in for a surprise, too. Of course, since you *do* know what happens when toddlers are given powder and liquid to pour, you need to conduct this experiment when you can tolerate a bit of a mess.

Whether parents keep their households free of toy guns and rifles is a decision for each family. But if reducing violence is the goal, the best way is to curtail yelling and hitting among family members. If parents want to discourage children from re-enacting violent scenes, eliminate the one object that is clearly associated with an increased preoccupation with blood, gore, and violence: the TV.

Art Box

Decorate a box and fill it with an assortment of nontoxic supplies:

Bows and pieces of ribbon
Coloring book
Construction paper
Cotton balls
Crayons or markers (washable)
Envelopes
Glue sticks
Paper or old newspaper
Paper bags, cups, and plates
Pictures from magazines, greeting cards, and postcards
Pipe cleaners
Stickers
Watercolor kit
Wrapping paper odds and ends
Yarn and string (16 inches or shorter)

Pull out the art box when you can enjoy it with your toddler. The possibilities are limited only by your imaginations! Younger toddlers can put stickers on paper plates and cups and dab markers onto newspaper. You can cut out the center of a paper plate to make a crown tots can decorate. Help older toddlers fold construction paper and glue on pictures or stickers to make greeting cards. Then drop them into an envelope and mail them to Grandma and Grandpa, who will cherish them more than store-bought cards. Here are some other crafty ideas:

- Punch small holes on each side of an upside-down cup and insert pipe cleaner arms. Do what you will to create a face. Glue on cotton for hair and beards.
- Glue magazine pictures onto paper plates to display on the refrigerator.
- Lunch bags make great hand puppets.
- Paper grocery sacks can be used to make masks. Cut oversized eyeholes.

Remember that toddlers don't care what they make as long as they get to roll, rub, pat, dab, and draw while they're making it. Adults might care about the finished product; little ones prefer just to putter.

Personalized Puppets

Cut out a picture of your child. Glue it onto a Popsicle stick, leaving room so the toddler can hold onto the bottom half. Voilà! Your child has a puppet of her favorite person! Create a family of dolls using pictures of other family members.

Dress Up

With so many garage sales around these days, it's easy to stockpile an array of wardrobe items befitting a queen, princess, mermaid, superhero, pirate, cowboy, or anything else your child likes. Keep your eyes open for cloth remnants, costume jewelry, hats, purses, scarves (pin them to shoulders; don't tie them around little necks), and shoes.

Kids will also appreciate things to put in the purse, such as an old comb or wallet. Applying a bit of color from half-used tubes of lipstick, eyeliner, and powder is a great accent for any outfit. (Make sure you supervise this part.) Turn your child into a superhero by pinning a pillow case cape to your child's shirt, bestowing a pizza pan shield, fashioning a tinfoil hat and wrist bands, providing a pair of gloves, and adding a plastic spatula to fend off the bad guys.

Water Fun

Kids love to play with water as much as parents dislike the mess. So open the dishwasher and place a dishpan filled with water on the open door. A lot of the splashes will run inside. Then, bring out the margarine- or yogurt-container boats, and add a cup of rice or dried beans (supervising to be sure she doesn't swallow them!) so she can scoop them into the cups. Add a touch of food coloring to the water—blue for a lake or green for the sea. When cleaning up, let the overflow drain into the dishwasher, but empty the dishpan in the sink.

ESSENTIALS
An empty plastic dish soap or shampoo bottle makes a great squirt gun. Travel-size bottles are easier for little hands to squeeze. (Squirt guns are great bathtub fun, too!)

For fun in the tub, toss in plastic water bottles, clean plastic soda bottles, or hand-lotion bottles. Punch holes in the bottoms of some of the bottles to create a tot-sized shower (or give them a plastic colander to play with). Cut a liter soda bottle in half, smooth the cut edges with sandpaper, and show your child how to use the top half for a funnel and the bottom half for a cup. After he's finished straining water in the colander, store his bath toys in it so they'll drain and dry.

Down 'n Dirty

Toddlers *know* they've landed in heaven when they're given a garden spade or some plastic kitchen utensils, a bucket or a few plastic whipped-topping or soft-spread margarine containers, and a chance to play in the dirt. Add to that a bucket of water, and they'll probably be more contented than with any other toy. It's a given that they'll end up with some around their mouths; the challenge is to keep younger ones from getting too much in their mouths.

Of course they'll get dirty—make that filthy—but it's got to be better for kids to wallow in nature than to stare passively at yet another video. Certainly it's easier to clean up their bodies than their minds.

If you prefer a down-'n-far-less-dirty experience, sand is cleaner and can be more fun for toddlers to play in than dirt. If a traditional sandbox is too expensive, try these alternatives:

- Dig a 6-inch hole, and line it with plastic. Punch holes in the plastic for the water to drain through, and fill the hole with sand until it's level with the ground. Cover it with another sheet of plastic weighted with rocks to help keep out the rain.

- If the homemade kind is too much work, look for a rectangular plastic storage bin at a discount store, pour 6 inches of sand in the bottom, and pop your toddler inside—leaving the lid off, of course!
- Fill an inexpensive plastic wading pool with sand.

FACTS

Some store-bought, time-tested toys help toddlers develop everything from visual/motor skills to imagination. Tinker Toys and Lincoln Logs will provide hours of fun for years to come. (Keep any pieces small enough to be swallowed out of reach until your child is older.) With classics, more is better, so add them to your child's birthday wish list, next to the other tried-and-true favorites: books.

Forbidden Toys

Some seemingly harmless objects that toddlers love are too dangerous to allow. Don't try to teach them that these are no-no's; to do so would be to risk an accident. Instead, keep the following items carefully out of reach:

- Any toy marked "not suitable for children under age three"
- Glitter, which has edges sharp enough to damage eyes when they're rubbed with glitter-speckled hands
- Plastic wrap and bags
- Small toys and objects that could be swallowed, such as buttons, marbles, Lego's, and deflated balloons
- String, yarn, cords, and long thin objects such as necklaces and bracelets, which can choke or strangle children
- Styrofoam products (cups, plates, bowls, and packing materials) that could be eaten

Outdoor Play

Playing outside is essential for children and parents. Fresh air and sunshine; room to run, yell, and tumble; and all sorts of things to explore make the out-of-doors a whole new world. Playing outside is also an opportunity to teach yard and street safety, and boundaries. The following games can be modified for city or suburban play as needed:

- Have your toddler lie down on the sidewalk. Trace his outline with nontoxic sidewalk chalk. Then have him draw in the eyes, ears, nose, and mouth.
- Place a series of parallel sticks on the ground spaced 8 to 12 inches apart. See if your toddler can walk through them without stepping on any.
- Play follow-the-leader: walk with one or both hands on your hips, above your head, while swinging your arms.
- Blow tufts off the head of a dandelion.
- Collect leaves and line them up on the sidewalk in a long chain.

Use the money you saved from making indoor toys on kiddie transportation your toddler can play with outside. Invest in a small shopping cart or toy stroller that your child can push. She'd love to peddle a tricycle or Big Wheels toy. Finally, don't underestimate the hours of fun he can have with a wagon. The Navigator Wagon won the People's Choice Award for spring 2001.

Check It Out!

When buying toys, be sure to check the targeted ages noted on the box. That should help ensure they are developmentally appropriate and safe. Also consider whether the toy needs batteries. If so, are they included? So many toys require them that investing in a battery charger can save not only money but also the headache of making frequent runs to the store.

The National Parenting Center's Seal of Approval program rates everything from games and crafts kits to kiddie computer hardware and software, as well as books, audio, and educational products. Look for its seal on packages or check out products at ✍ *www.tnpc.com.* Another source to check out is *Consumer Reports,* which evaluates everything from toddler toys and furniture to the pesticides in store-bought vegetables. Subscribe to the magazine by calling ☎(800) 208-9696, or to the on-line service at ✑ *www.consumerreports.org.*

To increase the chances that your toddler will be more interested in the toy you buy than in the box it came in, select those that have won Parents' Choice Awards. Unfortunately, there aren't many award-winners listed for toddlers at the Parents' Choice Web site, ✑ *www.parents-choice.org.*

The award-winning toys listed for this age group include Fisher Price Pull Up Ball Blast for ages nine months to three years, Brio Builder System Robot Set for ages 2 and over, and the Big & Small Chime Ball for ages six months to three years. Some of their recommended toys, like Imagibricks Giant CastleBlocks, should provide hours of educational fun for one- to six-year-olds.

Toys, Toys Everywhere

There are a number of compelling reasons why toddlers need to learn to pick up their toys—and not just to fulfill your desire for a neat house. Not only will toddlers break the toys by walking on them, but also possibly hurt themselves tripping or stumbling amid the rubble. In the process of learning to care for their possessions, toddlers learn to sort and organize. Little ones won't know how to do that, so plan on doing most of the work for quite some time.

Because toddlers slow things down to a snail's pace, it's often easier for parents to pick up everything. But when parents look ahead and consider that playthings will need to be picked up every day for the next eighteen years, they'll realize how important it is to work actively on teaching this skill now.

Toddlers do like to go back and forth between toys, playing with one for a while, moving on to another one, then returning to the first, so the strategy of insisting that one toy be put up before the next is taken out is too rigid. But to hold the chaos in check (which makes many toddlers, like many adults, feel scattered), to keep toys from becoming trampled on and broken, and to teach organizational skills, consider these guidelines:

- Only allow two or three different toys out at once, not counting that special truck, doll, or ball he wants to keep close at hand at all times.
- Keep the quantity down to items that can be carried to his room or piled into a container he can drag to the toy storage area in a single trip.
- Store toys that aren't being used much in the closet. Bring them out for a rainy day surprise.

Cleanup Games

When your toddler is looking for something new to play with, say, "Let's pick these up and find you a new toy." Then make the picking up of toys into a game. Ask, "How many of these can you carry?" Place one toy in her right hand, one in her left, tuck one under her arm, and another under her neck if she's a practiced walker. Keep up the fun by giving a quick tummy tickle and seeing if she can manage not to drop them.

If you're putting away toys in a carrier that a toddler can drag from room to room, toss a toy inside and then hand her one to toss inside and continue taking turns. Count aloud as you alternate placing toys in her box. Have a race and see who can pick up toys the fastest. Make the trek to her room pleasurable—this is a great time for a hiking song or a chorus of *Ten Little Indians*—though you might want to hold it to four Indians for such a short trip.

A Place for Everything . . .

Designate a special spot in the toddler's bedroom or toy storage area for each toy. Show young toddlers where to put each item, handing him one item at a time, while giving verbal instructions. "The clown goes on your bed." "The ball goes in this box." "The blocks go in this basket." When the toys are put away, gush your congratulations ("You did it!") and help him select a new toy or activity.

When a child is old enough to want to have a say in the matter (i.e., when he's going through the stage in which when you say, "Let's pick up the toys," he refuses, and if you say, "*Don't* pick up the toys," he proceeds to pick them up), defer to his need to make some decisions by asking him what goes where: "Where should I put the blocks?" "Where does your clown go?" If he's being "terribly two" and refuses to put away his toys, don't argue. But hold firm that no other toys can be played with until the other ones are picked up.

Toy Storage

Now that traditional toy chests have fallen from grace (see Chapter 7, "Safety First"), be more creative about designing toy storage that solves some of the problems big chests posed. For instance, consider these solutions to typical problems:

PROBLEM	SOLUTION
Small toys slip to the bottom of deep chests where they are lost or broken.	Use a shallow storage box.
Everything gets mixed together so toddlers can't find the toys they want.	Use a number of smaller containers rather than a few large ones to keep toys separated and organized. Remove the lids so toddlers can see inside. Place toys on open shelves low on the wall so toddlers can easily see and reach their toys.
Toys have to be carried to the chest a few at a time, requiring many trips back and forth when putting toys away.	Use small- to medium-size cardboard boxes, lightweight laundry baskets, or pillowcases that children can drag. They'll enjoy playing in them, too! Use gym bags or small suitcases with handles.

Store toys low to the ground so children can reach them, rather than on high shelves (which beg to be climbed), and beware of brick-and-board shelves that can topple! Try these other storage solutions:

• Make a stuffed animal holder from a fishnet or see-through beach bag and hang it on a low hook or hooks.

- Attach Velcro dots to the wall and to toys so your child can pull them down and stick them up.
- Store books in a plastic dish drainer.
- Attach wicker baskets to the wall (low so children can reach them) and drop toys inside.

Birthday Parties

At age two, children are old enough to be excited about the prospect of having relatives and/or friends over . . . of receiving presents . . . of eating cake and ice cream . . . of "Me birthday party!" To make sure your child's party is a success, keep these tips in mind:

1. Include your youngster in the planning, having him help select the refreshments and the theme.
2. Beware of guest appearances by a face-painted clown or mask-wearing magician; they tend to provoke more terror than mirth.
3. Remember that the Number One Rule is to keep it short, around two hours. The anticipation beforehand and the excitement of the party itself are apt to fray your child's nerves—not to mention yours!
4. Ask other parents to stay for the duration. It's hard for one parent to supervise a group and keep everyone safe.
5. Consider having your child open presents after the guests leave so they don't get upset about wanting presents, too.
6. Provide party favors to help everyone feel included.

CHAPTER 12
Parenting Tricks and Tactics

The easy definition of parenting is "raising a child." The complicated reality, however, involves providing a safe, loving, structured, and consistent environment in which your child can grow to be well adjusted, disciplined, sociable, confident, and happy. It requires as much hard work and discipline from you as it does from your child.

Misbehavior Management

The dictionary meaning of *misbehavior* is "to manage one's actions wrongly or badly." Most of toddlers' "wrong" and "bad" actions stem from their ignorance or lack of physical skill. It doesn't mean they are bad! Concepts like the proper timing for eating cake (after lunch or dinner but not before, and not before *or* after breakfast) and are very complex for a toddler. In addition, getting that cake from the plate to the tummy requires coordinating hundreds of muscles. Learning to do life isn't easy!

The following sections are a sampling of behaviors (not misbehaviors) that, with supervision and patience on your part, can be modified for your child to preserve his safety and your sanity.

Hitting Fido

Say, "Let me show you how to pet the dog." Clasp your child's wrist and make stroking motions while saying, "Be gentle with the dog, and pet him this way. Say, 'Good Fido.' Yes, that's right. See? He likes to be petted like this." Supervise tykes carefully until they learn. Be firm in correcting older toddler misbehavior too, so the child isn't bitten or scratched.

Pounding the Piano

Sit your toddler in your lap on the piano bench. Help her make fists and stretch out her index fingers. Clasp a fist in each of your hands. Help her strike the keys with her index fingers. Help her raise her hands high and drop them hard so she can get enough leverage to make a sound. If the pounding resumes when you remove your hands, say, "No, honey, that hurts Mommy's ears."

Rocking Chair Wildness

Say, "No, baby. You might fall over backward. Let me show you how." Place your hands on his shoulders and teach the correct motion by controlling the rocking. Hold the chair back and say, "Now you try." Stop the chair if he rocks too hard and explain, "That's too hard. Let me show you again." Give positive feedback: "Yes! You've got it! Now I'll let go, and you try it by yourself." Jazz up the practice session with a stuffed animal that needs to be rocked *gently*.

FACTS

Controlled rocking requires subtle flexing movements that are hard for toddlers. Practice sessions are good physical therapy, which help develop coordination and motor control. But if rowdiness persists, make the rocker off-limits and substitute an active game to burn off some high-octane toddler energy.

Emptying Drawers

You need to explain, "That drawer has to stay closed. The clothes will get dirty and wrinkled if you take them out." Let her open the drawer for a look inside. Then say, "Yes, see all your pretty shirts? Can you say 'shirts'?" Let her touch the shirts. Say, "No, don't pick them up." Put her hand in her lap if she grabs them. Say, "Now see if you can close the drawer gently. No, that's too hard. Try again, like this." Place your hand over hers to help close the drawer. Let her try by herself. Give positive feedback for successes: "Yes! That's the way to close a drawer!"

Younger toddlers won't understand much of what you're saying, so remember to say "yes" while smiling to signal permissible behavior and "no" when they're doing it wrong.

Grabbing in the Store

Remove his hand and say, "Ask if you can touch that first. Can you say 'Touch, please'?" If it's too fragile, say, "No, that might break." Find something else to practice on. Extend his index finger and guide it over the object, "Yes, use one finger so you don't break it."

Saying "No!"

Maybe tots can't yet say what they do want, but by saying "No!" they can at least exercise a veto. Reverse psychology can sometimes induce them to comply: "I changed my mind," a mother said in the midst of one losing battle to get her toddler into his coat and out the door. "Forget it. We'll just stay home." "No!" he screamed, trying to put on the coat he had thrown onto the floor a moment before. His mother replied, "Take your coat off!" as she helped him into it and added, "Whatever you do, do not put on your hat!"

You guessed the rest. He had his hat on and was out the front door and in the car faster than his mother could start the ignition and say, "Now whatever you do, don't buckle that seat belt!" Of course, if he'd said, "Okay," Mom would have been up the creek without a paddle.

Always in Trouble

There is a saying among psychologists that "negative attention is better than no attention." This is a hard concept for parents to grasp. "What child in her right mind would want to be yelled at?" they ask. The answer is, "A child who isn't getting enough attention." How much is "enough" depends on the child. Humans are social animals. Extroverted types with their outgoing dispositions desire constant interaction. They find having to spend time alone stressful. Meanwhile, introverts can happily entertain themselves for extended periods and too much social stimulation makes them cranky.

If pleas for parents to play pat-a-cake, read a story, or sing are ignored, it doesn't take toddlers long to fathom that one guaranteed way to get attention is to stir up a ruckus. When toddlers engage their parents by getting mischievous, they are not conscious of what they are doing. They don't harbor thoughts like "Dad will pay attention to me if I hit the baby." Research shows that when adults are rewarded for picking the "right" answers, they soon begin answering correctly— even if no one tells them what the problem is! Their intuition guides them long before they understand the rules of the game. Similarly, intuition guides toddlers toward rewards. If the choice is being ignored or being yelled at, they're likely to opt for the latter. In saying, "Shantal is only doing that to get attention," her father is acknowledging his daughter's need for attention. The trick is to give it for the right behavior.

Parents may feel too tired to keep little ones entertained. Yet when misbehavior develops, most summon the wherewithal to respond. If they had responded before problems developed, they could have expended less energy. It's hard to offer praise when a child is playing nicely by herself for fear she'll want you to play with her. But by ignoring children when they're entertaining themselves, parents discourage them from engaging in this important parental sanity-saving skill. So, when toddlers are playing quietly, lavish them with praise!

Hyperactivity

It's true that a few toddlers do *not* meet the criteria for attention deficit disorder and hyperactivity listed in the *Diagnostic and Statistical Manual of Mental Disorders,* the book professionals use to diagnose emotional and behavior problems. But most do—they're toddlers.

Yet when parents insist their tot is unmanageable, many doctors give in and write prescriptions. Unfortunately, instead of giving Ritalin (a substance chemically similar to amphetamines or "speed") to parents so they can keep up, they medicate little ones!

FACTS

The drugging of American youth is a national scandal. Millions of prescriptions for antidepressants and other mind- and mood-altering medications are written for increasingly younger children. Although psychiatrists may frequently prescribe psychotropic medications, as of this writing, none were FDA approved for this age group.

Don't request medication for your child; you might get it. Just as you might get antibiotics from a doctor who knows full well that they won't cure your child's virus and that the side effects pose a danger. Instead, try the following:

- If your child is running circles though the house, open the door so he can run circles in the backyard. Don't say it's too cold out. What do you think kids do in Alaska? They wear heavy coats!
- If she's climbing the walls, take her to the park so she can climb the jungle gym.

- If he breaks everything he touches, put the breakable stuff away and teach him how to handle objects gently.

If she doesn't nap and hardly sleeps at night, she's probably not getting enough exercise. If more vigorous play doesn't help, cut out junk food and eliminate stress, since kids get "hyper" when they're nervous just like adults. If that doesn't work, be happy for her! She'll have extra time every day for the rest of her life to work and play while the rest of the world is sawing logs. (See Chapter 13, Super Toddlers. The personalities of toddler geniuses and hellions can be hard to tell apart.)

Approaches to Discipline

Some simple parenting tactics can solve a wide range of behavioral problems. The following methods come highly recommended by a variety of psychologists, teachers, pediatricians, and parents.

Hear No Evil; See No Evil

A tried-and-true disciplinary technique psychologists recommend is to ignore problematic behavior. In reality, it's hard to turn a blind eye to the mud pies being constructed from the soil of your potted plants or to turn a deaf ear to the drum of a high chair tray being pounded with a spoon. Although you may be compelled to swoop in to rescue the plants to stop the destruction, there may be an advantage to ignoring the clanging kitchen band—assuming your strained nerves can last through the serenade.

At some point children must learn that spoons aren't drumsticks and loud noise at the dinner table is unacceptable, but some lessons are better postponed. It would be easy to spend all day, every day chastising more active, inquisitive, inventive toddlers, but it isn't good for them to have their failings and inadequacies constantly spotlighted. Since feistier personalities will learn to either tune out the never-ending litany of nagging harangues, or enjoy this sure-fire way to get attention, reprimands may not serve much purpose, either.

When parents ignore problematic behavior that they have attended to in the past, children escalate. Parents may have to react despite their determination to turn a blind eye and deaf ear to small crimes. In this case, they need to teach the child more acceptable ways to get attention. This may require parents to notice and respond when their child begins to act bored or restless, suggest activities that they can do together, and comment on behavior that pleases them.

Warm Fuzzies

If the loving, helpful things toddlers do are ignored, youngsters may give up trying to please. Further, negative parental comments teach children to attend to flaws, so toddlers learn to pay attention to things parents don't do for them and ignore the loving, helpful things that parents do. To keep from focusing on the bad at the expense of the good, set a kitchen timer to remind you to make a positive comment at least once every ten minutes:

- "Thanks for holding still while I change your diaper." (Even if the wiggling only stops for ten seconds!)
- "I'm glad to see you eating your peas." (Even if she's only swallowed one so far!)
- "I'm glad you told me you need to use the potty." (Even if this is the only time he's told you this week—and it was *after* he wet his pants.)
- "I appreciate you sitting still in the grocery cart." (Even if it's been briefly enough to classify as a pause.)
- "Thanks for helping to put away the toys." (Even if she only got one block into the basket and you did all the rest.)
- "I appreciate you waiting while I talked on the phone." (Even if it was only for the minute he ran into the other room to look for the cat.)

Bribes

It can be so easy to offer a cookie, treat, or toy to soothe tears, head off tantrums, and garner cooperation. And bribes often work—at least temporarily. But it's important to consider what children learn in the long run from this behavior management short cut:

- "When I'm upset, eating is the route to feeling better." This is the stuff of which modern eating disorders are made, not to mention plain, old-fashioned obesity.
- "When I'm upset, being given a toy or special activity cheers me up." Materialists are made, not born. If you want to set children on a course of seeking hugs from a human instead of items from a department store, the time to help set the pattern is now.
- "If Dad wants me to do something, he should make it worth my while." If you believe that family cooperation is its own reward and your child should do the right thing whether or not she's paid, avoid bribes! They will jeopardize your child's values.
- "If the reward isn't good enough, I won't cooperate." The problem with having to buy good behavior is that it can be very expensive!

When toddlers are developing a sense of themselves as people in their own right, the attractiveness of bribes may fall by the wayside. No reward is good enough, and *not* doing what a parent wants actually becomes more desirable than any reward.

Contracts

Although bribes ultimately reward bad behavior, contracts are arrangements between the toddler and parent to reinforce the "first things first" principle, as in, "*If* you pick up the blocks, *then* you can play with your dolls." The dolls aren't a reward; they're a privilege that can be exercised once business has been taken care of.

Decide in advance whether the toddler can in fact make a choice. Don't say, "If you'll put on your shoes, we can go out for pizza" if the toddler *must* get dressed because it is time to run errands. The toddler might decide the pizza isn't worth it!

Logical Consequences

One approach to discipline is to provide "logical consequences." This strategy requires parents to figure out what the consequences of misbehavior would be if committed by an adult and design similar consequences for the toddler. The goal is to teach responsible behavior and prepare little ones to deal with the realities of life. For example:

- In the "real world," adults must clean up their messes. So, instead of yelling at a toddler over spilled milk, having him get the rag and help clean it up teaches a basic skill.
- If cleaning up is so much fun that the toddler spills the milk on purpose, say, "I guess you're not thirsty," and take the milk away. A logical consequence of wasting food is having none.
- Adults can't eat according to their whims and must control their diets. So, instead of sending a toddler to her room for having dipped into the sugar bowl, the logical consequence might be that the youngster gets no dessert because she already ate her allotment of sweets.
- Adults are sent to jail to be contained if they're out of control. Send the toddler into time-out.
- Since mistreated possessions get broken and people lose the use of them, remove the toy a toddler is mistreating so he can experience what it's like to be without it.

Sometimes, parents try to impose logical consequences, but they often fail for the following reasons:

- The consequence has nothing to do with the crime. "If you eat that candy bar, no TV for you for the rest of the day!"
- The consequence accomplishes exactly what the child would like to have happen. "If you don't behave in the store, we're going home."
- The parent backs down rather than allowing the child to suffer the consequence. The child isn't supposed to get to hear a story because he was tearing up the books, but the parent reads one anyway.

- The parent sets consequences that can't be carried out. "If you take your coat off again, we're not going out." But the parent has to run errands and must take the child.

"The Big Cahoona"

Harlan was angry because his grandmother wouldn't take him outside to play. "Shut up, dummy!" he exclaimed.

"Harlan," she said gravely. "Have you forgotten? I am the Big Cahoona. You must never say 'shut up' or 'dummy' to the Big Cahoona."

"What dat Big C'oona?" Harlan asked nervously.

"That is me. *I* am the Big Cahoona."

"Why?" he asked.

"Because that's what I am," she answered. Harlan nodded gravely. "Why don't you play in the family room until it's time to go outside?"

Later, when Harlan began asking to go outside again, he was irritated and impatient but not disrespectful. At lunch when Harlan's grandmother told him not to pour milk onto his plate, he persisted.

"What did I tell you?" she asked.

He smiled. "Big C'oona," he said. He stopped pouring the milk.

Every toddler needs a Big Cahoona—a caregiver who is authoritative, firm, and in charge.

ALERT

Don't resort to hitting an unruly child. Take a behavior management course to learn physical containment ("holding") strategies. Many mental health professionals and therapeutic foster parents enroll to learn to contain volatile youngsters. Contact the Crisis Prevention Institute at ☎800-558-8976 or check their Web site at ✎*www.crisisprevention.com.*

Street Brawlers

Some children escalate to the point that even time-out doesn't settle them down. They leave the time-out area or destroy property. Parents must not allow destructive behavior. If children are out of control, parents need to control them. Biting cannot be allowed. The easiest cure is to give your little Jaws something she can safely sink her teeth into, like a sock or a thick rubbery something she can't shred or bite through.

Children must not hit parents, either! Sometimes it helps ground their energy to place your hand firmly on their forehead to hold them away from you. With your feet, and their feet, planted firmly on the ground, let them flail away. Don't smile at the "cuteness" of their impotent rage or otherwise reinforce this forbidden behavior.

If they persist:

1. Firmly say, "No! Biting/hitting me is not allowed!"
2. Send them straight to time-out.
3. Do not give them any additional attention; some children thrive on being yelled at, so don't waste your breath.
4. Do not comfort them when you release them from time-out.

The Basket Hold

The basket hold is a somewhat controversial measure of last resort after other, less drastic disciplinary techniques have failed. The following description is *not* a substitute for taking a course in physical containment techniques. Adults' anger is readily triggered and they can use too much force, which has resulted in children's injury and death. Adults themselves can be injured when a raging child kicks, hits, scratches, bites, or throws his head back. This technique is not appropriate for every child.

QUESTIONS?

What is the basket hold?
The basket hold is a containment technique used to restrain an out-of-control child. Putting toddlers in a basket hold is a powerful nonverbal technique that enables little ones to lose control without harming themselves or others. It also allows them to regain control while being lovingly, yet firmly, held.

If a child has been subjected to any sort of trauma, this technique can trigger disturbing memories. The child may need play therapy to help process the intense emotions that can arise. After taking and passing a course in physical containment strategies, consult a mental health professional and your child's health care professional to determine if the basket hold would be appropriate, and if so, under what circumstances.

The following description of the basket hold is meant for informational purposes only. Parents need to undergo training so they can practice it in a controlled setting.

1. Stand behind the child, reach around her, and cross her arms in front of her chest.
2. Loosely encircle the child's left wrist with your right thumb and forefinger, and encircle the child's right wrist with your left thumb and forefinger.
3. Do NOT squeeze the child's wrist; otherwise, you'll bruise her.
4. Hold the child's arms tightly enough to prevent her from getting enough leverage to hurl her upper body or head into your chest.
5. Do NOT pull the child's arms; this can readily dislocate a small shoulder.
6. Slide to the floor and place the child between your legs.
7. Put your legs over the child's legs to prevent kicking, but be careful not to crush the child's legs.
8. As the child rages and struggles (often spitting, cursing, and attempting to kick and bite—this is what causes some adults to lose their cool; tantrums can last from a minute to an hour), speak in soothing tones: "It's okay. You're all right. I'll keep you safe. I'll control you until you can control yourself. I'll let go when you settle down."
9. Don't release the child when the crying stops; continue the basket hold until the youngster is completely relaxed, often to the point of falling asleep.
10. Do not discuss with the child the events that lead up to the basket hold or what went on while the child was being contained. Instead, let the experience speak for itself.

It may be traumatic for children to be released from a basket hold before they are calm. They may feel they have overpowered their parent or believe that the parent was going to hurt them. They need to find out it is safe to be vulnerable and that parents can contain their intense emotions. On the other hand, parents *must* release a child if they are concerned about the child's safety or physical well-being!

After a toddler who has been placed in a basket hold several times hears the parent say, "It looks like you're losing control. Do you want me to hold you?" he may instantly cross his arms in front of his chest and sink to the floor in anticipation! It really scares children to be out of control, and they are relieved to be contained at that point. They must learn to regain control when they lose it!

Other Problems

Beyond the motor development and social skills that need constant encouragement are the emotional skills and traits that are unique to your child. Whether they are nervous and easily frightened, sensitive and easily upset, or impatient and easily frustrated, toddlers will need your patience and guidance as you both learn how to communicate what the problem is and find an effective solution for it.

Cry Babies

Toddlers are still babies, and some are more sensitive than others. Lots of crying is to be expected. Here are a few tips to help a little one whose faucets are constantly dripping:

- Encourage them to use words to express their feelings.
- Recognize that crying doesn't always signal sadness. Many children cry when they are angry. Model how to express frustration and irritation by using words when you are upset and by helping them say the magic words, "I'm *angry!*"
- Just let them cry! Tears can relieve tension. They're only a problem when parents work overtime to make them go away.

Whining

Whining drives parents nuts. So why do youngsters do it? Because parents who have ignored requests and demands suddenly respond when the plaintive pleas begin. To cure kids of whining, respond before they switch into their high-pitched, plaintive voice, if only to ask for a minute to think about it. Insist that the child ask again without whining. Say "Ask me nicely" or "Use your regular voice." Then try to comply with the request to reinforce your child's polite request.

Fears

Typical terrors that make young toddlers tremble are loud noises, large objects and buildings, something that has startled them, and strangers. Fear is instinctive—a response to a perceived threat that sends adrenaline surging through the body and mobilizes the muscles for flight. It is an inborn survival mechanism. Difficulty distinguishing reality from fantasy sets the stage for many toddlers' fears. If there's a monster in the toilet bowl on TV, what's to keep it out of the toilet bowl at home? (The possibility of your child seeing that commercial is reason enough to pull the TV plug or keep it tuned to PBS.) Standing in line for thirty minutes while other kids have their pictures taken with Santa is one thing, but you want her to sit in that hairy stranger's lap? Go back when she's three and she might consider it.

To help toddlers overcome fears, try the following:

- Confidently approach the frightening object yourself to show that it is safe.
- Let them cling, cry, and hide their faces.
- Say, "You're okay. You're safe" in soothing tones to desensitize them.
- Ask, "Are you afraid of that dog?" Toddlers must know that you have identified the correct danger to feel reassured.
- Do not urge or force toddlers to touch something that frightens them. Let them continue to trust their instincts rather than trying to teach them not to.
- Later, continue desensitizing them by encouraging them to talk about the scary situation. They should appear less traumatized each time.

Do not ridicule, shame, or tease frightened toddlers. Otherwise, they learn to hide their fears, not overcome them. Fears may also be relayed in nightmares, or the child may lose the ability to sense danger. The goal should be to develop courage, not to create a daredevil.

Bathtub Woes

Help a toddler overcome a fear of the tub by taking her into the shower with you or by joining you in the bath. Or consider this desensitization method (but note that it's dangerous because of the risk of falling!): Put her on the edge of the dry bathtub, keeping one hand on her at all times, with her legs dangling inside. Give sponge baths from a pail of water sitting in the tub. Sponge the hair, too, using very little shampoo. Put toys in the tub in hopes she'll reach for them. (Remember that wet feet make it easy to slip and fall!) If she does reach for a toy, see if she wants to sit in the dry tub for her sponge bath.

Then, follow a schedule something like this:

Days 1–2: Keep the tub dry.

Days 3–4: Put a splash of water in the tub before the child enters the bathroom.

Days 5–6: Add a few more splashes to the tub.

Days 7–11: Put a quarter inch of water in the tub.

Day 12: Put a quarter inch of water in the tub. Alternate between sponging water from the pail and from the tub.

Days 13–?: Add more water to the tub each day.

Self-Soothing

Children who have a hard time accepting physical comfort get upset more often and stay upset longer than children who readily accept it. Some youngsters may try to soothe themselves by rocking or clinging to a soft object. Others employ destructive strategies such as head-banging.

Physical pain can be soothing in that it distracts toddlers from their emotional pain.

If your child bangs her head, bites or claws herself, or inflicts other kinds of self-injury when she's upset, do the following:

- Hold her in your lap, rock her, and speak to her in a soothing tone.
- Tell her that you love her and don't want her to hurt herself.
- Tell her that when she feels like hurting herself she should come to you for hugs.
- Teach her other strategies for releasing intense emotions, such as pounding pillows.

Talking on the Telephone

It's totally predictable. The minute you pick up the telephone, your tyke suddenly appears at your elbow and tries to distract you. "She just wants my attention," irritated parents say. In a way, that's true, but the struggle for attention isn't as calculated as it seems. It is a toddler's attempt to restore a sense of connection to his beloved lifeline. Contact with a parent is so vital to a youngster's survival that he can become anxious when it disappears, however briefly.

There don't seem to be any good solutions for this age-old problem. You can try stroking the toddler's hair while chatting on the phone. The physical contact may quiet her down for a minute. Another idea is to set limits for the caller and the toddler. "I'll set the timer and when it rings, I promise . . ." The tot will know that the psychological absence will end soon. Finally, try offering your tot the chance-of-a-lifetime opportunity to jump on the beds, play in the dishwater, or tear up the plants while you talk.

Even that might not keep them content for more than two minutes. Threats and anger might be moderately effective, at which point your phone call has been derailed beyond recovery. The best solution may be to let Father Time usher the toddler to an age where he or she can tolerate not being at center of your universe. Typically, that's the stage also known as "adolescence," and by then the phone will always be busy and you still won't get to talk on it!

Attachment Issues

Children who have difficulty bonding fly into rages readily, and are notoriously difficult to soothe because of their inability to trust others. A combination of the basket hold (discussed earlier) with the following strategy to promote bonding has helped many youngsters. When a toddler is spent and exhausted from having been in a basket hold, or from a tantrum, follow this procedure:

1. Carry the toddler to a rocker and hold him as if nursing, maintaining eye contact if the child is willing.
2. Rock the toddler lovingly but avoid speaking, so the youngster can focus on the physical and emotional warmth and closeness.
3. Use your intuition to determine when the toddler is ready to re-engage with the world, or carry him to bed if he falls asleep.
4. Do not discuss what transpired before or during the basket hold or tantrum unless the toddler brings it up.

Once toddlers are familiar with the procedure, parents can ask, "Do you want me to rock you like a baby?" when a stressed tot is losing control. Often the tantrum suddenly ends and the child hurries to the rocker. (See Chapter 8, "Doling Out Discipline," for more on handling tantrums.)

Breaking the Pacifier Habit

If going cold turkey is too tough, some children have found it less traumatic to lose their pacifier a piece at a time. The parent pokes a small hole in the tip on day one. The next day, the hole is enlarged. On subsequent days, tiny pieces are cut from the tip to gradually shorten it. Children receive less pleasure from sucking as it disappears. After having been reduced to a nub, some parents report that their children lose interest and simply toss it aside.

Thumb-Sucking

Infants suck their thumbs in the womb. Toddlers suck their thumbs or fingers to soothe themselves. If a child is turning to his thumb for comfort, should parents worry? It depends on which expert you ask:

- Some experts say it is a harmless activity that usually disappears on its own.
- Some recommend trying to get toddlers to trade the thumb for a pacifier, blanket, stuffed animal, or doll for reasons of sanitation.
- Some warn that the seeds of addiction are sown when toddlers use oral stimulation to comfort themselves. The desire to suck should be parent's cue to nurse, hug, rock, or cuddle.
- Some say that thumb-sucking is positive in that toddlers comfort themselves rather than using something artificial like a pacifier.
- Some say that since the thumb is so readily available, it's hard to give it up; but plastic is preferable.

Most experts agree that parental nurturing is a healthier way to soothe. Try to increase toddlers' feelings of well-being by criticizing less, praising more, and resolving family and personal problems to reduce the household tensions that can make toddlers feel tense and insecure. (See also Chapter 5, "The Road to Independence," for details on a child's attachment to "comfort objects.")

FACTS

Use of thumbs, pacifiers, and bottles usually ends between ages three and four. If not, the social pressure of kindergarten is a powerful deterrent. Talk to your dentist to be sure that no damage is being done. There's not usually a threat until the permanent teeth start to come in.

Spoiling

Is Grandma spoiling her grandson by thinking he's the most wonderful child in the world? By providing unconditional love and acceptance? By showering him with sugary treats and expensive toys? By letting him jump on the sofa and generally get away with murder? Probably not, as long as when she does occasionally say "no," she holds firm.

Maybe she keeps him safe when he jumps on the sofa by standing at his side so she can catch him if he falls. Of course, that means he'll want his parents to provide the same, personalized service. Maybe she does allow foods you'd prefer he not eat, but only if he does a good job on his veggies first. Maybe she rarely says "no" because she works overtime to make most everything permissible.

ESSENTIALS

Will a toddler wish his parent would say "yes" to him as often as Grandma, buy him Big Wheels "just because," and let him jump on the beds at home? Of course. But that doesn't mean he's spoiled or that he loves her more.

That will make it harder for the parents, who fear they will be seen as the bad guys for holding to stricter rules at home. Indeed, toddlers may test limits when they return home to see if the rules have magically changed. And, given that toddlers only express their crankiness and irritability when they're with people they really trust, they may be a handful after spending time with a doting relative, just as they save up their less savory emotions at day care and explode when they get home or the parent appears.

Rather than attempting to control your child's relationships with others, try to let them work things out between themselves. Instead of controlling gift giving, respond to inappropriate gifts as you would to a neighbor. Thank the sender, and then put the gift away until the child is older, or give the gift away, or suggest that the gift remain at Grandma's house so Sonny can play with it there (if that wouldn't hurt Granny's feelings).

The Waiting Room Blues

If you use car keys to entertain your toddler whenever you're in a waiting room or office trying to conduct a bit of business, boredom will set in fast. All that fussiness and grabbing items from peoples' desks isn't because she's naughty. She's not misbehaving, either. Her goal is to relieve boredom, so her behavior is appropriate, if decidedly inconvenient. Before heading out on errands, drop some brightly colored plastic lids in your purse or pocket to entertain a young tot; for older toddlers, buy some small toys that can only be played with during errands.

FACTS

The solution to many problems becomes obvious once parents understand what is driving toddlers to act as they do. Don't assume that troublesome behavior stems from naughtiness, contrariness, or mindless negativity. Look at what toddlers are trying to achieve. Be flexible as you help them achieve their goals in an acceptable manner.

Dealing with Death

Toddlers can't comprehend that death means forever. They may appear unmoved when a beloved person or pet passes away. They may continue to anticipate that the person or pet will return, ask again and again when he or she is coming back, and require repeated explanations. Whereas talking is adults' primary vehicle for expression for coming to terms with difficult emotional issues, toddlers re-enact their confusion and upset in their play. Following a death, it is not unusual for them to replay any rituals to which they have been exposed, holding funerals for a stuffed animal, digging graves in the sandbox, or sending a doll off to heaven.

Many parents try to shield toddlers from the reality of death. This can backfire, precipitating more confusion and insecurity. The fact that no one seems to notice or care that someone special has disappeared may cause toddlers to worry about who might disappear next. Seeing adults cry and grieve helps make death more real to them, communicates that feeling sad is an appropriate response to loss, and enables toddlers to grieve, too.

If it is decided that attending a funeral might be too difficult or traumatic for a toddler, holding some sort of ceremony at home can help make the death more real and enable tots to say good-bye. It is hard to provide little ones with information that is accurate yet simple enough for them to understand, but that is what they need. However, some common ways to communicate may prove more upsetting than helpful:

- "He went bye-bye." Can trigger fears that parents won't return when they go bye-bye, too.
- "Fido went to sleep" or "We put Fido to sleep." Can instill fear of going to sleep.
- "God took him." Can instill fears that they or a loved will be taken next.
- "She was sick so she died." Can make toddlers worry that they'll die when they get sick.

Instead, try, "Grandma got so *very* ill that her body couldn't heal. She died, so no one can see her any more. I'm sad, because I will miss her." Toddlers need to hear explanations many times before they comprehend.

More Quality Time?

Forget it, because some experts are now saying that *quantity* is more important for toddlers. Fortunately, it can be easier to share more moments than parents may think:

Turn off the phone. At meals, try turning the answering machine on and the cell phone off. Ensure that you have uninterrupted time to interact each day. Turn off the TV, too, especially if no one is watching it. By hitting the off switch, parents eliminate the wall of noise separating toddlers from other family members. In fact, turn off the TV even if someone is watching. It's better to sacrifice shows than your toddler. It's better to be behind on the news than behind on your toddler's development. Be a good role model and find another way to relax, such as reading.

Sleep together. Sharing the family bed helps strengthen attachment and eliminates negative bedtime struggles that can eat up so much time (see Chapter 10, "Sleepy Time," for more on sharing beds).

Cook together. Inviting toddlers to play on the kitchen floor while parents are preparing the meals, instead of sending them to another room to play, puts youngsters where they belong: in the heart of the family. If parents can talk to their youngster while waiting for the water to boil and pause occasionally while stirring the eggs to look at those blocks she's stacking, that's about as engaged as toddlers need parents to be during play. Just learn to walk carefully as you make your way from counter to table so as not to trip over a toy or (heaven forbid!) your child.

Clean the house and do yard work together. Give your toddler a few drops of water in her pail and a sponge to use when you're washing the floor. Attach a broom handle to a box to make a kiddie broom or lawnmower.

Run errands together. Accept that a toddler shopping buddy will slow you down. Interact amicably while cruising the grocery store aisles. Notice that while most of the parents are tangling with their troublesome two-year-old, some are getting along well—because they're talking nonstop and enlisting the toddler's help at every turn.

Turn off the car radio. Little wigglers tolerate the confinement better and benefit from the time to and from day care if parents talk and sing to them in the car. Outings to the zoo and carnival are great, but it's more important to relate well to each other on an everyday basis.

ESSENTIALS

If you can't expand the quantity of time you spend with your child, improve the quality by carving out a twenty-minute slot to spend with your little one during which you studiously avoid teaching, disciplining, reprimanding, and controlling. Stick to singing, reading, tickling, and laughing!

And Toddler Makes Three

Caring for a toddler is so draining that it is easy for spouses to neglect one another. Marital satisfaction typically decreases during the toddler years. Worse, it continues to decrease until the children leave home. The risk of divorce is all too real. Children of all ages need their parents to live together, love each other, express genuine affection toward each other, and resolve any differences they might have.

Have your toddler unite rather than divide you and your spouse by sharing your toddler, working together to solve problems, supporting each other's disciplinary measures if you can or taking a hands-off approach if you can't, going on family outings, and becoming members of family-centered groups such as churches, museums, or parenting classes.

Friends and Lovers

Keep the friendship alive between you and your partner by expressing appreciation more, criticizing less, conversing on subjects besides your child, not taking out crankiness on each other (and apologizing if you do), holding a weekly family meeting to discuss issues, and seeing a counselor for help resolving differences you can't work out yourselves.

Keep the romance alive by getting a sitter and going on weekly dates, taking turns getting up early to make breakfast to serve each other in bed, finding out what pleases your partner and doing it more often, and finding out what displeases your partner and doing it less.

Divorce

Although divorce may be better for toddlers than living in an environment fraught with tension and anger, the loss is hard on them. Being shuttled back and forth between households is taxing given their need for predictable routines. At a time when youngsters are struggling to learn so many household rules, having to learn two sets is especially difficult. You can make the situation a little easier by doing the following:

- Coordinate schedules to create as much continuity as possible.
- Provide a comfort object toddlers can take back and forth.
- Don't grill toddlers about what goes on in the other home.
- Respect their love for their other parent.

- See a counselor to work out issues that affect the toddler.
- Communicate with your ex-spouse about what is happening in your toddler's life, including everyday events and special problems, so each of you can make sense of toddler conversation and behavior.

Parenting Styles

Different people have different styles of dealing with children. Work on learning to appreciate yours as well as your spouse's and discuss ways to help each other by minimizing the inherent drawbacks.

Permissive Pals

Give some youngsters a lenient, laid-back, anything-goes parent, and they flourish. Parents who adopt a hands-off approach to child-rearing may operate more like friends than authority figures. Their strength is their ability to enjoy tots as people in their own right, which can lead to exceptionally warm, joyful relationships. For some youngsters, a bit of parental advice now and then is enough to help them find the right path and stick to it.

However, most children need more solid guidance. When given a lot of freedom, instead of rising to the challenge, they crater. Open classrooms, all the rage in the early 1970s, were built on the philosophy that children would do well if given learning materials and the freedom to do their own thing. The results were mixed. Many students used the time to good advantage; some were lost in the shuffle and wandered aimlessly for years.

On the home front, too much autonomy and independence can translate into a very insecure, spoiled, out-of-control youngster who begins looking to siblings, friends, teachers, and eventually policemen and judges to set limits and contain her. Whether or not you adopt a firmer approach, don't undermine teachers and other adults who impose rules and limits, especially your partner. If people complain about your child's behavior, believe them!

Soldier Strict

Very strict parents believe that teaching the difference between right and wrong and obedience are the top child-rearing priorities. They are conscientious about communicating expectations, providing structure, setting limits, and following through with consequences if youngsters fail to tow the line. Their children may not like many of their rules and regulations, but they have the security of knowing what is expected and the consequences for failing to comply.

ESSENTIALS

Whatever your parenting style, if you need to expand your parenting skills, there's help available in the form of numerous books, workshops, classes, or even counseling. A good place to start is by talking with your child's pediatrician, doing a search on the Internet, or looking in the phonebook under "parenting."

Strict parents' emphasis on respecting authority may make it difficult for them to step out of the parenting role long enough to engage in lighthearted play, which can turn child-rearing into an eighteen-year chore. They may also overinvest time in work, where they feel more at ease because of the clarity of rules and roles.

Although strict parents have a sense of what they want their youngsters to accomplish, many are at a loss as to how to get them there. Being more comfortable in the role of police officer than teacher, the parent may assume children break rules and do things improperly because they are willful or lazy and may fail to see that little ones need to be taught. This can lead them to punish children to try to combat misbehavior when teaching is called for. Fearful children may develop an exaggerated sense of their own inadequacy as they fail in their efforts to please, while bolder types become increasingly defiant.

Authoritative Adults

Authoritative parents believe in taking children's individual needs into account when making child-rearing decisions. They include youngsters' opinions when making decisions but believe that adults must have the final say. They are flexible in the parent role, being strict or lenient as the situation dictates. Thus, they can engage in playful silliness one minute and quickly call a halt to the shenanigans if a little one is getting out of hand. They see themselves as teachers. They break goals into a series of manageable tasks to help little ones get where they need to go, one step at a time.

Authoritative parents' willingness to consider many factors when making decisions can backfire as little ones learn to use logic and advanced negotiating strategies. It may be in each child's interest to have a separate food menu each day, to have their parent help them paint, take them for a walk, and read their favorite books to them. It's also unrealistic. Unless such accommodating parents give sufficient consideration to their own needs, they run the risk of becoming drained and suffering from burnout.

CHAPTER 13
Super Toddlers

Some experts think that extra educational stimulation during the toddler years can boost youngsters' intelligence: If brain development depends on interaction with the environment, then a richer range of activities can translate into higher IQ. Other experts say that although a deprived early environment slows development, an exceptionally stimulating one can't necessarily do much to expand intellectual powers: Potential is dictated by genetics.

The Magic of Books

Your toddler is fussing for you to buy her something at the store. You're tempted to get her a book. After all, a book is better than candy, right? Perhaps . . . but good books nourish the mind just as good food nourishes the body. To decide what to serve your tot, read the labels! Look for stickers on covers (and on the boxes of videos and CDs) to locate winners of the Boston Globe–Horn Book Award, the Caldecott Medal, the Coretta Scott King Award, the National Book Award for Young People's Literature, the Newbery Medal, and the Parent's Choice Awards.

To find quality books for your child, you need to do your homework! Check the American Library Association Web site at ✐ *www.ala.org*. Or try the following:

- Read *Kirkus* and *Booklist* reviews in the book section of big-city newspapers.
- Check editorial and customer reviews at the Barnes & Noble Web site at ✐ *www.bn.com* or read them at ✐ *www.amazon.com*.
- Ask children's librarians for recommendations—they're experts!
- See if your bookstore has a section for award-winning children's literature.

FACTS

Research shows that reading to toddlers translates into better reading ability in elementary school; reading ability in elementary school is a prime predictor of school success; and school success is a predictor of lifelong achievement, occupational success, and overall life satisfaction.

Building Kiddie Libraries

Reading to tots provides great intellectual stimulation and teaches vocabulary. However, what matters most at this age is instilling a love of reading. To choose books:

- Identify your tot's special interests, be it dogs, dinosaurs, doctors, or dust.
- Get books with sturdy cardboard or plastic pages so young toddlers can "read" without damaging the pages and older children can tote them about without destroying their tomes.
- Look for books with exceptionally large print; although toddler vision is about the same as adults', some studies suggest bigger is better for learning to read at an early age.

Between twelve and eighteen months, tots begin to enjoy simple stories (though they don't often want to hear them from front to back; they spend most of the time studying the pictures), so get a mixture of board and regular books. For holiday gift giving, suggest relatives add a good volume of nursery rhymes, an alphabet book, and a counting book to add to your child's permanent collection.

Budding Bibliophiles

The secret to reading lots to tots is to keep it fun. The secret to keeping it fun is to keep it interactive. Don't expect toddlers to sit still or listen quietly. Follow their lead. If they want to start in the middle and look at two pictures before moving to another activity, let them! Let toddlers turn the pages. Teach them how to grasp a corner, pull it gently toward them, and lay it down. This requires a well-developed pincer grasp and fine motor coordination. Until they've developed the physical ability and have practiced, they use their entire hand, which means some wrinkling and ripping. Board books are better!

As you read to your child, keep the humor going! Tell older toddlers that the picture of a cat is a horse. So as not to confuse things, be sure your youngster gets the joke!

Give vocabulary "lessons" by pointing to the pictures and talking about them, so youngsters associate the object with the word: "See, this is a dog. This is a cat." Ask questions to keep them engaged: "Can you find the daddy duck?" Avoid drilling and grilling. If your child doesn't answer the question, answer it for him: "Here's the daddy duck!"

Teach your child to point by making a fist and extending an index finger. If a toddler points to a picture with a finger or hand, he is expressing interest and a desire to discuss it. The parent can say, "That's an elephant. He's eating peanuts. I wonder if he'd like a peanut butter sandwich? I would!"

As you and your child look at pictures in books, round out her education by pointing out:

Colors. "Look, here's a red hen. I think there's something else 'red' on the next page, too. Oh, here it is. The cat has a red bow."

Sounds. "The chicken says, 'Cluck, cluck.' The cow goes 'moo.'"

Categories of objects, such as clothes, foods, vehicles, animals. "The dog is an animal. Can you find another animal?" "Yes, the cat is an animal. And look, here's another one. A horse."

Numbers. Extend your child's index finger and help her count the bunnies, stars, French fries, or anything else.

Location. Point out the house, the barn, the haystack, the pond, and buildings or areas (such as the top, bottom, front, or back).

The Book Nook

To instill a love of reading in children, don't just read to them. Cuddle up with your books, too! If that sounds like a pipe dream amidst the chaos of toddler-rearing, make it a habit to curl up with your own book as your child's naptime approaches. Refrain from all conversation except to state (again and again), "Sorry, I can't talk to you now. I'm reading. We'll talk later."

When the terrible vision of you paying attention to something besides them compels youngsters to protest, clamor for a video, hurl a toy across the room, and otherwise let it be known that they need attention *now*, you can take the bait and lecture about the inappropriateness of throwing toys and the ill effects of video-watching. Or, you can avoid the call to battle by suggesting the toddler look at a book, too. Then keep your eyes glued to your book to drive the message home: "I'm busy. I'm doing something important! I'm reading."

Some children will escalate until parents are forced to close their book to tend to their tyke. But just as little ones hold tea parties because Mom cooks and push toy brooms because Dad sweeps the garage, if they see parents reach for a book when it's time to relax, they will begin to do the same.

Books Versus TV

Reading to a toddler for just fifteen to twenty minutes per day adds up to 168 to 224 hours from ages one to three. On the other hand, watching just 1 hour of TV per day adds up to 730 to 1,460 hours from ages one to three! Parents read an average of 8.9 books per week to toddlers, according to a 1994 study. Considering that toddler attention spans are under ten minutes, that probably means the average child spent less than ninety minutes per week with books—the equivalent of only three cartoon shows. Keep your priorities straight!

ALERT

Informative kids' shows, such as those found on PBS, are okay. But add *Mr. Roger's Neighborhood* to *Sesame Street*, and your child is already up to one hour of TV per day. Resist the allure of the electronic baby sitter. Your child can learn more from interacting with you.

Although television provides nonstop language exposure, experts agree that optimal learning occurs from experiencing the world firsthand. Watching others experience it on TV is a poor alternative. However, the children's TV show *Sesame Street* is an exception and should be fine for older toddlers. When compared to children who watched cartoons or other programs and to youngsters who watched little or no TV, *Sesame Street* viewers had significantly larger vocabularies in first grade. Toddlers who watch mostly cartoons score much lower in tests of vocabulary, paragraph comprehension, and letter and word recognition at age seven than those who watch mostly *Sesame Street* and other informative children's programs.

The Road to Reading

Toddlers can readily learn the rudiments of reading. Buy blocks in the shapes of letters and numbers. Turn on *Sesame Street* or another informational children's program. Then, when you play with your tot, focus on the *Sesame Street* letter of the day: "I'm giving *T* a ride in this car. Look out! Here comes *T!*" Buy or make a poster showing the letters of the alphabet. Position the poster so your child can see it when lying in bed. As part of your bedtime ritual, pick a letter and practice saying words that start with it: "Tuh-tuh-tuh-table! Tuh-tuh-tuh-turtle!"

Help your tot add a *T* page to his homemade alphabet book. Here's how to make the alphabet book:

1. Put twenty-six pieces of notebook paper in a loose-leaf notebook.
2. Print a different letter of the alphabet on each page.
3. Find a picture that starts with each letter, cut it out, and have your toddler paste it on the correct page.
4. Slip each page into a plastic protector.
5. Glue a picture of your child on the front of the notebook and include your child's name in the title: *Larry's Alphabet Book.*

P Is for Phonics

Teach children to recognize letters by pointing them out in books and teaching the sounds they make the same way you teach about animals and the sounds they make. It doesn't matter if a toddler isn't yet talking. All that matters is that youngsters listen and look.

Here's how one mom taught her four children their letter sounds and animals before they reached age four.

PARENTS' READING GAME

	ANIMAL RECOGNITION GAME	LETTER RECOGNITION GAME
Parent	"This is a duck. Can you say 'duck'?"	"This is an *m*. Can you say 'em'?"
Child	"Duck."	"Em."
Parent	"The duck says 'quack.' Can you say 'quack'?"	"The *m* says 'mmmm.' Can you say 'mmmm'?"
Child	"Quack, quack!"	"Mmmm!"
Parent	"Where is a duck?"	"Where is the *m*?"
Child	(Points.)	(Points.)
Parent	"That's right. Can you find another duck?"	"That's right. Can you find another *m*?"
Child	(Points.) "Duck!"	(Points.) "Em!"
Parent	"And what does it say?"	"And what does it say?"
Child	"Quack, quack!"	"Mmmm!"
Parent	"Look, the daddy duck is big. The baby duck is small. What do they say?"	"See? This is the big *M*. This is the little *m*. What do they say?"
Child	"Quack! Quack! Quack!"	"Mmmm!"
Parent	"And here's what I do when you say 'quack, quack, quack.' I tickle, tickle, tickle."	"And here's what I do when you say 'Mmmmmm.' I tickle, tickle, tickle."

Sight-Reading

To help a child progress from prereading to sight-reading when reading stories, point to each printed word as you say it, taking care not to block the child's view. Occasionally the child will follow your finger and glance at the text. After two years of having words pointed out as they're read, toddlers should be able to associate some spoken words with written ones.

The Leap to Reading

Point to a word that occurs often in a story that your child is very familiar with, such as "ham" in Dr. Seuss's *Green Eggs & Ham*. After pointing and reading the same word dramatically several times, focus your child's attention by pausing before you say it. Try to get him to say it with you. The next time the word comes up, pause but don't say the word.

Encourage your child to say it with you. Don't insist if your child resists! The point is to get him to notice your chosen word, not to ruin the story. If your child says the word on his own, praise lavishly: "Wow! My baby can read! You were exactly right! It says 'ham,' see?" Continue reading and pausing before saying the word to see if he can "read" it again. Write the word on a note card and have him wow other family members by reading it to them. On another day, add another word. Make another note card to add to his collection.

FACTS

If your child insists on the same story repeatedly, remember that hearing words in context is the best way to build vocabulary. The more words kids understand at age two, the better they read in first grade. When toddlers know a story by heart, it is easier for them to match the written words to the sounds as you run your finger along the text.

Or try this sorting game: Cut pieces of three different colors of cloth into triangles, squares, and circles. Show children how to match by shape and by color. As your child becomes more advanced, so can the card-sorts. Make (or buy) cards with pictures and "bits" of information on them. Show kids how to sort them into categories (such as house pet or farm animal), and create new categories (such as animals that give us food or animals you see at the circus).

Gifted Tots

Gifted tots develop skills in the same sequence as everyone else, but they do it faster. When the backgrounds of geniuses were examined, one study found that they had begun talking at an average age of nine months! And since that's an average, many began much earlier! Still, many were far less precocious, so even exceptionally late talkers aren't out of the running for a Nobel Prize.

Currently, it is not possible to assess intelligence in toddlers reliably. For older children and adults, genius means performing at an exceptional level in one or more of the following areas:

Linguistic intelligence. Exceptional abilities at speaking or writing characterize a genius orator or writer.

Logical-mathematical intelligence. Gifted scientists have special abilities to think and reason abstractly.

Spatial intelligence. Talented architects, choreographers, and engineers are able to visualize forms and shapes and comprehend spatial relationships.

Interpersonal intelligence. The hallmark of great leaders and therapists is their capability to understand and influence people.

Intrapersonal intelligence. The uncanny ability of some special people to plummet the depths of their own mind has transformed the world. Metaphysicists like Carl Jung and Jean-Paul Sartre are in this group.

Kinesthetic intelligence. Outstanding athletes and dancers possess special physical abilities.

Musical intelligence. The special talent of musical geniuses is the ability to tune into subtle nuances of sound and rhythm.

In one study on children ages 2½ to 12½ with IQs at the top of the chart, parents reported the following personality characteristics:

- 90 percent were described as "sensitive"
- 83 percent liked to concentrate on one activity at a time
- 79 percent had high energy or activity levels
- 50 percent needed less sleep than other children
- 44 percent were sensitive to clothing tags and other tactile sensations

Some studies have found that gifted children appear to have short attention spans because they become bored so easily. Others have found them to be overly excitable and unusually intense, with greater emotional extremes, including more compassion, sadness, and depression.

More intelligent toddlers are likely to have more frustrations to contend with than other youngsters. Their minds can concoct projects, problems, and solutions, but they are blocked by their physical limitations. For example, they can figure out how to solve a puzzle but lack the motor coordination needed to fit it into the proper place. Or they may have complex ideas to express, but don't have the verbal skills to communicate them.

FACTS

According to a quotation from writer Pearl S. Buck, "The truly creative mind in any field is no more than this: A human creature born abnormally, inhumanly sensitive. To him a touch is a blow, a sound is a noise, a misfortune is a tragedy, a joy is an ecstasy, a friend is a lover, a lover is a god, and failure is death."

The exquisite sensitivity that enables them to note subtle differences in texture, movement, color, and shape means that what others perceive as a blank wall can appear to them as a vibrant palette. Because they are constantly bombarded with sensory stimuli, they are more stressed. The extreme interpersonal sensitivity causes some tots to tune into other people's feelings. They are aware of hints of criticism and displeasure that other toddlers don't notice. Ironically, the combination of extreme sensitivity, high energy level, and reduced need for sleep are characteristics of children often diagnosed as "hyperactive." There may be a lot of very misunderstood toddlers out there!

Gearing Up for Greatness

Programs designed to nurture toddler genius, ranging from the Institute for the Achievement of Human Potential headquartered in Pennsylvania to the Yew Chung International Schools in China (see Appendix B, "Resources"), are firm that at this stage, the following should occur:

- Focus on the total child, including emotional, behavioral, and social development.

- Toddlers should be free to follow their own inclinations by having a range of materials available for them to explore.
- Toddlers should not be pressed to pursue structured learning activities.
- Use a loving and nurturing approach when working with toddlers.
- Participate actively; your role in learning is central.

Giving lessons is often a struggle. The time you both spend trying to get her to pay attention would be better spent if she worked on her own. Teaching children how to do puzzles and solve problems with toys actually inhibits learning, if you think about it. The ability to mimic someone else's solution to a problem doesn't require much intelligence. In-depth, complex, high-power thinking takes place as children struggle to figure things out for themselves. Anyone who says, "She's just playing" doesn't understand how toddlers learn! (For more tips on teaching toddlers, see Chapter 4, "Brain Power.")

Teaching strategies appropriate for older children actually inhibits toddler learning. Toddlers seem to have an innate sense of what they need to learn next; structured learning activities imposed by adults distract them from the work *they* know they need to do!

Genius Troubles

If your toddler is exceptionally difficult to manage, it could be because he's literally too smart for his britches! An estimated 20–25 percent of gifted children have social and emotional problems—twice the normal rate, according to Ellen Winner, Ph.D.'s article entitled "Uncommon Talents: Gifted Children, Prodigies, and Savants" (*Scientific American*, February 28, 1999). Meanwhile, for moderately gifted children, the rates of maladjustment were the same as for average children. Similar problems with hyperactivity and attention have been found among highly gifted (IQ from 140 to 154) and learning-disabled boys.

If your child truly is a handful, don't think Ritalin. Think Harvard!

Early Achievement

In this same study, reported characteristics of genius toddlers included:

- 94 percent were very alert as infants
- 94 percent had a long attention span as an infant or toddler
- 91 percent showed early language development
- 60 percent showed early motor skill development
- 48.9 percent were ambidextrous at some period of their development
- 37 percent had imaginary playmates

It's also interesting to note that the age at which mothers of gifted children gave birth was much older than average—30.8 years. Is that because older moms tend to be more patient and tolerant than younger ones and work with them more? No one knows.

Special Gifts

Regardless of whether parents suspect giftedness, they should provide a wide range of learning experiences to stimulate brain development. They also need to respect toddlers' choices about how to spend their time. Pushing and pressuring can propel toddlers down the path of rebellion, burnout, or the trap of molding themselves to fulfill someone else's dreams.

Children's abilities differ. Some are intellectually superior; most are average; and some are clearly slow. When intelligence is very limited, the challenge for parents may be learning to appreciate their youngster's other special gifts.

Rest assured—each child has them. For instance, the typically loving natures and sunny dispositions of children with Down's syndrome remind the rest of us about the importance of pausing in our self-absorbed, busy lives to share a heartfelt smile with a stranger, and grace an acquaintance with an affectionate hug.

Look for your child's strengths, and cherish them!

At This Age: What Toddlers Are Learning

AGE TWELVE TO EIGHTEEN MONTHS

LANGUAGE

Responds to own name

Knows the meaning of "mama," "dada," and "no"

Repeats words and imitates sounds

Jabbers, hums, and "sings"

Identifies two pictures in books

Communicates needs by pointing and making sounds

Points to a part of the body

Responds to one-step commands (e.g., "Come here.")

COGNITIVE/INTELLECTUAL

Understands that a hidden object still exists

Explores via touch and taste

Dumps things out

Takes things out of a container and puts them back in again

Tears paper

Repeats actions to learn cause and effect

Sorts simple objects by shape

Does 3-D puzzles (e.g., insert a block into a square hole)

Remembers some things they saw or heard hours or days ago

PHYSICAL/MOTOR

Stands alone

Lowers themselves from standing to sitting

Walks alone

Walks while carrying toys

Bends over and picks something up

Claps

Points with index finger

Picks up small objects with thumb and index finger

Puts an object in a container

Scribbles

Opens drawers and cabinets

Tosses or rolls a ball

Throws a ball

Stacks two to four blocks

Stirs with a spoon

Climbs 1–2 foot objects

SOCIAL

Imitates demonstrations

Initiates simple games

Looks to caregiver for praise

Is proud of accomplishments

Signals a need for help

Waves "bye-bye"

Shows affection

Smiles at favored objects and people

SELF-CARE

Washes hands

Takes off an article of clothing

Drinks from a cup with a lid

Uses a spoon

AGE EIGHTEEN TO TWENTY-FOUR MONTHS

LANGUAGE

Understands the meaning of "don't"

Knows names for familiar people and objects

Uses fifty words (if talking)

Makes two-word sentences ("Go bye-bye")

Listens to short books and nursery rhymes

Points to six parts of the body when asked

Speaks in gibberish that has the cadence and rhythm of speech

Identifies four pictures in a book with words (if talking)

Follows a two-step command ("Get your coat and come here.")

COGNITIVE/INTELLECTUAL

Categories (e.g., "toys," "books," "foods," "people")

Points to specific pictures in books when asked

Tries different ways to do something

Figures out how to do things by trying different strategies

Learns from looking at books

Pretends (e.g., the piece of play dough is a snake)

Focuses on an activity for five minutes

Chooses (between two things)

Inspects something by looking (not tasting or touching)

PHYSICAL/MOTOR

Runs

Stacks six blocks

Rides a toy by pushing on the floor with alternating feet

Walks up steps

Kicks a ball forward

SOCIAL

Has an impact by saying "no" or resisting

Feels concerned when someone is crying

Tries to comfort someone who is very upset

Handles simple responsibilities

Is interested in other children

Feeds a doll

SELF-CARE

Drinks from a cup without a lid

Uses a spoon and fork (still has trouble turning the hand)

Washes and dry hands

Takes off some clothes

Puts on an article of clothing

Puts arms and legs through holes when being dressed

AGE TWENTY-FOUR TO THIRTY MONTHS

LANGUAGE

Speaks in two-to three word sentences (if talking) | Has short conversations (if talking)

COGNITIVE/INTELLECTUAL

Listens to books with simple stories | Identifies one color

Understands the concepts "one" and "two" | Plays make-believe and fantasy games

PHYSICAL/MOTOR

Draws | Kicks a ball forward

Matches objects that are the same | Throws a ball

Makes play dough or clay snakes and balls | Stands on one foot (briefly)

Stands on tiptoes | Climbs low ladders

Stacks eight blocks | Leans forward without falling

Pedals a tricycle | Goes up and down stairs using alternate feet

Jumps forward

SOCIAL

Plays next to other children | Participates in interactive games

Categorizes people as boy or girl | Identifies a friend

SELF-CARE

Puts on a pull-over shirt | Puts on or pulls up pants

AGE THIRTY TO THIRTY-SIX MONTHS

LANGUAGE

Says the names of pictures in a book when asked (if talking)

Names six body parts (if talking)

Describes what two objects are used for (if talking)

Makes three- to four-word sentences (if talking)

Speaks so that others understand him most of the time (if talking)

Says fifty words (if talking)

Understands most of what is said to him

COGNITIVE/INTELLECTUAL

Follows a two-step command ("Find your hat and put it on.")

Reasons through problems themselves

Counts to two

Identifies four colors

PHYSICAL/MOTOR

Copies a straight line

Copies a circle

Confines coloring to the paper

Balances on one foot (two seconds)

Stacks eight blocks

SOCIAL

Says "please" and "thank you" when prompted

Takes turns (with guidance)

Asserts rights with peers

Knows not to bully other children

Contributes to joint activities and discussions

Negotiates and compromises

Asks for information

Approaches other children to play in daily care setting

Plays with other children

SELF-CARE

Uses the potty

Eats with minimal assistance

Dresses themselves

Fixes a bowl of cereal

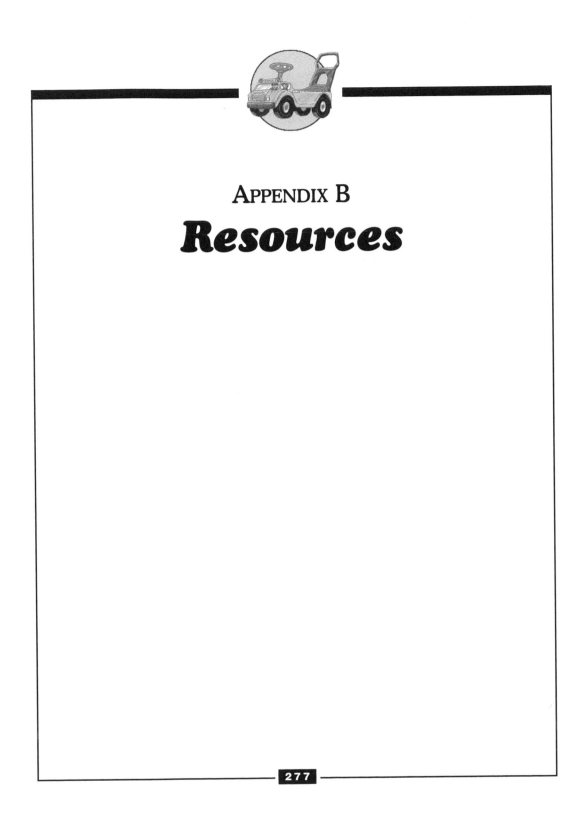

APPENDIX B

Resources

Books and Magazines
For Parents

Books

Brazelton, T. Berry. *Touchpoints: Your Child's Emotional and Behavioral Development.* Cambridge, MA: Perseus Publishing, 1994.

Faber, Adele, and Elaine Mazlish. *Siblings Without Rivalry: How to Help Your Children Live Together So You Can Live Too.* New York: Avon Books, 1987.

Feldman, Robert S. *Child Development.* New Jersey: Prentice Hall, Inc., 2001.

Garcia, W. Joseph. *Sign with Your Baby: How to Communicate with Infants Before They Can Speak.* Seattle: Northlight Communications, 1999.

Iovine, Vicki. *The Girlfriends' Guide to Toddlers.* New York: Perigee Books, 1999.

Nathanson, Laura Walther. *The Portable Pediatrician for Parents.* New York: HarperPerennial, 1994.

Smutny, Joan Franklin, ed. et al. *The Young Gifted Child. Potential and Promise, an Anthology.* Cresskill, NJ: Hampton Press, 1998.

Smutny, Joan Franklin, et al. *Your Gifted Child: How to Recognize and Develop the Special Talents in Your Child from Birth to Age Seven.* New York: Ballantine Books, 1994.

Spock, Benjamin. *Baby and Child Care.* New York: Pocket Books, 1976.

White, Burton L. *The New First Three Years of Life.* New York: Fireside, 1995.

Zand, Janet, et al. *Smart Medicine for a Healthier Child.* Garden City, NY: Avery Publishing Group, 1994.

Magazines

- *Parents,* www.parents.com
- *Parent & Child,* www.scholastic.com
- *Parenting,* www.parenting.com/parenting
- *Mothering,* www.mothing.com

For Children

Books

Barrett, Judi. Illustrated by Ron Barrett. *Cloudy with a Chance of Meatballs.* New York: Aladdin Paperbacks, 1982.

Brown, Margaret Wise. Illustrated by Clement Hurd. *Goodnight Moon*. New York: Harper, 1947.

Carle, Eric. *The Very Hungry Caterpillar*. New York: Putnam Publishing Group, 1984.

Dr. Seuss. *Green Eggs & Ham*. New York: Random House, 1960.

——*Dr. Seuss's Sleep Book*. New York: Random House, 1962.

——*Hop on Pop*. New York: Random House, 1963.

——*Fox in Socks*. New York: Random House, 1965.

——*One Fish Two Fish Red Fish Blue Fish*. New York: Random House, 1981.

Frankel, Alona. *Once upon a Potty*. New York: HarperCollins, 1999.

Gomi, Taro. *Everyone Poops*. New York: Kane/Miller Book Publishers, 1993.

Martin, Bill Jr., and Carle, Eric. *Brown Bear, Brown Bear, What Do You See?* New York: Henry Holt and Company, 1983.

Paterson, Bettina. *Potty Time*. New York: Grosset & Dunlap, 1993.

Sendak, Maurice. *Where the Wild Things Are*. New York: HarperCollins, 1988.

Viorst, Judith. Illustrated by Ray Cruz. *Alexander and the Terrible, Horrible, No Good, Very Bad Day*. New York: Aladdin Paperbacks, 1987.

Web Sites

- *www.4everythingnanny.com*: Learn the ins and outs of in-your-home child care at a Web site devoted to nannies.
- *www.abcparenting.com*: Get help on thorny issues like day care, weaning, and potty training. There's also information for parents of multiples and discussion groups for everyone.
- *http://babyparenting.about.com*: Here's a Web site with great smoothie recipes, potty training tips, and the chance to network with other on-line moms and dads.
- *www.disney.go.com*: Check out the activities, music, and stories. Games teach toddlers basic concepts like matching, but the sounds and graphics provide great sensory stimulation whether or not they care to play.

- *www.drsonna.org*: Read the online articles and get personal answers to your toddler questions at my Web site.
- *www.kidsdoctor.com*: This site contains a wealth of information on health, nutrition, parenting, and behavior.
- *www.kidsfree.com*: Check the toddler section to download free software for kid friendly games, stories, and keyboard bangers. Well, maybe not that kid friendly; parents will still need to supervise.
- *www.kidsource.com*: If you have a toddler health-and-wellness question, they've got the answer. Read the articles or post your question to a forum.
- *www.nccic.org*: When you want child care information, go for the best at the National Child Care Information Center. It has a searchable database, too.
- *www.parentcenter.com*: Here's a site that offers a wealth of tips and how-to's to enhance toddler learning, health, and better behavior.
- *www.parents-choice.org*: Find out which books, toys, videos, software, and TV shows get the thumbs-up from other parents.
- *www.parentstv.org*: Parent's Television Council Green Light Seal of Approval identifies TV shows that exhibit positive values and/or educational content for families. Phone: ✆(213) 629-9255.
- *www.pbs.org/barney*: Color with BJ, make music with Baby Bop, and play games with Barney.
- *www.pbs.org/rogers*: Hear the songs, learn the facts, listen to the stories, and color in the on-line coloring book while visiting Mr. Rogers Neighborhood.
- *www.pbskids.org/teletubbies*: Make Tinky Winky, Dipsy, Laa-Laa, and Po talk while touring their Teletubbie homeland.
- *www.tnpc.com*: Before you buy a children's product, check the recommendations and recalls at the National Parenting Center's Seal of Approval Web site.

Videos

Elmo's Musical Adventure: The Story of Peter and the Wolf. Sony Wonder, 2001. (Ages 1–5)

Elmo's World: Flowers, Bananas & More. Sony Wonder, 2000. (Ages 1–5)

Little Bear: Little Sherlock Bear. Paramount Studio, 2001. (Ages 2–6)

Richard Scarry's Best Sing-Along Mother Goose Video Ever. Sony Wonder, 1994. (Ages 2–5)

Thomas Trackside Tunes and Other Thomas Adventures. Anchor Bay Entertainment, 2001. (Ages 2–6)

Zoboomafoo: Play Day at Animal Junction. PBS Home Video, 2001. (Ages 2–5)

Programs and Associations

- Achievement of Human Potential has educational products and programs that teach toddlers to read, do math, and acquire knowledge. It has a program for brain-injured children, too. ✆ (800) 344-MOTHER, ✍ *www.iahp.org*

- The International Parenting Association offers free, downloadable educational materials and publishes *Child Genius* magazine. Contact P.O. Box 1152, Emigrant, MT 59027, ✍ *www.ycsi.net*

- The National Association for Gifted Children, 1707 L Street, NW Suite 550, Washington, DC 20036, ✆ (202) 785-4268, ✍ *www.nagc.org.*

- A Web site that has collected links to other sites with information on early giftedness: ✍ *www.baycomputer.com/ebeth/*

- To join an e-mail list in which parents and educators discuss the needs of gifted children, see ✍ *www.ri.net/gifted_talented/lists.html*

- If you are interested in genius, learn more about Mensa, the exclusive international group, ✆ (800) 66-MENSA, ✍ *www.mensa.org*

- National Association for Down Syndrome, P.O. Box 4542, Oak Brook, IL 60522, ✆ (630) 325-9112, ✍ *www.nads.org*

- National Association of the Deaf, 814 Thayer Avenue, Silver Spring, MD 20910, ✆ (301) 578-1788, ✍ *www.nad.org*

- National Federation of the Blind, 1800 Johnson Street, Baltimore, MD 21230, ✆ (410) 659-9314, ✍ *www.nfb.org*

- United Cerebral Palsy, 1660 L Street, NW, Suite 700, Washington, DC 20036, ✍ *www.ucpa.org*

Index

A

abuse
  corporal punishment, 158
  domestic violence, 124
  sexual, 54–56
accidents, *see* safety
agility, 37
airbags, 132
alcohol, driving and, 132
Alexander and the Terrible,
  Horrible, No Good, Very
  Bad Day (Viorst), 85
allergies, to food, 165
"All gone!" concept, 65
alphabet book, how to make, 264
American Heart Association
  Web site, 137
American Library Association
  Web site, 260
American Red Cross Web site,
  137
anxiety, *see* fears
appetite, 164, 177
aromatherapy, 206
art box supplies, 224–225
artificial colorings, 213
artificial respiration, 137–138
associations, list of, 281
attachment issues, 249

attention
  negative, 236–237
  positive, 253–254
  see also comfort
authoritative parenting, 257–258
autism, 33, 183
automobile safety, 131–132
awards, for quality books, 260

B

Baby's Colors (Ricklen), 69
baby talk, 19–20
balance, 36–37
Barrett, Judi, 182
basket hold technique, 243–245
bathrooming, *see* toilet training
bathroom safety, 8, 124–125
bathtub
  overcoming fears of, 247
  seats for, 124–125
bedrooms, 202
beds, *see* toddler bed
bed-wetting, 116–117
bee stings, 131
behavior management, 234–237
  emptying drawers, 235
  grabbing, 235
  hitting of pet, 234

hyperactivity, 237–238
misunderstandings and, 41–42
negative attention and,
  236–237
pounding of piano, 234
rocking chair wildness,
  234–235
saying "no," 235–236
see also discipline
"Big Cahoona," 242
birthday parties, 232
biting, 243
blocks, homemade, 220
body, *see* physical growth
books
  about toilet training, 109
  awards for quality, 260
  concept of categories and, 68
  how to choose, 260–261
  list of useful, 278–279
  television vs., 263–264
  vocabulary development and,
    30
  Web sites for, 260
  see also reading
booster seats, 186–187
bottled water, 173
bowel movements, *see* toilet
  training

boxes, as toys, 218–219
Boynton, Sandra, 205
boys, *see* gender issues
Brazelton, T. Berry, 167
breast-feeding, 164–165
bribes, 239–240. *See also* rewards
Brown, Margaret Wise, 205
Brown Bear, Brown Bear, What Do You See? (Carle), 69
bubbles, 221
Buck, Pearl S., 268

C

caffeine, 212–213
calcium, 170, 173
calories, 168–169
candy, 184–185
cardiopulmonary resuscitation (CPR), 137
online video of, 137
Carle, Eric, 69, 182
carotid artery, 138–139
car safety, 131–132
catching, 41
categories, concept of, 66–71
colors, 69–70
learning from books, 68
locations, 70–71
shapes, 70
sorting game, 266
chemical poisoning, 127–130
chest compressions, 138–139
child abuse, *see* abuse

childproofing, 123, 147, 203
choices, for toddler, 150–151
choking, 45, 175
how to treat, 139–141
climbing, 38
Cloudy with a Chance of Meatballs (Barrett), 182
clumsiness, 41, 42–43
coins, swallowing of, 141
colors, 69–70
comfort
from contact, 84–86
from special objects, 86–87
words of, 89–90
communication tantrums, 162
complex carbohydrates, sources of, 171
consequences, logical, 241–242
Consumer Project Safety Commission hotline, 126
Consumer Reports Web site, 228–229
containment (holding) strategies, 242–245
contracts, 240
cooing, 13
cooking, as joint activity, 254
corporal punishment, 153, 157–159
cosmetics, 129–130
cotton diapers, 102–103
Count! (Fleming), 62
CPR, 137
online video of, 137

crafts, 64–65
cravings, for strange foods, 185–186
crawling, 38
crib, 197
Crisis Prevention Institute, 242
criticism, 90
cruising, 38
crying, 245

D

daily living skills, 58–60
danger, *see* safety
death, dealing with, 252–253
depression, of parent, 76
destructive behavior, 242–243
development, *see* emotional growth; physical growth
developmental aphasia, 33
diapers, 102–104
diet, *see* nutrition
dirt, playing in, 226–227
disabilities, speech and, 33–34
discipline, 145–162, 238–245
attachment issues, 249
bathtub fears, 247
"big Cahoona," 242
bribes, 239–240
contracts, 240
crying, 245
destructive behavior, 242–243
fears, 246–247
ignoring behavior, 238–239

impatience, 251–252

logical consequences, 241–242

pacifiers, 249

positive reinforcement, 239

praise, 153–155

saying "no," 146–151

spanking, 157–159

spoiling, 250–251

tantrums, 159–162

telephone interruptions, 248

thumb-sucking, 250

time-outs, 156–157, 158

whining, 246

see also behavior management

distraction, of toddler, 149, 151

divorce, 255–256

docosahexaenoic acid, 172

dolls, 48–49

homemade, 221

domestic violence, 124

Dr. Seuss's Sleep Book (Seuss), 205

drawer emptying, 235

dress up game, 225

drowning, 124–125, 133

drumming, 218

E

eating disorders, 184, 185–186

echolalia, 33

elective mutism, 33

emergency list, 136

emotional growth, 77–100

comfort objects and, 86–87

contact comfort and, 84–86

delaying of gratification, 93–98

developing of initiative, 91–92

feelings and, 88–90

independence and, 98–100

parent's role in, 81–83

routine and, 78–79

sleep and, 210

stranger anxiety and, 83–84

toilet training and, 104–105

trust and, 79–80

emotional intelligence, 94

encopresis, 118–120

errands, as joint activity, 254

Everyone Poops (Gomi), 109

exercise, sleep and, 204, 238

exercise class, 39

exploration, *see* learning

expressive language disorder, 33

exquisite sensitivity, 268

eye, how to treat chemicals in, 129

F

facial muscles, 44–45

false memories, 73

fat sources, 171–172

fears

overcoming of, 247–248

sleep and, 211–212

of strangers, 83–84

feelings, 88–90. *See also* emotional growth

fiber, 173

fine motor coordination, 43–45

finger foods, 166

finger paints, homemade, 222–223

finger-play poetry, 74–75

fire ants, 130

firearm safety, 123–124

fire safety, 133–135

first-aid kit, 141–142

Fleming, Denise, 62

flexibility, 37

food, *see* nutrition

food allergies, 165

sleep and, 213

Foot Book, The (Seuss), 71

foreign language, 21

Fox, Mem, 205

Frankel, Alona, 109

Freud, Sigmund, 104–105

fruits, 172

frustration, tolerance of, 97–98

G

galloping, 39

gardening, 179

gases, dangerous, 131

gender issues, 47–51

genius, *see* gifted children

gibberish, 20–21

gifted children, 266–270
  categories of, 267
  characteristics of, 270
  handling troubles with, 269
  ways to encourage, 268–269
girls, *see* gender issues
Going to Bed Book, The
  (Boynton), 205
Gomi, Taro, 109
Goodnight Moon (Brown), 205
grabbing, in store, 235
grammar, 31
gratification, delaying, 93–98
gross motor skills, 40–41
growth, *see* emotional growth;
  physical growth
gun safety, 123–124

H
hand washing, teaching of, 59
Harlow, Harry, 82–83, 84, 86
hazardous substances, list of, 128
head banging, 247–248
Head Start, 76
health issues
  bathroom hygiene, 112
  dental checkup, 45
  hearing, 25–26
hearing, speech development
  and, 25–26
herbs, 144
high chairs, 186–187
hitting

by toddler, 234
of toddler, 242
see also abuse
hopping, 39
hornet stings, 131
housecleaning, as joint activity,
  254
hygiene, 112
hyperactivity, 237–238, 268, 269

I
impatience, 251–252
independence, *see* emotional
  growth
initiative, developing, 91–92
insects, poisonous, 130–131
insomnia, *see* sleep
intellectual development, *see*
  learning
intelligence, *see* gifted children;
  learning
interpersonal intelligence, 267
intrapersonal intelligence, 267
ipecac syrup, 127
iron, 173

J, K
juices, 172
jumping, 3, 39
kicking, 40
kinesthetic intelligence, 267
kitchen

helping in, 179–181
utensils from, as toys, 217

L
language, *see* speech
lead poisoning, 128
learning, 57–76
  of "All gone" concept, 65
  of categories, 66–71
  of daily living skills, 58–60
  exploration and, 2–5
  of math skills, 61–62
  memory and, 71–76
  of problem-solving skills, 60–61
  of self-esteem, 62, 63
  teaching and, 63–64
  toilet training readiness and,
    105–108
  toys and, 64–65
  see also reading
learning stages
  12 to 18 months, 272
  18 to 24 months, 273
  24 to 30 months, 274
  30 to 36 months, 275
left vs. right-handedness, 44
lifesaving skills, 136–141
  artificial respiration, 137–138
  chest compressions, 138–139
  choking treatment, 139–141
  CPR, 137
linguistic intelligence, 267
liquids, importance of, 173

lisping, 25
listening
    by toddler, 12, 19–20, 21–23
    to toddler, 30
Little Squirt diaper sprayer, 103
locations, teaching about, 70–71
locomotion skills, 38–40. *See also* walking
logical-mathematical intelligence, 267
lowering, of self, 38
low-fat diets, avoiding, 167, 171

M

magazines, list of useful, 278
manipulative tantrums, 160–162
marshmallow, lesson of, 93–94
mathematical-logical intelligence, 267
math skills, 61–62
medication safety, 142–144
memory, 71–76
    gaps in, 75
    rhymes and, 74–75
Michael, Walter, 93
milk, 167, 203, 206
misbehavior, *see* behavior management; discipline
molestation, 54–56
Montessori, Maria, 58
music, at bedtime, 213
musical intelligence, 267

N

names, using proper, 20
naps, 190, 204
National Parenting Center Web site, 228
negative attention, 236–237
nightmares, 211–212
"No"
    saying by toddler, 235–236
    saying to toddler, 146–148
noisemaking, 234
nudity
    of parents, 54
    of toddler, 53
    toilet training and, 108, 111–112, 114
nursing, 164–165, 203
nutrition, 163–188
    appetite and, 164, 177
    basics of good, 167–173
    minimum diet requirements, 167–168, 174
    outside the home, 187–188
    RDAs, 174
    safety and, 175, 186–187
    solid foods and, 165–166
    struggles over, 181–186
    tips for encouraging eating, 175–181
    vitamins and, 174
    weaning and, 164–165

O

offensive language, 53–54, 109

Once upon a Potty (Frankel), 109
outdoor play, 227–228

P

pacifiers, 249
pajamas, flame resistant, 135
parentese, 19–20
parenting styles
    authoritative, 257–258
    permissive, 256
    strict, 256–257
Parents' Choice Web site, 229
parents, relationships of, 254–256
"Pat-a-Cake" poem, 75
perfume, 130
permissive parenting, 256
personal pronouns, 20
phonics, 264–265
physical growth, 35–56
    central nervous system and, 36, 41–42
    gender issues and, 47–51
    physical skills and, 36–45
    sexual abuse and, 54–56
    sexuality and, 51–54
    teeth, 45–46
physical skills, 36–45
    fine motor, 43–45
    gross motor, 40–43
    locomotion, 38–40
    see also walking
Pica, 185
pigeon toes, 5, 6

pincer grasp, 43–45

plants, dangerous, 130

play, importance of, 7. *See also* toys

play dough, homemade, 221–222

playpens, 126

Poison Control phone numbers, 122

poisoning
  chemical, 127–130
  cosmetic, 129–130
  gases, 131
  insects, 130–131
  list of hazardous substances, 128
  plants, 130

positive reinforcement, 239

positives, in discipline, 147–148

potty, *see* toilet training

potty mouth, 53–54

praise, 153–155

prescription drugs, avoiding, 237–238

problem-solving skills, 60–61

pronunciation errors, 25–27

protein sources, 170–171

psychotic language, 33

pulling self up, 38

pull toys, homemade, 219–220

puppets, homemade, 225

puzzles, 220–221

R

radio, in car, 254

rattles, homemade, 219

reading
  game to encourage, 265
  to toddler, 261–263
  by toddler, 264–266
  see also books

receptive language disorder, 33

recommended daily allowances (RDAs), 174

Red Cross Web site, 137

redirection, of toddler, 149–150

restaurants, 187–188

rewards, for toilet training, 111, 114–115, 119. *See also* bribes

rhymes, 74–75

Ricklen, Neil, 69

right vs. left-handedness, 44

Ritalin, 237

rituals, before sleep, 204–205

rocking chairs, 234–235

rolling, 41

Rountree, Bob, 174

rumination disorder, 185–186

running, 39

S

safety, 121–144
  automobile, 131–132
  basics of, 122–123
  bathroom, 8, 124–125
  chemical, 127–130
  discipline and, 151–153
  emergency contact list and, 135–136

fire, 133–135

firearm, 123–124

first-aid kit and, 141–142

food, 45, 175, 186–187

gases, 131

herbal remedies, 144

insects, 130–131

lifesaving skills and, 136–141

medication, 142–144

plants, 130

playpens, 126

sleep, 195, 197, 202

stairs, 7–8

strollers, 126

swimming pool, 133

toy chests, 125

toys, 216, 227

walkers, 5–6

sandbox, homemade, 226–227

science "magic," 223

seat belts, 132

second language, 21

self-esteem, 62–63, 91–92
  praise and, 154

self-soothing, 247–248

Sendak, Maurice, 85

separation anxiety, 207–208

Sesame Street, 263–264

Seuss, Dr., 71

sexism, *see* gender issues

sexual abuse, 54–56

sexuality, 51–54

shapes, 70

shoes, fit of, 9–10

show-and-tell, discipline and,

148–149

sight-reading, 265

sign language, 14–18

silly putty, homemade, 222

skipping, 40

skull, 45

slapping, 153. *See also*
    spanking

sleep, 189–214
    after learning to walk, 3, 10
    amount needed, 190–192
    of children with parents,
        193–197, 253
    cycles of, 206
    exercise and, 204, 238
    getting ready for, 202–204
    handling problems with,
        207–214
    importance of schedule for,
        192–193
    insomnia and, 212–214
    as learnable skill, 205
    moving from crib to bed
        and, 197–202
    safety and, 195, 197, 202
    tiredness and, 191

*Smart Medicine for a Healthier
    Child* (Zand, Walton, and
    Rountree), 174

smoke detectors, 134

snacks, 181–182, 183
    to induce sleep, 213–214

sock puppets, 221

socks, 9, 10

soft spot, of skull, 45

solid foods, 165–167

sorting game, 266

spanking, 157–159

spatial intelligence, 267

speech, 11–34
    correcting errors in, 25–27, 31
    development of, 12–14, 19–21,
        23–25
    disabilities and, 33–34
    hearing and, 25–26
    inappropriate words in,
        53–54, 109
    parental help with, 13–14,
        19–20, 21–23, 27–31
    sign language and, 14–18
    stuttering and, 31–32

spiders, 131

spoiling, 250–251

stairs, 7–8

storage, of toys, 230–232

stranger anxiety, 83–84

strangulation hazard, 141

strength, 37

stress
    sleep and, 204
    tantrums and, 159–160

strict parenting, 256–257

striking, 40

strollers, 126

stuttering, 31–32

sugar, 177, 184–185
    sleep and, 213

swimming lessons, 43, 133

swimming pools, 133

syrup of ipecac, 127

T

talking, *see* speech

tantrums
    communication, 162
    constructive strategies for,
        243–245
    manipulative, 160–162
    from stress, 159–160

teaching, art of, 63–64

teeth, 45–46

telegraphic speech, 24

telephone interruptions, 248, 253

telephone numbers
    Crisis Prevention Institute, 242
    poison control, 122
    U.S. Consumer Project Safety
        Commission hotline, 126

television
    books vs., 263–264
    language development and, 19
    sexuality on, 51
    turning off, 253
    violence on, 223

"This Little Piggy" poem, 75

throwing, 40

thumb-sucking, 250

tibial torsion, 6

Time for Bed (Fox), 205

time-outs, 156–157
    for adults, 158

avoiding bedroom for, 202
Time to Sing (Center for Creative Play), 75
Tinkle Toonz musical toilets, 114
tiptoe walking, 5
toddler bed, move to, 197–202
toilet training, 101–120
  bedwetting and, 116–117
  bowel problems and, 117–120
  outside the home, 116, 120
  personality development and, 104–105
  process of, 109–115
  readiness for, 105–108
  rewards and, 113, 114–115, 119
  terminology and, 109
Touchpoints: The Essential Reference (Brazelton), 167
toy chests, 125
toys, 215–232
  cleanup of, 229–230
  homemade, 219–227
  household objects as, 216–219
  outdoor play and, 227–228
  safety and, 216, 227
  storage of, 230–232
  store-bought, 227, 228–229
training pants, 111
trampolines, 126
trust, emotional development and, 79–80
tryptophan, 213

U

U.S. Consumer Project Safety Commission hotline, 126
"Uncommon Talents: Gifted Children, Prodigies, and Savants" (Winner), 269
urination, *see* toilet training

V

vegans, 175
vegetables, 172
  growing of, 179
  sugar on, 177
vegetarians, 175
Very Hungry Caterpillar, The (Carle), 182
videos, list of, 280–281
Viorst, Judith, 85
vitamins, 174
vocabulary, *see* speech
vomiting, when not to induce, 127

W

waiting, *see* gratification, delaying; impatience
walkers, dangers of, 5–6
walking, 1–10, 39
  behavior changes after, 78
  learning and, 2–5
  safety and, 5–9
  shoes and, 9–10
  statistics about, 3
  see also locomotion skills
Walton, Rachel, 174
wasp stings, 131
water, bottled, 173
water games, 225–246
weaning, 164–165
Web sites, 137, 228–229, 242, 260, 279–280
weight, of toddler, 167, 184
Where the Wild Things Are (Sendak), 85
whining, 246
Winner, Ellen, 269

Z

Zand, Janet, 174

THE EVERYTHING® MOTHER GOOSE BOOK

By June Rifkin

The Everything® Mother Goose Book is a delightful collection of 300 nursery rhymes that will entertain adults and children alike. These wonderful rhymes are easy for even young readers to enjoy—and great for reading aloud. Each page is decorated with captivating drawings of beloved characters. Ideal for any age, *The Everything® Mother Goose Book* will inspire young readers and take parents on an enchanting trip down memory lane.

Trade paperback,
$12.95 ($19.95 CAN)
1-58062-490-1, 304 pages

OTHER *EVERYTHING*® BOOKS BY ADAMS MEDIA CORPORATION

BUSINESS

Everything® **Business Planning Book**
Everything® **Coaching and Mentoring Book**
Everything® **Fundraising Book**
Everything® **Home-Based Business Book**
Everything® **Leadership Book**
Everything® **Managing People Book**
Everything® **Network Marketing Book**
Everything® **Online Business Book**
Everything® **Project Management Book**
Everything® **Selling Book**
Everything® **Start Your Own Business Book**
Everything® **Time Management Book**

COMPUTERS

Everything® **Build Your Own Home Page Book**

Everything® **Computer Book**
Everything® **Internet Book**
Everything® **Microsoft® Word 2000 Book**

COOKBOOKS

Everything® **Barbecue Cookbook**
Everything® **Bartender's Book, $9.95**
Everything® **Chinese Cookbook**
Everything® **Chocolate Cookbook**
Everything® **Cookbook**
Everything® **Dessert Cookbook**
Everything® **Diabetes Cookbook**
Everything® **Low-Carb Cookbook**
Everything® **Low-Fat High-Flavor Cookbook**
Everything® **Mediterranean Cookbook**
Everything® **Mexican Cookbook**
Everything® **One-Pot Cookbook**
Everything® **Pasta Book**

Everything® **Quick Meals Cookbook**
Everything® **Slow Cooker Cookbook**
Everything® **Soup Cookbook**
Everything® **Thai Cookbook**
Everything® **Vegetarian Cookbook**
Everything® **Wine Book**

HEALTH

Everything® **Anti-Aging Book**
Everything® **Diabetes Book**
Everything® **Dieting Book**
Everything® **Herbal Remedies Book**
Everything® **Hypnosis Book**
Everything® **Menopause Book**
Everything® **Nutrition Book**
Everything® **Reflexology Book**
Everything® **Stress Management Book**
Everything®**Vitamins, Minerals, and Nutritional Supplements Book**

All Everything® books are priced at $12.95 or $14.95, unless otherwise stated. Prices subject to change without notice.
Canadian prices range from $11.95–$31.95, and are subject to change without notice.

HISTORY

Everything® **American History Book**
Everything® **Civil War Book**
Everything® **Irish History & Heritage Book**
Everything® **Mafia Book**
Everything® **World War II Book**

HOBBIES & GAMES

Everything® **Bridge Book**
Everything® **Candlemaking Book**
Everything® **Casino Gambling Book**
Everything® **Chess Basics Book**
Everything® **Collectibles Book**
Everything® **Crossword and Puzzle Book**
Everything® **Digital Photography Book**
Everything® **Family Tree Book**
Everything® **Games Book**
Everything® **Knitting Book**
Everything® **Magic Book**
Everything® **Motorcycle Book**
Everything® **Online Genealogy Book**
Everything® **Photography Book**
Everything® **Pool & Billiards Book**
Everything® **Quilting Book**
Everything® **Scrapbooking Book**
Everything® **Soapmaking Book**

HOME IMPROVEMENT

Everything® **Feng Shui Book**
Everything® **Gardening Book**
Everything® **Home Decorating Book**
Everything® **Landscaping Book**
Everything® **Lawn Care Book**
Everything® **Organize Your Home Book**

KIDS' STORY BOOKS

Everything® **Bedtime Story Book**
Everything® **Bible Stories Book**
Everything® **Fairy Tales Book**
Everything® **Mother Goose Book**

EVERYTHING® KIDS' BOOKS

All titles are $6.95
Everything® **Kids' Baseball Book, 2nd Ed.** ($10.95 CAN)
Everything® **Kids' Bugs Book** ($10.95 CAN)
Everything® **Kids' Christmas Puzzle & Activity Book** ($10.95 CAN)
Everything® **Kids' Cookbook** ($10.95 CAN)
Everything® **Kids' Halloween Puzzle & Activity Book** ($10.95 CAN)
Everything® **Kids' Joke Book** ($10.95 CAN)
Everything® **Kids' Math Puzzles Book** ($10.95 CAN)
Everything® **Kids' Mazes Book** ($10.95 CAN)
Everything® **Kids' Money Book** ($11.95 CAN)
Everything® **Kids' Monsters Book** ($10.95 CAN)
Everything® **Kids' Nature Book** ($11.95 CAN)
Everything® **Kids' Puzzle Book** ($10.95 CAN)
Everything® **Kids' Science Experiments Book** ($10.95 CAN)
Everything® **Kids' Soccer Book** ($10.95 CAN)
Everything® **Kids' Travel Activity Book** ($10.95 CAN)

LANGUAGE

Everything® **Learning French Book**
Everything® **Learning German Book**
Everything® **Learning Italian Book**
Everything® **Learning Latin Book**
Everything® **Learning Spanish Book**
Everything® **Sign Language Book**

MUSIC

Everything® **Drums Book (with CD), $19.95 ($31.95 CAN)**
Everything® **Guitar Book**
Everything® **Playing Piano and Keyboards Book**
Everything® **Rock & Blues Guitar Book (with CD), $19.95 ($31.95 CAN)**
Everything® **Songwriting Book**

NEW AGE

Everything® **Astrology Book**
Everything® **Divining the Future Book**
Everything® **Dreams Book**
Everything® **Ghost Book**
Everything® **Meditation Book**
Everything® **Numerology Book**
Everything® **Palmistry Book**
Everything® **Psychic Book**
Everything® **Spells & Charms Book**
Everything® **Tarot Book**
Everything® **Wicca and Witchcraft Book**

PARENTING

Everything® **Baby Names Book**
Everything® **Baby Shower Book**
Everything® **Baby's First Food Book**
Everything® **Baby's First Year Book**
Everything® **Breastfeeding Book**
Everything® **Father-to-Be Book**
Everything® **Get Ready for Baby Book**
Everything® **Homeschooling Book**
Everything® **Parent's Guide to Positive Discipline**
Everything® **Potty Training Book, $9.95 ($15.95 CAN)**
Everything® **Pregnancy Book, 2nd Ed.**
Everything® **Pregnancy Fitness Book**
Everything® **Pregnancy Organizer, $15.00 ($22.95 CAN)**
Everything® **Toddler Book**
Everything® **Tween Book**

PERSONAL FINANCE

Everything® **Budgeting Book**
Everything® **Get Out of Debt Book**
Everything® **Get Rich Book**
Everything® **Homebuying Book, 2nd Ed.**
Everything® **Homeselling Book**

All Everything® books are priced at $12.95 or $14.95, unless otherwise stated. Prices subject to change without notice.
Canadian prices range from $11.95–$31.95, and are subject to change without notice.

Everything® **Investing Book**
Everything® **Money Book**
Everything® **Mutual Funds Book**
Everything® **Online Investing Book**
Everything® **Personal Finance Book**
Everything® **Personal Finance in Your 20s & 30s Book**
Everything® **Wills & Estate Planning Book**

PETS

Everything® **Cat Book**
Everything® **Dog Book**
Everything® **Dog Training and Tricks Book**
Everything® **Horse Book**
Everything® **Puppy Book**
Everything® **Tropical Fish Book**

REFERENCE

Everything® **Astronomy Book**
Everything® **Car Care Book**
Everything® **Christmas Book, $15.00 ($21.95 CAN)**
Everything® **Classical Mythology Book**
Everything® **Einstein Book**
Everything® **Etiquette Book**
Everything® **Great Thinkers Book**
Everything® **Philosophy Book**
Everything® **Shakespeare Book**
Everything® **Tall Tales, Legends, & Other Outrageous Lies Book**
Everything® **Toasts Book**
Everything® **Trivia Book**
Everything® **Weather Book**

RELIGION

Everything® **Angels Book**
Everything® **Buddhism Book**
Everything® **Catholicism Book**
Everything® **Jewish History & Heritage Book**
Everything® **Judaism Book**

Everything® **Prayer Book**
Everything® **Saints Book**
Everything® **Understanding Islam Book**
Everything® **World's Religions Book**
Everything® **Zen Book**

SCHOOL & CAREERS

Everything® **After College Book**
Everything® **College Survival Book**
Everything® **Cover Letter Book**
Everything® **Get-a-Job Book**
Everything® **Hot Careers Book**
Everything® **Job Interview Book**
Everything® **Online Job Search Book**
Everything® **Resume Book, 2nd Ed.**
Everything® **Study Book**

SELF-HELP

Everything® **Dating Book**
Everything® **Divorce Book**
Everything® **Great Marriage Book**
Everything® **Great Sex Book**
Everything® **Romance Book**
Everything® **Self-Esteem Book**
Everything® **Success Book**

SPORTS & FITNESS

Everything® **Bicycle Book**
Everything® **Body Shaping Book**
Everything® **Fishing Book**
Everything® **Fly-Fishing Book**
Everything® **Golf Book**
Everything® **Golf Instruction Book**
Everything® **Pilates Book**
Everything® **Running Book**
Everything® **Sailing Book, 2nd Ed.**
Everything® **T'ai Chi and QiGong Book**
Everything® **Total Fitness Book**
Everything® **Weight Training Book**
Everything® **Yoga Book**

TRAVEL

Everything® **Guide to Las Vegas**

Everything® **Guide to New England**
Everything® **Guide to New York City**
Everything® **Guide to Washington D.C.**
Everything® **Travel Guide to The Disneyland Resort®, California Adventure®, Universal Studios®, and the Anaheim Area**
Everything® **Travel Guide to the Walt Disney World Resort®, Universal Studios®, and Greater Orlando, 3rd Ed.**

WEDDINGS

Everything® **Bachelorette Party Book**
Everything® **Bridesmaid Book**
Everything® **Creative Wedding Ideas Book**
Everything® **Jewish Wedding Book**
Everything® **Wedding Book, 2nd Ed.**
Everything® **Wedding Checklist, $7.95 ($11.95 CAN)**
Everything® **Wedding Etiquette Book, $7.95 ($11.95 CAN)**
Everything® **Wedding Organizer, $15.00 ($22.95 CAN)**
Everything® **Wedding Shower Book, $7.95 ($12.95 CAN)**
Everything® **Wedding Vows Book, $7.95 ($11.95 CAN)**
Everything® **Weddings on a Budget Book, $9.95 ($15.95 CAN)**

WRITING

Everything® **Creative Writing Book**
Everything® **Get Published Book**
Everything® **Grammar and Style Book**
Everything® **Grant Writing Book**
Everything® **Guide to Writing Children's Books**
Everything® **Screenwriting Book**
Everything® **Writing Well Book**

Available wherever books are sold!
To order, call 800-872-5627, or visit us at everything.com

Everything® and everything.com® are registered trademarks of Adams Media Corporation.